Derrida and Feminism

See 28

Derrida and Feminism

Recasting the Question of Woman

edited by

Ellen K. Feder,

Mary C. Rawlinson,

and Emily Zakin

ROUTLEDGE
New York and London

Published in 1997 by

Routledge
29 West 35th Street
New York, NY 10001

Published in Great Britain in 1997 by

Routledge
11 New Fetter Lane
London EC4P 4EE

Printed in the United States of America
Design: Jack Donner

Library of Congress Cataloging-in-Publication Data
Derrida and feminism : recasting the question of woman / edited by Ellen K. Feder,
    Mary C. Rawlinson, and Emily Zakin
Includes bibliographical references and index.
ISBN 0–415–90916–3 (hc: alk. paper). — ISBN 0–415–90917–1 (pbk.: alk. paper)
    1. Feminism.   2. Derrida, Jacques—Views on women.   3. Feminist theory.   I. Feder, Ellen K.
II. Rawlinson, Mary C.   III. Zakin, Emily.
    HQ1154.D425   1996
    305.42—dc20   96–28730
                                                                                        CIP

Contents

Acknowledgments

The editors gratefully acknowledge Miami University, the State University of New York at Stony Brook, and Vassar College for institutional support. We thank Corinna Roth for her splendid work preparing the manuscript (and index), and Dinh Tran for his assistance. Alison Shonkwiler and Laska Jimsen at Routledge provided gracious and capable assistance at the project's beginning and culmination, respectively. Finally, we wish to extend our thanks to our editor, Maureen MacGrogan, for her patience and steadfast support of this volume.

Abbreviated Citations
for Derrida Text

ANU "The Almost Nothing of the Unpresentable" (1995) Peggy Kamuf, trans. in *Points*, Elisabeth Weber, ed. Stanford: Stanford University Press.

A *Aporias* (1993) Thomas Dutoit, trans. Stanford: Stanford University Press.

AT "At This Very Moment in This Work Here I Am" (1991) Berezdevin, trans. in *Re-Reading Levinas*, R. Bernasconi and S. Critchley, eds. Bloomington: Indiana University Press.

CH "Choreographies" (1982) reprinted in *The Ear of the Other*.

CI *Cinders* (1991) Ned Lukacher, trans. Lincoln: University of Nebraska Press.

CS "Circumfession" (1993) in *Jacques Derrida*, Geoffrey Bennington, trans. Chicago: University of Chicago Press.

D "Différance" in *Margins of Philosophy*.

DI *Dissemination* (1981), trans. Barbara Johnson. Chicago: University of Chicago Press.

EM "The Ends of Man" (1982) in *Margins of Philosophy*.

EO *The Ear of the Other* (1985), trans. Kamuf and Ronell. McDonald and Lévesque, eds. Lincoln: University of Nebraska Press.

FL "Force of Law: The 'Mystical Foundations of Authority'" (1992) in *Deconstruction and the Possibility of Justice*, Cornell, Rosenfeld, and Carlson, eds. New York: Routledge.

GE "*Geschlecht*: Sexual Difference, Ontological Difference" (1983) in *Research in Phenomenology* 13.

GD *The Gift of Death* (1995) David Wills, trans. Chicago: University of Chicago Press.

G *Glas* (1986) Leavey and Rand, trans. Lincoln: University of Nebraska Press.

GT   *Given Time: I. Counterfeit Money* (1992) Peggy Kamuf, trans. Chicago: University of Chicago Press.

LG   "The Law of Genre" (1980) Avital Ronell, trans. *Critical Inquiry* 17:1.

MP   *Margins of Philosophy* (1982) Alan Bass, trans. Chicago: The University of Chicago Press.

M   *Memoirs for Paul de Man* (1986) Lindsay, Culler, and Cadava, trans. New York: Columbia University Press.

NY   "A Number of Yes" (1988) Brian Holmes, trans. *Que Parle* 2.

OG   *Of Grammatology* (1976) Gayatri Chakravorty Spivak, trans. Baltimore: The Johns Hopkins University Press.

ON   *On the Name* (1995) Thomas Dutoit, ed. Stanford: Stanford University Press.

O   "Otobiographies" in *The Ear of the Other.*

PA   "Passions: 'An Oblique Offering'" (1995), David Wood, trans. in *On the Name.*

PF   "The Politics of Friendship" (1988) Gabriel Motzkin, trans. *The Journal of Philosophy* 85.

P   *Positions* (1981) Alan Bass, trans. Chicago: The University of Chicago Press.

PC   *The Post Card: From Socrates to Freud and Beyond* (1987) Alan Bass, trans. Chicago: The University of Chicago Press.

PR   "The Principle of Reason: The University in the Eyes of its Pupils" (1983) *Diacritics* 13:3.

PS   "Psyche: Inventions of the Other" (1989) in *Reading de Man Reading*, Waters, Godzich, eds. Minneapolis: University of Minnesota Press.

SN   "Sauf le nom" (1995) John P. Leavey, Jr., trans. in *On the Name.*

S   *Spurs: Nietzsche's Styles/Eperons: Les Styles de Nietzsche* (1979) Barbara Harlow, trans. Chicago: The University of Chicago Press.

SSP   "Structure, Sign, and Play in the Discourse of the Human Sciences" (1978) in *Writing and Difference.*

UG   "Ulysses Gramophone: Hear Say Yes in Joyce" (1984) in *James Joyce: The Augmented Ninth*, ed. Bernard Benstock. Syracuse: Syracuse University Press.

WM   "White Mythology" (1982) in *Margins of Philosophy.*

WB   "Women in the Beehive" (1984) reprinted in *Men in Feminism,* Jardine and Smith, eds. New York: Methuen, 1987.

WD   *Writing and Difference* (1978) Alan Bass, trans. Chicago: University of Chicago Press.

Introduction

Ellen K. Feder, Mary C. Rawlinson, and Emily Zakin

In philosophy the history of the question of woman is an ancient one. Plato broaches it in his discussion of the ideal state when he includes women as members of the guardian class. The inclusion is equivalent to an abolition of the social roles of gender among philosopher-rulers, constituting a political indifference to the biological difference of sexual reproduction. Children would be reared in common, each related to the other so that the differences of male/female and man/woman would make no difference. The mother, along with the family, disappears in the ruling element of the state.

It is Aristotle, however, who decides the question of woman by placing her and figuring her in a way that continues to hold sway. In Aristotle's text, woman is rendered, literally, as the nourishing medium which receives the enformed sperm, and figuratively, as the body, nature, or unformed and irrational matter; she functions as the other to man and his rational activity. Aristotle elaborates spheres of politics and friendship in which woman is not naturally suited to participate. As Irigaray remarks, woman supplies the "place" for man's reproduction and creative act: he works on/in her. This decision of the question is disseminated in (Judeo) Christianity in a profusion of highly differentiated images, from Eve to the Holy Family and the marriage of the female saints to Christ.

In philosophical modernity this decision acts on the question of education and on the problem of the relation of sexual difference to concrete social institutions. In the works of Kant and Rousseau, for example, the formation of human subjectivity is said to be marked by this difference, and each elaborates practical plans which might guide the institution of this difference. Both assign certain kinds of formative activity as proper to one sex or the other, and insist that the rational order of society requires this institution. They thereby advance a division which excludes women from the realm of political action.

Hegel makes this decision of the question intrinsic to the self-unfolding of Absolute Spirit: both to its self-reflection in language and to its embodiment in practical activity and social forms. To the woman belongs the care of the body and blood, the domain of the family and funeral rites. To the man, whose body the woman properly tends—as Antigone tends first her father, then her brother—belongs the public domains of action, science, politics, and philosophy. Even language, the universalizing medium, is said to be foreign or opaque to her. The system of Absolute Spirit depends upon this division of labor and life.

Psychoanalytic theory supplements and extends the tradition's decision of the question of woman by demonstrating how gendered subjects are produced in and through the family. Moreover, psychoanalysis explicitly develops the concept of normalization, of, for example, "normal" female sexuality. Articulating the conditions for the formation of a "normal" human subjectivity, psychoanalysis mediates between the regulatory force of social practices and institutions, such as medicine and law, and the philosophical tradition within which the program of subjective constitution is laid down. Through it the philosophical decision is deployed on actual human bodies.

It was *our* gamble, the gamble that inaugurated this collection, that Derrida—following certain clues in Nietzsche—had undecided all this and put woman into question again. The results of that gamble, this collection, have not proved us wrong. Derrida has certainly not been alone in reopening this question; however, his practice of reading and writing have made it possible to articulate the logic of this move in a particularly clarifying way. Derrida's reading/writing is a "strategic science" which operates upon a text so as to expose how its own limits and margins are inscribed within it, how the decision of the other or the exterior is intrinsic to and marked within the system of identity or logic of concepts. Derrida advances, then, not concepts, which would grasp the truth of some preconceptual given in a word, but "levers of intervention" which assist in the text's subversion and transgression of itself. Woman is an exemplar of such a lever, and is measured by/manifest in her effects.

Reopening the question of woman releases a whole program of questions: If "woman" is not a concept, i.e. refers neither to actual women, nor to the practices and institutions by which they are formed, then how does it operate? Does it refer at all, or is it, rather, an undecideable figure, an *aporia* that will not let us decide the question and put woman in her place? What difference does it make to philosophy and its archive of concepts that the question of woman has been undecided? What effects does this operation have upon concepts of the other, ethics, responsibility, subjectivity, agency, and decision? What is the relation, then, of such a practice of reading and writing, to the domain of life and the formation of women? What might this practice contribute to the practical struggles that have gone on under the heading of "feminism"?

Derrida himself remarks that the "practical struggles" of feminism have resulted in a shaking and loosening of the decisive logic of identity and the concept, making possible a multiplication of possibilities in the field of sexual difference, and providing an opening for interrogations of closure, presence, and truth. To what extent, then, is Derrida indebted to feminism, both theoretical and practical, as that which has given him the gift of this opening? And what ironies and impossibilities lurk within Derrida's desire to "write with the hand of a woman" and his inscription in his texts of explicitly female interlocutors, who appear to write the text? Does Derrida fall prey to the danger he himself identifies, namely that in attempting to intervene in the language of metaphysics and disrupt it, one risks merely repeating? Is Derrida's use of woman one more appropriation in philosophy's long history on this question?

The papers collected here are only more or less decisive and operate more to complicate and amplify these questions than to close them down. Jane Gallop's essay establishes the scene in which feminist theorists engage with Derrida. Gallop reads Derrida "in history," to note his engagement with a certain essentializing feminism characteristic of the Second Wave, or what she calls the "era of 'women.'" In "Women in Spurs and Nineties Feminism," Gallop argues that "[a]s Derrida dreams of 'sexual difference' which would not be contained within a binary opposition, of 'sexual differences' which would not be singular, his text trips over, catches in passing only to quickly forget other 'sexual differences,'" i.e. the differences among the formulations of "woman" in Nietzsche's work rendered *femme* in Derrida's text. Reading the mark of property in the possessive use of *frau*, or "wife," or the distinction between *frau* or "lady," and the base *weib* or "female" in *Spurs*, Gallop dates Derrida's text, marks it as invested in the assumptions of the 1970s feminism of which it is critical. If seventies feminism "envisioned a singular unity which could be collectivized under the name of woman," Gallop offers what she identifies as a nineties gloss on the figuration of Derrida's 'woman,' recognizing that "these sexual differences which cannot be called gender construct 'women' in diacritical distinction not to the opposite sex but to another class or sexuality or age."

Ellen Feder and Emily Zakin propose a reading of *Spurs* which attempts to occupy a dual, perhaps even "undecidable" position. In "Flirting with the Truth," they recognize both Derrida's betrayal of, and his participation in, the structures of masculinity which perpetuate the sexual violence of philosophy. The equation of Truth and Woman makes of both possessions to be exchanged. Feder and Zakin argue that while Derrida's equivocations between truths and women contest this dynamic of desire, it nonetheless remains necessary to address the dangers of seduction and appropriation which face women readers of *Spurs*. Lured by the notion of feminine style, the authors find themselves entangled in the persistent relegation of women's identities to metaphors, shadows, concepts, and bodies. The essay concludes by exploring the difference between the Question of Woman and women's questions, suggesting that it is only the latter which can begin to generate the possibility of a feminine subject.

Kelly Oliver interrogates Derrida's autobiographical essay "Circumfession" in quest of its absent maternal body. She asks whether Derrida's address to his own mother (among others), while seemingly an effort to regain recognition from her, might not actually be a denial of recognition which "turns the mother into silent nature." In posing this question, and listening to the text for answers, Oliver uncovers a re-naturalization of the mother, and a displacement of her, both of which occur through a speaking that "belongs to the maternal tongue." In the end, Oliver finds that the mother's blood exceeds Derrida's ritualistic writing even while her tongue—the mother-tongue—secures the system that separates nature from culture and expels her body into the former.

Mary Rawlinson's "Levers, Signatures, and Secrets" demonstrates how Derrida's "intervention" into the Hegelian text is subversive in its revelation of woman as necessary and illicit, even impossible, in the logic of the *Aufhebung*. This intervention, Rawlinson argues, opens up the possibility of rethinking alterity and perhaps, of disrupting the link between this logic of the concept and processes of normalization. Guided by the figures of the "mother tongue" and the "living feminine," Rawlinson explores the themes of the gift, the signature, and the play of life and death. It is in these themes that Derrida develops the thought of a singular other whose mortality gives rise to responsibility, i.e., to an ethics not governed by the state and the family. Rawlinson ends, however, by questioning Derrida and his choice of certain sites of intervention, e.g., friendship and the name of God; she wonders whether these concepts do not ineluctably return us to the dialectical logic of the same and the mastery of the other.

Tina Chanter's treatment of Derrida and his interlocutors is not intended, as she writes, to produce another "competing reading," an approach she characterizes as "[s]till governed by oppositional thinking." She seeks rather to interrogate the very "rules of engagement," i.e., the conventions which govern or regulate interaction with the text, in order to ask what it could mean "to read otherwise." In her consideration of the contradictions for providing a reading that is "responsible" to the text, Chanter introduces the trope of "interruption" to thematize Derrida's method and her own. For Chanter, the strategy of interruption—Derrida's with regard to the history of philosophy, its determination of the question of "the other" (or difference), and his participation in this determination, and Chanter's with regard to Derrida and to her own position—suggests the possibility of disrupting what has been constructed as an opposition between feminist and deconstructive methods.

The relation between feminism and deconstruction is also the concern of Ewa Ziarek's contribution, in which she argues that this is an alliance which needs continually to be "invented." Ziarek contrasts Judith Butler's theory of sex as performativity with a Lacanian depiction of sex as a "radical failure of signification." While both theories recognize sex as compulsory, only the theory of performativity explains it "in terms of the internal relation between the force and the law." Ziarek presents an argument against the Lacanian position, maintaining that the failure it describes in fact ensures the "permanence of sexual difference." She then proceeds to analyze the role of performativity in Butler and Derrida's work, linking their projects together in calling for an ethical response to sexual difference.

In his essay, John Caputo continues this theme of the relation to the Other in his pursuit of a Derridean ethics. He claims that understanding the conditions of justice with regard to sexual difference means imagining the possibilities of a sexual difference which "exceeds the number two." Caputo aims to supplement the Nietzschean reading of Derrida with a Levinasian approach, and toward that end he turns to the work of Drucilla Cornell who clarifies Derrida's commitment to "the claim of the other." While questioning Cornell's formulation of deconstruction as "a philosophy of the Good," Caputo engages the notion that "deconstruction is justice," contrasting it with that of the Law which functions as a Monster. Caputo concludes that the justice of sexual difference lies "beyond" our gendered destinies.

Drucilla Cornell's project in "Where Love Begins: Sexual Difference and the Limit of the Masculine Symbolic" is to explore the meaning of an ethical relationship to the other understood as radical alterity. Cornell argues with Derrida that "Lacan does not fully apprehend the otherness of the Real as 'truly' beyond the symbolic." To this extent, Lacan recuperates feminine Otherness as the guarantee of the masculine Symbolic, while his conception of law demands the denial of this otherness. Cornell maintains that, in contrast to Lacan, the force of *differance* promises for Derrida the possibility of an ethical encounter with the Real, because it "disrupts any conception of the law of law." In thereby recognizing a beyond to the Symbolic, Cornell concludes that "deconstruction is justice."

Each of the essays in this volume marks out a strategy of engagement, an intervention that has as its ambition to investigate Derrida's work with and against the insights of feminism. What we see in these diverse essays are theorists grappling with the question of woman: inventing, interrupting, collaborating, flirting, and recasting. Some of the authors address the body, blood, maternity. Others address language and what is "beyond" language. Together they comprise a revisioning of Derrida's corpus which suggests the importance of reading Derrida, and of reading him under the scrutiny of women's questions.

"Women" in *Spurs* and Nineties Feminism   1

Jane Gallop

Derrida first presented the paper I will call *Spurs* at the 1972 symposium entitled "Nietzsche Today?"[1] Derrida interpreted the second word of the symposium title by choosing to speak on Nietzsche and women. *"La femme—le mot fait epoque,"* Derrida said in 1972 (S 60). The French expression *"faire epoque,"* my French-English dictionary tells me, can be rendered by the English expression "marks an era." The era marked by the word "woman" was the "today" in which Derrida speaks.

A generation ago, Derrida began his talk with a dateline: "From Basel in seventy-two (The Birth of Tragedy) Nietzsche writes to Malvida von Meysenbug" (S 35). These are the very first words of *Spurs*. Derrida goes on to quote a few sentences from Nietzsche's 1872 letter to von Meysenbug as a sort of epigraph, what he and his American translator call an "exergue." An "exergue," my English dictionary informs me, is "a space on a coin, token, or medal ... often containing the date." Speaking in 1972 at a conference on "Nietzsche Today?" Derrida casually dates Nietzsche's letter as "seventy-two," taking to heart the question "today?" in his assignment to talk about Nietzsche. Twenty years later, invited to write about Derrida and feminism, my subject might be "Derrida Today?"

This paper is, in particular, written for, to, and because of Ellen. Ellen is a "nineties feminist," a feminist of the generation that I, a seventies feminist, teach. I call her "Ellen" because that was the guise in which I encountered her the first time I found myself "teaching Derrida" in the nineties.

Spurs is Derrida's response to seventies feminism. As such, despite its apparent opposition to certain feminist positions, *Spurs* shares some presuppositions with the specific feminism it would critique, correct, and/or seduce. Like the feminism with which it was contemporary, *Spurs* belongs to the era of "woman."

The second sentence of *Spurs/Eperons* announces: *"woman will be my subject/la femme sera mon sujet"* (S 36). This is the first appearance of "woman" in *Spurs*, but it is not the first instance of the word *"femme"* in *Eperons*. The exergue contains the word *"femme"* but not "woman." Where the French version of the letter tells of the upcoming visit of *"Wagner et sa femme,"* Barbara Harlow's English translation announces the visit of "Wagner and wife." In French unlike English (but not unlike some other languages), the generic word to refer to an adult human female also denotes a particular legal, economic, and sexual status (wife), a subset of the category "woman." Synechdochally, in French (but not just in French), the word for part of the group of women stands for the whole.

This is certainly not the *"femme"* who made an epoch. This exergual use of *"femme"* is certainly marginal to Derrida's consideration of Nietzsche and women. My insistent use of "certainly" is, of course, ironic: meant to wink at Ellen, who knows that Derrida has deconstructed precisely that move which would cordon off the margins, keeping the center simple and pure, who knows that Derrida generally directs us to look seriously at such textual marginalia as exergues. But that is not all.

The inseparability of wife from woman in the *Spurs* inscription of *la femme* might be connected to the figure of the hymen which appears there and elsewhere in Derrida's work. Or we might remark the possessive adjective in the phrase *"Wagner et sa femme."* The possibility of a man's possessing a woman recalls not only Nietzsche's pronouncements—"Woman wants to be taken and accepted as a possession"[2]—but also *Spurs'* consideration of "propriation" as central to thinking about women.

Derrida's quotation of the French translation of Nietzsche's 1872 letter draws particular attention to the phrase *"Wagner et sa femme"* by preceding it with the German original—*"Wagner mit Frau."* *Eperons* frequently supplements the French translation of Nietzsche with the original German. The exergue alone does this nine times. But—while the other eight German phrases are in either parentheses or brackets following the French text—*"Wagner mit Frau"* not only precedes the French but is laid out as if part of the French text, set off only in commas. Like the French *"femme,"* the German *"Frau"* can mean either wife or woman. In Richard Schwaderer's German translation, *Sporen*, Derrida writes: *"Die 'Frau'—das Wort macht Epoche"* (S 49).

Ellen, a U.S. graduate student enamored of "theory," reads French and German. "Ellen" reads like a bad bilingual pun: the French female pronoun (*elle*) pluralized in German (*en*). "Ellen will be my subject," I might say, translating *Spurs* in the nineties. Where, a generation ago, Derrida put "woman," I might replace the noun with a female bilingual plural pronoun.

Bilingual: a word not quite in any language but marking the junctures and disjunctures between them, thus making language knotty and thick, blocking the view. A pronoun: marking the inadequacy or excessiveness of any name while standing in the place that demands a noun. Not a name and not in any mother tongue, yet despite and because, still female and plural: the subject of nineties feminism, as dreamt in *Spurs*.

If the epoch-making word in 1972 was "woman," by 1982 it was "women," emphasis on the plural. Seventies feminism envisioned a singular unity which could be collectivized under the name of woman. Woman in *Spurs* is figured as insistently plural. Derrida, through Nietzsche, criticizes feminism's desire for a singular concept of woman. Through the eighties, the feminist response to *Spurs* either used Derrida to criticize a restrictive and too singular conception of woman or criticized Derrida for speaking only of woman and not caring about women or, and often, both.

Spurs works to make sure that Nietzsche's figuration of woman is not seen as singular. The text centers around a numbered list of three different positions for women in Nietzsche.[3] This is probably the most often cited part of *Spurs*, the numbered paragraphs functioning as a mnemonic device, a ready-made format for note-taking. The typology is, to be sure, hedged around with recognitions that it is reductive, but although three may not be enough, it will at least ward off the collapse into a single conception of woman. Yet the same word names these different positions: all three are called "woman," or taken in their plural, they are all "women."

In French: "1. *La femme . . . comme figure . . . de mensonge. . . . 2. La femme . . . comme figure . . . de verite. . . . 3. La femme . . . comme puissance affirmative*" (as figure of falsehood, as figure of truth, as affirmative power). In the German translation: "1. *Die Frau . . . als Bild . . . der Luge. . . . 2. Die Frau . . . als Bild . . . der Wahrheit. . . . 3. Die Frau . . . als affirmative . . . Macht.*" When Derrida's reading of Nietzsche is translated into German, Nietzsche's various statements about women are all grouped under the word *"Frau."* Even though the statements do not all use that noun.

At least two readers of *Spurs* have had occasion to comment on the German word *"Frau,"* placing it in diacritical distinction not to a word for man, but to another word for woman. In his 1980 reading of the four-language edition of *Eperons*, Alexander Argyros interrupts his quoting of an English translation of Nietzsche after the word "women" and inserts (in brackets): "[actually 'ladies'—*frauen*, not *weiben*]."[4] Reading Derrida on Nietzsche and women, Argyros is distracted by something not in the text, by the thought of *"weiben."* Like "ellen," *"weiben"* is not a German word, but a pseudo-German plural. Sensitive to a distinction in German, Argyros feels a need for a similar distinction in English. *"Frauen"* is not an exact equivalent of the

English "ladies"—the translator is not incorrect in using "women"—but like Argyros we might want to remember the "ladies" (as earlier we recalled the "wife") and interrupt the too smooth progress, whether in translation or otherwise, to the word "women."

"Ladies" don't appear in *Spurs*, except once. The English translation states: "In its maneuvers distance strips the lady of her identity and unseats the philosopher-knight" (S 53). "Lady" here translates the French *"femme,"* where the German translation puts *"Frau."* Called by the proximity of "knight," the "lady" reminds us that the best equivalent of "femme" may not always be "woman." The identity the lady here loses is, in Derrida's French, *"l'identité propre de la femme."* The lady's rare appearance is, appropriately, on the side of the "proper." If one of the figures of woman in *Spurs* would be proper, might we not be tempted to call her a "lady?"

A few years after Argyros, another reader of *Spurs* pauses over the German word for "women." At the beginning of her account of Derrida's paper, Alice Jardine supplies Nietzsche's German *"die Frauen"* in a parenthesis after "women." She adds a footnote: "The alternations in Nietzsche's texts between *Frau* (which has noble, wifely connotations) and *Weib* (the 'female'—at most, a prostitute) would need to be sorted out to untangle fully 'woman' . . . in his text."[5] Responsive to the same distinction as Argyros, Jardine suggests not "ladies" for *"Frauen"* but "female" for *Weib.* If *"Frauen"* can be translated by "women," we need another, lower noun for *"Weib."* While it is not entirely correct to say that *"Weib"* is "at most, a prostitute," groping like Argyros for a way to express the hierarchy in the *Frau/Weib* distinction, Jardine recalls the classic polarization of women into either wives or prostitutes. (Yesterday I saw a movie poster with the line: "In 1866 a woman had two choices . . . she could be a wife or she could be a whore.")[6] Although they do not exactly succeed in mapping the German words onto the available English vocabulary, these two eighties commentaries recognize in the *Frau/Weib* distinction something which also functions in English: a hierarchy dividing and classing "women" according to an inextricable combination of sexual and economic position.

Both Argyros and Jardine slip in their attempts to translate the *Frau/Weib* distinction. It is no wonder. What is to their credit is that they notice it at all. Excellent readers of Derrida's French, Argyros and Jardine encounter Nietzsche's German in Derrida's text. Derrida, himself an excellent reader of Nietzsche's German, gives his readers no help with this aspect of the German text. Argyros and Jardine (like the present author), trained in French, barely know German. But they notice what Derrida ignores.

Some of the quotations from Nietzsche in *Spurs* use the word *"Frau"*; others use the word *"Weib."* Sometimes these German words are even inserted parenthetically into the French or English quotations in the text. But nowhere in *Spurs* does Derrida comment upon these words. Derrida often comments not only upon Nietzsche's vocabulary, but even on his punctuation (for example: "once again the play here of both the quotation marks and the hyphens should be noted"—69). The entire texture of *Spurs* teaches us to attend to the specificity of Nietzsche's text, rather than reduce it to its conceptual positions. But with all the attention to the fine points of Nietzsche's writing, nowhere in this essay on Nietzsche's women does Derrida remark on what even those of us who barely know German nonetheless can see from the quotations in his text: that Nietzsche sometimes speaks of *Frauen,* sometimes of *Weiber.*

Argyros and Jardine trip over the German terminology and then let it slide. Both notice the *Frau/Weib* distinction parenthetically but their brilliant and careful readings of *Spurs* do not comment further upon it. Nor would I have, a decade ago. Nor could I until faced with Ellen.

The same "female" Jardine suggests as a translation for *"Weib"* makes a significant appearance in *Spurs.* Discussing "The History of an Error" (*The Twilight of the Idols*), Derrida writes: "In each of its . . . epochs . . . there are certain words underlined. And in the second epoch, Nietzsche has underlined only the words *sie wird Weib, elle* [l'Idée] *devient femme".* Harlow translates Derrida's last phrase, his translation of *"sie wird Weib,"* as *"it becomes female."*[7] In this instance where *"femme"* clearly translates as *"Weib,"* Harlow chooses to translate *"femme"* by "female" rather than "woman." For the next few pages the English refers to the "becoming-female" of the Idea when the French has *"devenir-femme."* Schwaderer's German translation, which generally translates Derrida's *"femme"* by *"Frau,"* gives us *"Weib-werden"* for this phrase (69ff).

Immediately following this appearance of the "female" in *Spurs,* we read: "Heidegger cites this sequence, even respects its underlining, but . . . he skirts the woman . . . all the elements of the text are analyzed, without exception, except the idea's becoming-female *(sie wird Weib).* In such a way does one permit oneself to see without reading, to read without seeing. But if we ourselves should take a closer look at this *"sie wird Weib"* we would not be proceeding in a way *counter to* Heidegger's (such a counter direction is in fact his own)." As a reader of Nietzsche, Derrida places himself in the tradition of Heidegger which prides itself on "analyzing all the elements of the text." Derrida points out that Heidegger neglects the woman and, no less in Heideggerean tradition, Derrida skips the *"Weib"*—so I point out, carrying on.

I want to read the "wife," the "lady," and the "female" in *Spurs.* Yet they appear, not in Derrida's (French) text, but in its English translation. Focusing on the four-language edition of *Eperons* whose format foregrounds translation, Argyros writes: "Derrida's work clearly seeks to trouble the various 'centrisms' at work in any glib notion of translation. . . . Derrida *is* his prolongation, in stylistic mimicry or in translation" (S 27–28). It may be that the work of translation, the necessity of thinking on the level of word choice, carries Derrida's "femme" into a more finely articulated space—more divided and pluralized—than is possible in an all too familiar language.

And of course Derrida's French text was always already in translation—not just in the general or banal Derridean sense that every text is, but specifically in its many quotes which are translations of Nietzsche's German. And although we cannot pick up a "wife" or a "lady" in the French, we can encounter a "female" there, precisely at a moment when Derrida pauses over Nietzsche's word choice. Quoting the translation of *Ecce Homo* where Nietzsche claims that he *"connaît bien les femmes,"* immediately after the word "femmes," Derrida writes (in brackets): *"[ou plutôt la femelle, Weiblein]"* (S 104). The English translation closely renders the bracketed remark as "[or rather, the female, *Weiblein*]." Here Harlow's "female" translates not *"femme"* but *"femelle,"* an actual cognate of "female." Although Nietzsche's alternation between *"Frau"* and *"Weib"* never causes Derrida to hesitate over the use of *"femme,"* here—registering that Nietzsche is using another word for women—he is prompted, in a gesture reminiscent of Argyros, parenthetically to correct the translation.

And, like Argyros, Derrida here trips a bit over the plural, correcting the translation's plural *"femmes"* with the singular *"femelle."* Nietzsche's German reads *"die Weiblein,"* the definite article marking as plural a word *("das Weiblein")* which is otherwise unchanged in the plural. As Derrida's *"Weiblein"* recalls Argyros's *"weiben,"* I begin perversely to imagine the power of the grammatically incorrect plural to express something not yet fully contained and domesticated in the correct, singular woman. From wom*en* to wei*b*en to ell*en*: "Ellen will be my subject"—here where "ellen" is a bad plural of *"elle,"* as we are trying to read between three languages.

If *"Weib"* is lower than *"Frau"*—in the entangled terms of class position and sexual propriety—*"Weiblein,"* the diminutive of *"Weib,"* is more insistently low: dismissive, derogatory, condescending. Derrida feels it necessary to mark that lowness with *"femelle,"* the diminutive of *"femme,"* a word which itself is, according to my French dictionary, both pejorative and low-class in usage.

Frau/Weib/Weiblein: we have here not a binary opposition, but an active and fluid lexical distinguishing between "women" which is not at all restricted, even just in the quotes from Nietzsche in *Spurs,* to these three terms. At stake in such lexical distinctions, which can also be found—albeit differently skewed—in English and French (among other languages) are always intermingled connotations of class and sexuality. As Derrida dreams of "sexual difference" which would not be contained within a binary opposition, of "sexual differences" which would not be singular, his text trips over, catches in passing only to quickly forget other "sexual differences." These sexual differences which cannot be called gender construct "women" in diacritical distinction not to the opposite sex but to another class or sexuality or age. Because differences "between women" have been sexualized, no less than the difference between the sexes, distinctions of class or age operate as sexual difference.

Ellen recognizes these categories as among those which nineties feminism insists we do not collapse back into a model in which gender is the only difference that matters. "Ell/en" recognizes that as we cross between languages we run into those differences. "Women" here always designates not just gender, but also class and sexuality and age.

I added the category of "age" to my list because of the German word *"Frauenzimmer"* which, although it can have sexual or class connotations, always implies youth.[8] If Nietzsche's *"Weiblein"* causes Derrida briefly to hesitate in his use of "women," Nietzsche's *"Frauenzimmer"* truly gives him pause. Quoting the opening of *Beyond Good and Evil*—"Supposing truth to be a woman"—*Spurs* comes to Nietzsche's question of whether philosophers' clumsy ways of approaching truth are not inept means *"pour prendre une fille"* (S 54). Derrida inserts a parenthesis after the word *"fille"*—*"(Frauenzimmer, terme méprisant: une fille facile)."* (The English translation of Nietzsche gives us "winning a wench," after "wench" Derrida's parenthesis is translated: "(*Frauenzimmer* is a term of contempt: an easy woman)".) There is a double paragraph break immediately after the *"Frauenzimmer"* parenthesis and then we read the title of the next section.[9] After the title, the new section begins by quoting the very next sentence from *Beyond Good and Evil*; thus the section break actually interrupts the quotation. It is as if *"Frauenzimmer"* occasions not just a parenthesis but an actual break in the text, as if *Spurs* not only hesitates but stops short and has to start up again.

"Frauenzimmer" reappears in another parenthesis later in *Spurs*, in a quotation from *The Gay Science* which Derrida later interrupts to remind us (in brackets) to note "the play of both the quotation marks and the hyphen" (S 68–69). I want to pay at least as much attention to Nietzsche's slightly archaic *"Frauenzimmer,"* here translated by *"filles"* in French and "women" in English. *"Frauenzimmer"* appears here in a discussion of women that begins *"Endlich* [finally] *die Frauen:"* and ends with the assertion *"Das Weib ist so artistisch,* Woman is so artistic," with the German included (without brackets, italics or parentheses) in the French (and English) text. Situated

between *"Frauen"* and *"Weib," "Frauenzimmer"* here marks a place in *Spurs* where the French equivalent for "women" is not *"femmes"* but *"filles."*

"Fille," the French word for daughter, is also the word for girl, "a child or a young person of the female sex." But *"fille"* can also mean a "young woman *(femme)* who leads a debauched life (especially, a prostitute)." In fact, the word *"fille,"* used without any qualifier, implies this secondary meaning, a woman of loose morals. In order to refer to a proper young female, in French one must use the pleonasm *"jeune fille"* (literally, "young young person of the female sex") so as to avoid the sexuality suggested by an unaccompanied *"fille."* Between the age definition and the sexual definition, my French dictionary tells me that, in a usage either archaic or rustic, *"fille"* means "an unmarried [female] person (as opposed to *'femme')."* Under this definition, we find that the somewhat oxymoronic term *"fille-mère"* (literally, "daughter-mother") means an unwed mother and the common but no less oxymoronic *"vieille fille"* (literally, "old young person of the female sex") means a likewise oxymoronic "old maid."

This dictionary *(Le Petit Robert)* likes to explain meanings through opposition or antonymy, when possible. For example, it parenthetically glosses the two primary meanings of *"fille"* with "as opposed to 'son'" and "as opposed to 'boy.'" With this old-fashioned or provincial sense of *"fille,"* the dictionary uses the same antinomous formulation: "as opposed to *'femme.'"* The distinction *femme/fille,* presented most directly in this usage, suggests that to become a woman, one must marry; otherwise one remains in a minoritized and/or improper state. In this usage—but I would argue also implicitly in its other senses—a *"fille"* is *elle*-who-is-not-*femme.* And, I would further argue, that difference, the distinction *femme/fille,* is—no less than the opposition daughter/son or girl/boy if otherwise—a sexual difference.

Nietzsche's *"Frauenzimmer"* brings Derrida to the *femme/fille* distinction. Its first appearance, in the quote from *Beyond Good and Evil,* introduces the *"fille"* into *Spurs.* Immediately thereupon, Derrida breaks the text, ending a section. Or we might say (picking up *Spurs's* nautical motif) that, unable to continue in the path of the *"fille,"* Derrida comes about (*virer:* changes tack, veers, turns around). When the next section begins (under a new heading), the same passage from *Beyond Good and Evil* continues. But first Derrida states: "At this moment, the truth of woman *(femme)* . . . Nietzsche turns it about *(virer)"* (S 54–55). Derrida's comment ends with a colon, following which the quotation from Nietzsche continues.

By thus breaking up the quotation, making it span two sections of the text, and reintroducing it with this short commentary, *Spurs* turns from the *"fille"* and returns to the *"femme."* When the quotation continues with "[c]ertainly she has not let herself be won," Nietzsche repeats the verb from the preceding sentence (German *"einnehmen,"* French *"prendre"*), but, as framed in *Spurs*, "she" seems to refer to the *"femme"* of Derrida's introductory phrase and not the *"fille"* who ends the previous section (*"prendre une fille"*), the *"Frauenzimmer"* of Nietzsche's preceding sentence. Derrida immediately follows the quotation with the assertion, *"[l]a femme ne se laisse pas prendre* [does not let herself be won]," reinforcing the sense that the creature who resists capture is called *"femme,"* although in fact the verb *"prendre"* refers back to the phrase which ends the preceding section: *"prendre une fille."*[10]

Derrida's celebration of the woman who cannot be taken is, to be sure, an affirmation of what slips away from our inept attempts to pin her down and name her. Ironically, "at this moment," the *"fille"* he encountered for the first time slips away, leaving him with the same old *"femme."* Ironically, the *"fille"* who got away is, by the philosopher's own account, "easy": "easy" implying one who can be taken. But "easy" may also imply a female who, unlike the wife, does not have a good name, is not possessed under a man's name. As the Nietzsche quotation passes from one section of the text to another where it literally appears *under* another name (under the title of the new section, "Truths"), the *fille* becomes a *femme*, a passage which normatively entails a change of name.

Spurs goes on to assert: "That which . . . does not let itself be taken *(prendre)* is—feminine, which should not, however, be hastily translated by femininity, by woman's feminini*ty*, by feminine sexuali*ty*, or other essentializing fetishes which are just what one thinks one is capturing *(prendre)* when one has not escaped the foolishness of the dogmatic philosopher . . . or the inexperienced seducer" (S 54–55).

"That which does not let itself be taken" refers back to Nietzsche's "she has not let herself be taken," whose "she" refers back to Nietzsche's *"Frauenzimmer"*—*"fille,"* "wench," *"fille facile,"* "easy woman." Derrida takes Nietzsche's phrase, transforming the feminine pronoun (*sie, elle,* she) into the neuter construction in order to say that all we know about "that" is that it is "feminine," meaning first of all that "it" is represented by a feminine pronoun. When Derrida says that "it" is feminine, he is saying, among other things, that the word for truth, in German and French (*"die Wahrheit," "la vérité"*), is feminine. Derrida notes the word's gender and then warns us against proceeding too quickly from that to some more substantive femininity.

Perhaps because I am thinking about *"elle,"* I hear Derrida warning us not to move too quickly to any noun. "Femininity" makes a noun out of the adjective "feminine," gives it a proper name, we might say. By underlining the endings, he lays scornful emphasis on the nominalization of the feminine. All the "essentializing fetishes" he lists are nouns, as if here the process of essentializing were synonymous with nominalizing, with the making of nouns from adjectives and pronouns—the noun, the name, the substantive as fetish. It would be foolish to think one could capture her with any noun; all he can say is that there is something feminine, what we could call *"elle."* This attack on essentializing feminine fetishes is certainly a central message of *Spurs*, and the term "essentializing" is recognizable as part of a campaign against a certain seventies feminism.

"Essentializing"—the word marks an era. Ellen is an anti-essentialist feminist and her anti-essentialism has learned from Derrida. Facing Ellen, I'm pleased to notice that the move he warns us against, the move from an indefinite feminine *(elle)* to a name or substantive, is here termed hasty translation. I am further amused to note, in the bilingual edition of *Spurs*, that the English translation puts this as "should not be hastly [sic] mistaken." "Mistaken" here renders the verb *"traduire,"* a perfectly good equivalent of the English "translate." And, as if to enact both haste and translation as mistake, a letter is left out of "hastily."

The pauses to consider the difference between *Frau* and *Weib* or *femme* and *fille* (often marked by a bracketed intervention in a translation) could be considered defenses against what Derrida here calls hasty translation. And this particular quotation allows me to begin to dream of some solidarity between the suspicion of "essentializing feminine fetishes" and the insistence that we slow down for the bumps in passing from one language to another.

A hasty translation wants to take as little time as possible. If we would resist essentializing, we must take time. Commenting on *Spurs* at the beginning of the eighties, Argyros wrote that "Derrida *is* his prolongation . . . in translation." If translation is prolongation, hasty translation is mistaken. Translation extends Derrida in time. The present essay has been an attempt to translate *Spurs* into the nineties.

Translation in time, however, cannot be translation out of time. In responding to the question "Nietzsche today?" Derrida spoke in, for, and of the era that was 1972. By prolonging *Spurs* into the nineties, I am trying not so much to update it but to date it. Prolonging the passage of translation, I often found reason to linger among what the dictionary calls "archaic." Nietzsche's *"Frauenzimmer"* was (already in the nineteenth century) old-fashioned, which is why one English translator chose to render it with "wench." (And probably why another chose the more contemporary "woman.") The dusty path of *"Frauenzimmer"* led to two "archaic" usages of *"fille,"* one debauched and the other rustic. Momentarily excited by the debauched *"fille,"* I found the rustic definition particularly fertile. For there—out of touch with the modern era, out of step with modern woman—was made plain the assumption that a *"femme"* was someone married to a man. To lean thus upon the archaic is to recognize that language exists in time, that it carries a history in it, and that in it we can read traces not just of its history but of history.

The refrain of anti-essentialism has moved feminism to a slow dance with history. Where, in the seventies, we hastily scanned history for "woman," filtering out local differences, now we try to attend precisely to those local differences, describing the varying situations of women in place and time. Nineties feminism is the context where we must see that "women" (or some close equivalent of that word in other languages) is defined differently at different moments of the language. Vocabulary carries traces of how actual living females were defined, constrained, considered, and treated. For example, historians of the British Victorian period have called our attention to the sexualized class identities marked by words like "lady" and "female," so that we cannot blithely speak of "women" in that period as if there were any group defined solely by gender. Not to deny differences between the English and the German in the late nineteenth century, still, one might assume similar assumptions are operative in Nietzsche's context. Although I do not have the knowledge of German language and history to pursue the connotations of Nietzsche's various terms for "women," I hoped here to open up the possibility of reading his vocabulary not only as the creative choices of a singular genius but also, because it is language, as necessarily part of a sociolect, inflected by communal understandings which he might take for granted, but which become visible through passage to another language or another time.

In our U.S. context, feminists have learned not only that race was intrinsic to the definition of a "lady" in the nineteenth century but, perhaps more painfully, that it functioned likewise to define the "woman" who was liberating herself in the 1970s. The latter is part of the recognition that seventies feminism was functioning in history, that we not only envisioned a future but also spoke in archaicisms. The critique of our "essentializing fetishes" has led us to historicize but has not made us less anxious about our own inevitable embedding in history. Not only is "woman" not a timeless universal, but neither are feminists: we cannot be endlessly up-to-date.

Facing Ellen I recognize that I teach in time. How do we transmit our learning in history? When we recognize that knowledge is not timeless and unchanging? In the seventies my feminist certainties were shook up by something I would call learning in an encounter with something we might call Derrida. I fantasize that Derrida might have had similar encounters with what he calls Nietzsche. And that would be why he would want to transport Nietzsche into 1972, into dialogue with seventies feminism. Most of what I have to teach I might have learned from Derrida, whom I read for the first time in 1972. If I would teach what as a seventies feminist I learned from *Spurs*, I must for the moment transmit it in the nineties.

In 1992 I saw Ellen while I read *Spurs*. Ellen prized *Spurs* for the way it put seventies feminism in its place. I wanted to "show her," by putting *Spurs* in its place, showing how behind it was from the point of view of nineties feminism. Derrida seemed suddenly out of it, stuck on a single, binary notion of sexual difference when we could see multiple sexual differences all around. Did I make Derrida look old-fashioned in order to appear up-to-date myself?

Spurs today? Derrida's timely intervention called into question a certain essentializing of woman in seventies feminism. No longer in that era, we can see that, however much it questioned seventies "woman," *Spurs* was not beyond what it questioned but in engagement with it, sharing the assumption that, in thinking about women, what we since have called gender was the only pertinent category and that the only difference that was sexual was the distinction male/female.

This dates *Spurs*. To read Derrida as if he were writing outside of history would not only put him in the position of timeless master, but also and in the same gesture render him obsolete. Derrida took pains to date his text and I want to read rather than erase those marks. He wrote in, for, and of the era marked by the word "woman," and I want to read that word as the mark of an era.

Notes

1. Originally entitled "La Question du style," the paper was first published in the proceedings of that colloquium, *Nietzsche Aujourd'hui?, V. 1 Intensites* (Paris: Union Generale d'Editions (Collection 10/18), 1973), 235–87. In 1976, retitled *Eperons: Les styles de Nietzsche*, the paper was republished as a book in four languages—the original French alongside translations into Italian, English, and German (Venice: Corbo e Fiore Editori). The French version alone was published as a book in 1978 by Flammarion. The French and English versions from the 1976 four-language edition were published in 1979 by the University of Chicago Press as *Spurs: Nietzsche's Styles/Eperons: Les Styles de Nietzsche*. The English translation by Barbara Harlow for the 1976 four language edition reappears in the 1979 American bilingual edition. All references, unless otherwise noted, will be to the 1979 bilingual edition. Cited as S

2. Nietzsche, *The Gay Science*, 363, quoted in *Spurs*, 154–55, n. 9/14.

3. Derrida, *Spurs*, 96. The numbering of the paragraphs is in the French text as

well as the Italian and German translations; it is oddly omitted from the English translation (see 1976, 76–77).

4. Alexander Argyros, "Daughters of the Desert," *Diacritics* 10, 3 (Sept. 1980), 33.

5. Alice Jardine, *Gynesis: Configurations of Woman and Modernity* (Ithaca: Cornell University Press, 1985), 193 n. 64.

6. Advertisement for *The Ballad of Little Jo*, by Maggie Greenwald, 1993.

7. Jardine, *Gynesis*, 184–85. Italicization and brackets, Derrida's. Harlow adds the French quotation marks to her translation of the italicization. The word "époque" appearing twice in this passage is the same found in the earlier *"La 'femme'—le mot fait époque."*

8. I am grateful for discussion with Marcus Bullock, of the University of Wisconsin at Milwaukee German department, about Nietzsche's various words for "women." Marcus is not responsible for my inevitable misuses of the observations on these words he so generously shared with me.

9. The 1979 French/English edition of *Spurs* is divided into thirteen sections, each headed by a title. The title of the section which ends with *"Frauenzimmer "* is "Veils/Sails"; the next section is called "Truths." In the 1978 French edition, each section begins on a new page and the section titles appear in the running heads. Here in the monolingual edition the sections are chapters, perhaps in order to make the paper into a "book." The sections are in neither the 1976 four-language edition nor the original 1973 publication of *"La Question du style."*

10. The English translation makes it hard to follow Derrida's emphasis on the verb *"prendre."* This verb appears for the German *"einnehmen"* in the quoted French translation of Nietzsche. The quoted English translation of Nietzsche renders *"einnehmen"* with "win," but the English translation of Derrida uses "pin down" (and a bit later, "capture") for *"prendre,"* making it difficult to catch Derrida's repetition of Nietzsche's verb. The simplest English equivalent of *"prendre"* would be "take."

Flirting with the Truth   2

Derrida's Discourse with 'Woman' and Wenches

Ellen K. Feder and Emily Zakin

> If woman is truth, she at least knows that there is no truth, that truth has no place here, and that no one has a place for truth. And she is woman precisely because she herself does not believe in truth itself, because she does not believe in what she is, in what she is believed to be, in what she thus is not.

Jacques Derrida, *Spurs*

Supposing masculine philosophy didn't conceptualize truth as 'Woman,' what then? Might not both women and truth have escaped the violent duels which erupt in pursuit of the possession of these objects of desire? In *Beyond Good and Evil*, the interrogative metaphor suggested by Nietzsche—"Supposing truth is a woman?"—is directed toward a critique of ontological dogmatism. Similarly, when Derrida recapitulates this metaphor by inverting its terms—"if woman is truth . . ."—he endeavors to provide a critique of consolidated identity. Derrida's inversion bespeaks his recognition that gender identity is always, already implicated in essentializing ontological claims. Philosophic discourse constitutes femininity as inessential, as a lack which indicates women's inadequacy before its dictates, but the discourse thereby becomes dependent upon this alterity. By determining women's identities to be derivative of an already circumscribed masculine subjectivity, equated with the universal human position, philosophy is itself predicated upon the very process of othering that it regulates. As a truth-determining enterprise fueled by masculine reliance upon the feminine, logocentrism must be understood always, already to be phallogocentrism. Phallogocentrism thus presupposes the lack by which it is supported and which it must veil in order to maintain the semblance of stability and closure. Once claims to ontological certitude are revealed to be reliant upon this concept of femininity, the position of femininity within ontological discourse may have the capability to undermine the axioms which found logocentrism.[1] Yet, if woman is truth, then truth is castrated.[2]

Metaphysics and the Exchange of Women

If 'Woman' *is* truth, but also the inessential, truth is both grounded in her identity, and released from any grounding, paradoxically making it possible to end the coherence of woman and truth with one another. Derrida's critique of logocentrism in *Spurs* capitalizes on this paradox by reinvoking the equation of truth and woman. By casting 'Woman' as the one who "knows that there is no truth, that truth has no place, and that no one has a place for truth," Derrida shows that "if woman is truth," she has no truth (S 53). Nietzsche's metaphor collapses in upon itself: truth cannot be possessed and identity cannot be fixed. The metaphor of "Woman as truth" therefore not only inscribes but also undermines phallogocentrism. Derrida's metaphor challenges the logocentric history of philosophy by exploiting the instabilities which reside in the insistence on and enforcement of sheer opposition without regard to gradation or variation.

In tracing the implications of a truth which is gendered feminine, while its possessors are gendered masculine,[3] *Spurs* exposes the girders which bolster an apparently self-supporting system. That "the history (of) truth (is) a process of propriation," indicates the imbrication of this process with the history of sexual difference which it inaugurates and by which it is supported. Derrida clarifies this relation by noting that "not only is propriation a sexual operation, but before it there was no sexuality" (S 111). With this seemingly fantastic locution, Derrida suggests that sexual difference is nothing but the naturalized (i.e., symbolic) division of society into two distinct groups, of which one, women, is exchanged in order to sediment the symbolic organization of the other, men.[4] Sexual difference therefore depends upon propriation and the sexual dimension of propriation signifies that truth is inseparable from the dynamics of sexual domination. Derrida's aim is to dislocate truth from the duality and violence of sexual categories hypostatized by a system of meaning that requires unitary identity from its subjects. We can conclude that for this endeavor to succeed, the reliance of sexuality on propriation, i.e., the exchange of women, must be undercut. *Spurs* draws its force from this betrayal of sexual violence. Such a reconfiguration would depend in turn upon portraying the gap between women and femininity, the disjuncture where in feminine "style" can occur. This latter is a necessary element in undoing women's status as an exchange value because it is this disjunctive possibility that clarifies the notion of 'Woman' as an ontological deceit, that is, as factitiously substantive. At stake therefore in both the deconstructive project and women's stylizations is the status of the normative insistence on a world composed only and always of men and women.[5]

The opposition between man and woman relies upon the prior assumption of a necessary connection between woman and femininity. If femininity is conceived as a natural and necessary emanation of a pre-discursive and essential identity (i.e., woman), then it becomes reasonable to suppose that this primordial identity is opposed to that of man who would instead emanate a masculine (or human) character. But, as *Spurs* and *The Gay Science* make clear, women may or may not behave in a manner characterized as feminine. If women fail to embody feminine habits, or conversely, if women successfully appropriate feminine traits, the presumptive status of gender as preceding and underlying our subjectivity is incontrovertibly sullied. We can instead recognize gender as an accomplishment.[6] Acting like a woman, as a woman is enjoined to act, betrays the possibility that we may accede to or refuse roles designated us. Such dramatization of femininity (i.e., women acting like women) reveals precisely that the roles are *designated*, and not natural, that women are not simply tied to their identites. Once the causal link between woman and femininity is broken, the opposition between woman and man is also shown to be neither natural nor essential. If the normative relationship between gender and sexual role-play can be effectively subverted through a recognition that the relation *as* normative is not natural, but rather naturalized, then the stronghold of logocentric discourse is also undermined.

Within the dominant hierarchies, it remains an imperative for women to become feminine, even while such an injunction reveals the divergence between woman and femininity.[7] The norm is at odds with itself, wanting to be a natural law, but working as a regulatory ideal whose power resides in convincing its subjects to *act as though* it were a natural law. In taking itself as ineluctable, the ideal of sexual difference ontologizes the identity of every gendered person. Laws of subject formation, which produce substantive identity, demand that we assume the mantle of a coherent gender. Derrida casts light upon this mandatory assignation:

Although there is no truth in itself of the sexual difference in itself, of either man or woman in itself, all of ontology nonetheless, with its inspection,

appropriation, identification and verification of identity, has resulted in a concealing, even as it presupposes it, this undecidability. (S 103–5; see also 139)

Metaphysics is grounded upon, at the moment it obscures, a lawless abyss,
a discrepancy whose correlative activity is characterized by what Derrida
calls style, the enactment or representation of dissonant possibilities. Such
dissonance sabotages any notion of a substantive identity by signalling the
refusal of diverse particularities to be subsumed under the predicate of
identity. It is from this discord that deconstruction takes its cue, revealing
the abyssal structure of any ontological order, whose work it is to erect
bridges over what is undecidable.[8]

The appearance of an opposition between man and woman is an effect of
ontological categories which, despite their inadequacy in containing identity within their borders, nonetheless succeed in characterizing sexual difference as a binary relation. We might then understand sexual difference, as
Nietzsche understood subjectivity, as a grammatical structure[9] which
appears to ineluctably form our gendered identities. This is not to suggest
that such a structure is merely nominal in character. Indeed, it enacts a
material violence and brutality in the very constitution of our selves. The
reified category of 'Woman' has operated historically to circumscribe
women's lives and maintain our devalued status within patriarchal hierarchy. But it does indicate that discursive categories ground and foster our
identifications, hailing us as gendered beings.[10]

Flirting with 'Woman'

Spurs uncovers the tension between the undecidability of gender on the one
hand, and its monolithic realization on the other. Derrida's analysis challenges the structural apparatus that sustains the reproduction of patriarchy.
Nonetheless, the style of *Spurs* clearly betrays its masculine signature, and
thereby participates in this reproduction. By addressing itself to those similarly positioned (i.e., men), *Spurs* rehearses patriarchal privilege. Throughout Derrida's discourse, there is a reliance on, and an invitation to the
unidentified "one," the subject-position of he who theorizes 'Woman.' As
such, it is a discourse which makes insecure any woman's position as its
interlocutors, while also securing Derrida's privilege to ask "the question of
woman." While both Nietzsche's original metaphor and Derrida's variation
on it destabilize the idea of an essential woman, and therefore of truth, we
must ask whether the position of women remains where it has always been:
in the service of masculine philosophy. Any feminist reading of Derrida
depends on attending to this question. To evade it means to risk recapitula-

tion to our traditional role as tools of philosophical analysis, central as its objects of discourse, yet marginal as its subjects. Insofar as *Spurs* participates in this history and positions women at the margins, its women readers are themselves cast as peripheral to the conversation. In order to determine our own position, we must engage in liminal combat with the authorial power that displaces us, aiming to undermine its dominion. If we therefore fail to put the question of feminine service to the text, we have no meaningful position from which to read it. This suggests that the question is solicited by the text itself: *Spurs* interpellates us as such interlocutors. We can then infer that *Spurs* is structured by its own ambivalence toward women, both locating us at the margins of its discourse and summoning us to challenge that positioning.

We aim to distill from Derrida's text its feminist potential to dismantle gender, but also to indicate Derrida's own lapse into a masculinist appropriation of women through recourse to 'Woman.' We will argue both that 'Woman' *is* the mechanism by which Derrida deconstructs the solidity of gender categories, and that this utilization of 'Woman,' integral to Derrida's project, is also necessarily a recapitulation of masculine violence, making of 'Woman' an object of exchange between men.[11] Derrida joins the discourse of masculine philosophy in order to undermine its terms; but in taking advantage of 'Woman,' he cannot help but remain within the fraternal circuit of reproduction even as he renders it apparent. So, although his appropriation of 'Woman' is not the same as his predecessors', it does not entail substantially different effects.

Perhaps we can characterize the distinction between the positions of Derrida and of metaphysics as one between flirting and seduction. Nietzsche makes clear the attitude of traditional philosophy toward women: the aim of philosophy is winning the wench, capturing truth, and truth therefore, like 'Woman', is the prize of seduction. Derrida assumes a different attitude toward both truth and woman, recognizing instead both truths and women, no longer symbols to be exchanged, but parries with which to interrupt symbolic circulation. Under Derrida's gaze, woman and truth lose the singularity demanded by those who would possess them; they are not functions of "the process of *propriation* (appropriation, expropriation, taking, taking possession, gift and barter, mastery, servitude, etc.)" (S 109), by which Derrida characterizes metaphysics. Derrida does not view women as conquests; his aim is not possession. If masculine and feminine identities have been inscribed through the relation of ownership (possession and barter), then the evasion of ownership, the refusal of the role of seducer, might also undermine those fixed identities. In these circumstances, it may be possible for women and truths to emerge from behind the ontological veil which obscures multiplicity and difference in the production of identity. This non-proprietary stance is precisely what marks Derrida's discourse as flirtatious rather than seductive.

Flirting positions women differently than does seduction. Where the levity of flirting could entail a suspension of established binary categories into which men and women fit in matters sexual, e.g., those of active/passive, seduction on the contrary is always presumptuous in its ascription of a symmetrical desire just waiting to be elicited.[12] In fact, it is often convenient for the seducer to read woman as the one who seduces. If a man is enchanted by a woman, it is because of "her beguiling song of enchantment." If a man is spellbound by a woman, it is because of the "spell of her fascination" (S 49). His attraction is a sign of *her* desire; she is singing the siren's song, casting a spell. Women are seen to exhibit desire, to seduce, by virtue of their femininity, i.e., their castration or lack (S 61). In this way, men disclaim responsibility for their own desire; they are seduced by her charms. Derrida might call such an ascription an "abduction" of woman (S 141), imprisoning her in the role of seducer. Such an abduction effectively conceals the masculine propriation of woman by inverting the terms of possession: *she* asked for it, *she* is master. Similarly, as we have seen, the propriation of truth makes truth into a temptress, so alluring the philosopher cannot resist taking her.

Faced with seduction, and its concomitant assignation of her desire, women must either fulfill the expectations of another or suffer the obloquies which put into question their ability to fulfill such expectations; in other words, women have only the binary possibilities of "yes" or "no" in response to the other's desires, and the latter is never recognized as legitimate, since a desired woman has already by definition exhibited her own desire. Moreover, success in seduction confirms men's masculinity insofar as it proves their potency and right to possession. It affirms and substantiates the ontological order of sexuality so that each is assured that "everything is in its place and all is right with the world."

Flirting suspends this ontological security provided by seduction. Indeed, in Derrida's text, flirting is designed to undermine the gravity of philosophic pursuit and capture. In the initial stages of *Spurs*, the text moves back and forth between the representation of 'Woman' and the question of style. While the former is regarded by Derrida as the antithesis of style in its pretensions to demarcate and close the borders of identity, the latter is conceived as illuminating and opening its horizons. Derrida takes on the elements of metaphysics (Woman, veils, distances). He deflects their use in the service of 'that which goes without saying' by beguiling them into confessing themselves affectations assumed by poseurs of the real. The graceful maneuvers by means of which flirtation sustains active exchange do not demand the assumption of preordained positions. By contrast, the rigid script of seduction successfully exhorts its participants into ready-made positions of activity and passivity, where "woman's appearance takes shape according to an already formalized law" (S 109). Flirting forestalls this fetishization of gender by playing with seduction in such a way as to continually defer it. Its aim is not a teleological satisfaction, but simply to enjoy the game of desire.

However, the danger of flirting is not forgotten in *Spurs*: Derrida might be read as a seducer, just another masculinist philosopher trying to get at Truth. As he says, "it is impossible to resist looking for her" (S 71). The danger is in fact twofold, corresponding to the possibilities of "yes" and "no" that seduction offers. On the one hand, Derrida will have seduced us, as readers, convinced us of his truth, that Derrida is right and now we have it. Derrida, in his critique of Nietzsche, anticipates this potential of flirting to slip into seduction, allured by woman's "captivating inaccessibility, the ever-veiled promise of her provocative transcendence" (S 89), and thus reconstituting the singular Truth he had aimed to deconstruct. At the same time he recognizes that deconstruction, too, must entail risks in order not to assume its own ontological security; he needs to meet the challenge of this danger in order to deflect it. On the other hand, Derrida will not have seduced us. We will walk away, not only not seduced, but not interested, refusing the game. The danger here is that the ontological predicates of gender identification will go unchallenged, and hence unchanged, because they are taken too seriously. Once Derrida has been read as a seducer, danger cannot be avoided.

This possibility necessitates that we be attentive to the status of *Spurs'* women readers. We also are in danger. The dangers women confront correspond to those Derrida faces. On the one hand, we might be seduced; in this circumstance, it is possible to mistakenly assume that if the category of 'Woman' has no ontological validity, neither does it have political efficacy. To err on this account, to assert that there are no women,[13] is to refuse to acknowledge that in our society, things happen to women because they are women, and is instead to revert, unreflectively, to the neutral and universal subject. On the other hand, we might not be seduced; we will over-invest in identity and dismiss Derrida on this basis. This investment may reify the ontological stasis which subjects us as women. When *Spurs* is read by women, it is therefore a dangerous interaction for all concerned.

Though flirting is not seduction, it carries similar risks. As a deferral of seduction, it continues to participate in the sexual meanings necessarily constituted by the system of gender difference, grounded inevitably in the presumption of heterosexual desire. In spite of the possibilities for flirting to evade confirming binary categorization, Derrida's flirtatious stance nonetheless (re)constitututes Derrida's masculinity and continues to inter-pellate women as objects of desire. Thus, it is in his own reproduction that Derrida makes clear the heterosexuality of masculine philosophy, from which his own cannot be excluded. Insofar as heterosexuality remains com-pulsory, its categories constrain any attempt to locate oneself beyond them.[14] In other words, any serious attempt to destabilize the categories of sexual difference would require that it be aimed at the systematization of heterosexuality in order to undermine the basis for those categories. Der-rida's project remains libidinally heterosexual because he retains an implicit commitment to male access to women: Derrida still wants to do it, but he wants to do it in style. This project thereby also forces its women readers into a heterosexual model of desire: *Spurs* does not allow us to conceptual-ize women among ourselves.[15]

Given these considerations, certain questions become salient. First, con-cerning Derrida: does, or to what extent does, *Spurs* constitute Derrida as breaking out of this matrix which positions him as seducer? Even if he is no longer interested in winning the wench, nor even in seducing her, is it pos-sible for him to renounce the patriarchal pleasure of exchange? Second, concerning women: can women surmount the dangers of reading this text? What are women to make of *Spurs* if we are the objects of its exchange?

These questions necessitate that we theorize our own position. We have entered men's discourse on woman, but in what way? Are we its objects? Or are we its interlocutors? It seems clear that we are both. 'Woman' is that con-cept which is bandied about by men in the conversation of philosophy. Truth is what is sought: "winning the wench." Yet 'Woman' and wench are not commensurate terms; they may in fact be in tension with one another, a tension which corresponds to that between idea and matter. When Niet-zsche calls truth a wench, he is ridiculing dogmatic philosophers by ridicul-ing their object of desire. Dogmatists think they seek the pristine concept but cannot help but to chase after the dirty bodies of wenches. At the same time, wenches are what evade philosophy. Embodied, they resist character-ization as conceptual tools, and so always fail to adequately render 'Woman' incarnate. Nietzsche's metaphor, "truth is a woman," is both a denigration of dogmatic philosophers' quest and a revaluation of worldly truths, i.e., truths enacted in the profusion of material existence. In this guise, truths are not objects to be had, but rather forces which do not admit of conceptual reifi-cation. These truths are wenches in their refusal to be taken or exchanged. Nietzsche's own identification of philosophy's objects as wenches and as 'Woman' affords us a doubled entrée into the masculine conversation that is

Spurs. We must be duplicitous in our reading, inhabiting the Trojan horse of 'Woman' in order to steal inside the gates of the textual economy and emerge as wenches. Our emergence disrupts this economy, founded as it is in the exchange of women. We therefore interrogate *Spurs* from this dual perspective.

We have structured our interrogation to disclose the possibilities of two kinds of feminine play operative in *Spurs*, one which has its "proper place," and the other which subverts the propriety of the essentialized meaning which determines that place. In scrutinizing established metaphors both for their mythologized content and for their implosive potential, we seek to comprehend both women's systemic oppression as it is perpetuated through philosophic discourse, as well as the redemptive possibility inherent in the ambiguity of metaphor. Metaphor can transform predetermined meaning, pushing us beyond thought circumscribed by binary arrangements.[15] To engage in metaphorical discourse is to make an is/is not identity claim, i.e., it is at once to say that there is a significant and particular connection between the subject and predicate of a metaphorical association, and it is to deny the ontological validity of this connection. When, for instance, one asserts that "Truth is a Woman," there is contained in this statement both a declaration of identity and a repudiation of such. It is thus only and precisely within ambiguity (rather than identity) that metaphor has meaning. The effect of asserting that 'truth is a woman' is to disembody *women* in rendering *her* singular—'Woman'—and so of symbolic use. By condensing the two terms in a statement of equality, women are occluded. This produces a tension demanding release. The equivocation present in *The Gay Science* between the metaphor of the "shadow" and that of the "body" of 'Woman' plays upon a similarly stressed dehiscence, as we will argue. The shadow of 'Woman' obfuscates the bodies of wenches.

Veils and Sails

Spurs displaces the metaphor of 'Woman' in a gesture which juxtaposes 'Woman' with "the feminine" and thereby destabilizes the mythological conceptualization of women within philosophical discourse. By approaching *The Gay Science* in this manner, Derrida is able to be both critical of Nietzsche's misogyny and redemptive of his playful affirmation of the feminine. We will begin by illustrating some of Nietzsche's aphorisms and developing them in a Derridean manner. Pivotal to this task is the explication of the relationship, in Nietzsche's text, between the metaphors of sail and veil, whose meanings are better exemplified, for Derrida, in the ambivalence of the French word, *voile*, which means either or both (veil and sail).

Among the aphorisms concerning women in *The Gay Science*, Derrida takes up and discusses in conjunction, numbers sixty, "Women and their action at a distance," and sixty-four, "Skeptics." The former envisions Nietzsche as artist embroiled in and overwhelmed by the "lowest depths," the immediacy of "the waves at his feet," the nearness of the "earth-shaking beat" (Nietzsche 1974, §60). This imagery represents for him the horror and immanence of daily life. "Then, suddenly," he writes, "as if born out of nothing, there appears before the gate of this hellish labyrinth, only a few fathoms away—a large sailboat, gliding along as silently as a ghost." Here, Nietzsche speculates, lies "my happier ego, my second, departed self." Elusive and illusive, this ghost in the distance glides away. This is the ghost of 'Woman,' the enchanted one who seems to promise men transcendence, or even deliverance from life. Nietzsche, too, is tempted by her "magic," but resists the desire to succumb to the spells of metaphysics. In these shadowy realms, "the magic and most powerful effect of women is, in philosophical language, action at a distance." Here 'Woman' acts as a shadow of herself in the service of philosophy.

Nietzsche also writes of a different woman. Aphorism number sixty-four, "Skeptics" makes oblique reference to aphorism number fifty-nine, "We artists," in which the beloved woman is always also the materially repulsive woman, whose vulva, or "pudendum" is veiled as "a matter of decency and shame" (Nietzsche 1974, §64). This act constitutes a veiling of truth as well, reflecting that "they [the old women] consider the superficiality of existence its essence" (§64), and find more value in frivolity than in woman's "natural functions." Nietzsche, with these old women, "looks contemptuously at nature" (§59) and, as artist and as lover "prefer[s] not to think of all this" (§59): although the proximity of woman's materiality is present, the veil proves sufficient in rendering it absent. The gruesome and excessive proximity of woman is perceived as repulsive from the lover's viewpoint because her "physiology" would reveal that she is "something more than soul and form" (§59), and she herself must then learn to make of her body a shadow.

We have seen in these aphorisms two distinct uses of 'Woman,' one as ideational shadow, the other as embodied excess. From afar, the philosopher may dream of the invitation into the supersensible realm which she extends to him; too close, the philosopher dreads the immersion into the hypersensible which her body presents and insists upon. This play of distance and proximity, this dissemblance of "*des voiles*" (S 37), partakes of sails and veils; that which conceals, pushes one forward, just as that which is concealed, recedes into the distance. The veil that conceals is at once the sail that moves into other realms, just as that which is concealed by the veil is that which is left in the sail's wake. "'Truth' and 'Woman' each function in this way. The metaphor of woman is thus both a veil and a sail. It is relevant to remark at this point that in the French, *des voiles* is gendered: veil is masculine, while sail is feminine. Accordingly, the male philosopher "covers" the woman, and the woman gets him off. This disjuncture takes 'Woman' twice: she is both veiled and sailed. In concealing the materiality of woman, her metaphorical abuse allows the discourse of philosophy to continue, but insofar as women are concealed, we are left behind by philosophy, rendered absent, even as our image serves its purposes.

The apparent fissure effected by this counter-metaphysical maneuver positions women in a double-bind: whether we are shadows or bodies, we are figured as that against which Nietzsche formulates his critique of philosophical dogmatism. Nietzsche is repelled by the body of woman and attracted to the shadow of truth, yet he recognizes this temptation as the lure of a transcendent metaphysics and so resists it. Nietzsche seeks to escape the pursuit of Truth, moving beyond its metaphysical promise captured in the opposition contained in the figure of woman. This flight from metaphysics, while not remaining within the same terms of sexual difference, nonetheless reinscribes in a new configuration the sexualized metaphor that degrades the feminine. Derrida takes up the Nietzschean operation in order to expose the way in which Nietzsche continues to rely upon the degradation of woman embedded in his metaphors. Representations of woman tend to bifurcate woman in untenable ways. But women are neither the conceptual essences signified by ghosts, nor the natural functions that characterize her as an excessive body, nor some combination of the two; women are, as *Spurs* reveals, undecideable. Therein lies the possibility of evading these categories that prefigure us.

Desire and Dogmatism

The metaphorical linkage between truth and woman epitomized in Nietzsche's query, "supposing truth is a woman—what then?" (Nietzsche 1968, 192; S 55) casts suspicion upon both insofar as they operate as concepts within philosophy. Dogmatic philosophers speculate about Truth in such a way that the ontological presuppositions of their search remain veiled, thus preserving the "integrity" of their pursuit. Their inquiries concerning an underlying Reality necessitate a conception of Truth which would be its absolute representation. This metaphysical undertaking is productive of power precisely because it naturalizes the effects of an interpretive activity. Truth is as natural as a woman, hard to catch but ultimately attainable, not constituted by philosophy but preceding and conditioning (even demanding) its search. In so positing a world which is self-manifesting, philosophy maintains its ability to grasp Truth. Invoking Woman in his critique of Truth, Nietzsche equates the presumption of an attainable Truth with that of the accessible woman. At the same time he problematizes the relationship, noting that the dogmatists who can't reach the absolute are the same dogmatists who can't get laid. Derrida quotes Nietzsche: "the gruesome earnestness, the clumsy importunity with which they have been in the habit of approaching truth have been inept and improper means for winning a wench" (S 55). Graceless and wholly without finesse, these philosophers project their lack upon women and truth, imagining them to be equally without style. Such grim desires frustrate any possible delight in a proliferation of meanings: illusory mastery prevents the realization of compulsive urges toward uniformity even as it generates them. Additionally, this fantasy naturalizes cultural forms of desire, placing constraints upon the proliferation of meanings for both truths and women, demanding Truth and Woman.

The construction of desire as univocal, as phallic,[17] dictates and delineates who women can be. Women are bound by the masculine economy wherein we are commodified and within which we are "valued." This economy obscures the way in which identity is produced because it assumes identity to be a natural fact; it thus denies the activity of commodification while simultaneously identifying women as commodities, thereby reifying our status as such. The effect of this cultural operation obfuscates the activity of constructing, thus naturalizing itself in the moment of its production by norms of dominance. It takes itself to be given. But if identities are always, already culturally produced, then we must understand the concept of identity itself as an effect of philosophy. This means that to search for or even to "discover" the essential identity of anyone is always already to presuppose the ontological category of substance or essence as determinative of Truth.

It is in the equivocal equation of 'Truth' and 'Woman' that Derrida locates the redemptive possibility in Nietzsche's work for a "new choreography of difference," that is, a new configuration of gender. As Woman's equation with Truth becomes women's equivocation with truths, the central positions of Truth and 'Woman,' as objects of Western philosophy, are displaced. It is no accident that Derrida begins his discussion of "the question of style," with an inverted reproduction of this displacement: He recounts that "The title for this lecture was to have been *the question of style*. However—it is woman who will be my subject" (S 35–37). If philosophy is founded on the othering of Woman, then it must be a displacement which makes of her a subject. In addition, the dual implications of the word "subject" indicate to the reader that Derrida includes himself among those philosophers who make of woman an object even while he renames 'Woman' as subject. This doubled signification disrupts the very place of man as subject: it both assumes responsibility for the historical subjection of women in philosophy and it displaces man as subject of philosophy. Derrida thus recapitulates a Nietzschean move, making subjectivity itself his subject and thereby throwing it into question.

The idea of the subject presupposes that of an essential Being hiding beneath all appearances, presenting, as Nietzsche writes:

> all activity as conditioned by an agent—the "subject"... but no such agent exists; there is no "being" behind the doing, acting, becoming; the "doer" has simply been added to the deed by the imagination. (Nietzsche 1956, I §13)

Since the imputation of subjectivity equally posits a divide between subject and object, Nietzsche throws the hypostatized meaning derived from this split also into question. He indicates that meaning is instead active and relational, not a result of the instrumental operation of a subject upon an object. Meanings are perspectively engaged, but there is no substantive being from which these manifestations emanate. The imputation of substance or subjectivity is the metaphysical activity par excellence.

At the same time, metaphysics has traditionally characterized "Woman" as the inessential (the Other), casting Man as the determining agent of identity, as he who philosophizes through her. Man fantasizes that he possesses the phallus: that he can therefore possess both Truth and 'Woman.' It is precisely his belief in this phallic possession which obscures the phantasmatic basis of his entitlement claims (to both Truth and 'Woman'). Yet, if in this discourse 'Woman' is ontologically (i.e., substantively) characterized as the inessential, might we not find in this reification the very possibility for women's escape from this conceptual construct? There is clearly a paradox in essentializing the inessential, reifying it. From this impossible positioning, women might devise other unthinkable matrices within which to engage in emancipatory thought and practice. Since 'Woman's proper place cannot be occupied without contradiction, it is an identity which fragments itself, and hence cannot be represented within the system which takes identity logic as its basis. Derrida suggests that this is so in his claim that

> That which will not be pinned down by truth is, in truth—*feminine*. This should not, however, be hastily mistaken for a woman's feminin*ity*, for female

sexual*ity*, or for any other of those essentializing fetishes which might still tantalize the dogmatic philosopher, the impotent artist or the inexperienced seducer who has not yet escaped his foolish hopes of capture. (S 55)

It is not that 'Woman' is essentially inessential; 'Woman's inessential character is not our Truth. Rather, what is inessential is 'Woman'—the idealized image of women—and metaphysical Truth, the very foundations of dogmatic philosophy, the substantive metaphors through which philosophy takes place. In affirming the inessential, Derrida affirms the "feminine," that which designates the "untruth of Truth" (S 51). The Truth which we know to be untrue is the possessive illusion that both results from and gives rise to castration anxiety, the insecurity through which patriarchy is maintained. But, Derrida writes, "Woman knows that castration does not take place" (S 61).

In this thesis, Derrida makes use of a Lacanian vocabulary wherein 'Woman' figures castration and lack. Lacan has contended that the masculine Symbolic (which is the only Symbolic) is premised upon the castration anxiety which brings the male child to the closure of his Oedipal Complex and to his submission to the Law, identifying with the Father and deferring (but not renouncing) possession of women and phallic access. But castration anxiety is the belief that the phallus can be taken away which is in turn predicated upon the belief that the phallus exists, a belief which is of Imaginary origin. Castration assumes that an ideal wholeness is both possible and present. Motivated by this anxiety, the Imaginary/Symbolic matrix constructs protective barricades, language and laws, which offer the illusion of security. These cultural institutions can be designated as the Symbolic Order, or at least its material form; although the masculine Imaginary is itself illusory (the phallus does not exist), its Symbolic *value* is actually experienced through these structual apparati. It is in the Symbolic that the masculine Imaginary gains meaning and power so that the phallus can appear to exist and men can appear to have it. The Symbolic retrospectively takes up and reconstructs the desire for phallic access in the form of gender identification and division, the constitutive norm of men and women which, once discursively inscribed, is perceived to be necessary. This division is the Symbolic mode of phallic access because it positions women as accessible, as commodities to be traded among men.[18] It is a division between subjects and objects of desire. Through the material power of laws and institutions, illusion constitutes reality, the penis becomes (acts as if it were) the phallus, and the myth is realized. Nietzsche writes in aphorism number sixty-eight, "Will and willingness,"

[I]t is man who creates for himself the image of woman, and woman forms herself according to this image . . . will is the manner of men; willingness that of woman. That is the law of the sexes—truly, a hard law for woman. All of humanity is innocent of its existence; but women are doubly innocent. (Nietzsche 1974, §68)

A correlation is achieved between the reality of social processes and the Symbolic appropriation of the masculine Imaginary, precisely because the phallus is taken to be true and natural and thus its normative consequence for gender does not appear as a regulatory law at all. Man will then be innocent, or ignorant, of this law because it is the acceptance of its analytic truth, the very acceptance which obscures its normativity, that allows him to feel secure in the world ordered by this same law, to feel certain he is not castrated.

Woman, however, is "doubly innocent": within patriarchy, she shares with man the everyday ignorance of the Law of the Father, which is exerted equally over men and women. Both are compelled to follow its dictates concerning their proper role. But the Law operates upon and against *her*; as disenfranchised and exchanged, women are unequally bound by a role which is limited and degraded in a way that man's is not. Both men and women are thrown into this world where the Law is already in effect. In this sense both are its innocents. Yet women's innocence is an achievement gained only through forgetfulness, a displacement of the conviction that she could be "other-wise." Her innocence is doubled because it is an effort of effacement, an effort not exacted from men.

The Masquerade of Femininity

Derrida claims that in a patriarchal society produced through men's fear of castration, women's playful knowledge that men do not, in fact, possess the phallus, and therefore cannot be castrated, is a form of power. This is the power of dissimulation.[19] It takes two forms. In the first, which we will designate the masquerade of femininity, dissimulation conceals or veils what is (not), depicting essential femininity. We understand this play as a necessary function of women's survival, one which all women enact. Derrida describes this process in a positive light, valuing the laughter within necessity:

She who, unbelieving, still plays with castration, she is 'woman.' She takes aim and amuses herself with it as she would with a new concept or structure of belief, but even as she plays she is gleefully anticipating her laughter, her mockery of man. (S 61)

Patriarchy requires that women enact ourselves as seductresses, that is, that we play the game of desire while continuing to follow patriarchy's rules. It is in this sense that Derrida says, "unable to seduce or give vent to desire without it, 'woman' is in need of castration's effect" (S 61). Women's play is contingent upon, but not wholly determinable by, the Symbolic order; within this set of given principles, we have a modicum of agency though not of the sort which could transform the customary, hierarchical dominion. This agency then functions within a system of multiplicitous and overlapping imperatives whose very plurality can be negotiated, or perhaps exploited, to establish a measure of self-determination.[20] This masquerade, however, perpetuates the idea that there is something to be unveiled, something behind the pretense, an ontological reality. Its effect is to confirm man's faith in the naturalized order of "that which goes without saying." We might then call this masquerade "artifactual" since it reproduces the myth of substantive femininity as an enduring fact, a found object whose history implies its inevitability, while simultaneously veiling femininity as a product of culture and the result of women's artistic endeavors.

Not all women who assume the habits of femininity in their daily lives do so in a naturalized manner. There are some who are quite aware of the scripted nature of their roles. This does not mean, however, that these women are either automatons, mechanically obeying the dictates of cultural direction, or that they are feminist revolutionaries, writing their own futures. Rather, it testifies to the expression of agency in their lives. A woman dependent upon her husband for economic stability, for example, may be able to manipulate the possibilities within the marriage, while unable to change the terms of the heterosexual contract. In order to secure the material conditions necessary for her relative comfort, she may provide her husband with goods produced in virtue of her femininity. In this manner, such a woman might present herself as the ideal 'Woman' while recognizing her own impersonation, i.e., she might perform her life dramatically, according to the Imaginable range of scripts given her by patriarchy. It is because the Symbolic *value* of the Imaginary is real that this play has not only meaning, but power; her enactment, however, does nothing to subvert the patriarchal order itself. As Nietzsche writes in aphorism number sixty-six, "The strength of the weak,"

All women are subtle in exaggerating their weaknesses; they are inventive when it comes to weaknesses in order to appear as fragile ornaments who are hurt even by a speck of dust. Their existence is supposed to make men feel clumsy and guilty on that score. Thus they defend themselves against the strong and "the law of the jungle." (Nietzsche 1974, §66)

These devices are the medium through which women modulate circumstances so as to sustain ourselves; yet these devices are both a result of and an avenue to women's acclimation to patriarchy, and thus also serve to defend the boundaries of patriarchy, reinforcing its (l)imitations.[21]

The artifactual woman benefits from the script of 'Woman' by exploiting 'Woman's' parasitic relationship with denigrated others. This divison between women has a similar function to that upon which masculine subjectivity relies in constituting itself. It is a division which functions by promoting an image of the "bad" woman as a contrast against which the "good" woman is formulated as a meaningful identity. This process is analogous to that which men engage in advancing the image of 'Woman.' In either case, the dualism produced corresponds to that which philosophy produces between the shadow and the body of women: 'Woman' serves a conceptual function, while 'bad' women figure materially. The woman who appears to adequately represent 'Woman' shores up her identity by observing and enforcing categorial boundaries at the expense of those women who are determined as failing at such representation. In this way, the conceptual ghost of 'Woman' is contained; she reinforces the demarcation of borders. She will assume her "proper place."

Because the artifactual woman presents the facsimile of 'Woman,' her practices do not offer a critique of masculine dogmatism, but rather confirm and sustain the metaphysical project by veiling the scripted nature of her enactment and reifying it as essence. Her alignment with 'Woman' thereby goes unchallenged, and furthermore consolidates the notion of a knowable feminine identity. Her exploitation of 'Woman' is thus complicit in a kind of conceptual violence whose effects are evidenced in the very formulation of her own identity. She recapitulates herself as the relic or remnant of metaphysics.

The Artificial Woman

By reenacting the same old scripts, the artifactual woman, as actress, accepts the direction of another; there is however, another enactment, that of the artificial woman. This second form of dissimmulation both conceals and reveals (veils/unveils) what is (not), privileging neither moment. Without teleologically tending toward revelation, she reveals that there is "nothing" to be revealed: if "nothing" is revealed, there is "nothing" to conceal. This artifice enacts the multiplicitous potentialities of identity. In refusing to be pinned down, its practitioner evades categorization; she is, as Derrida writes, "no-where" (S 121). This play of identity, unlike the paradigm of which we spoke above, might thus possess the gift of destabilizing the phallic order, ridiculing in its activity the Truth of the essential Subject. Refusing to participate in any drama which relies on the essential equilibrium of the given Order, which merely simulates an already determined identity, this second style instead fashions the dormant means with which patriarchy might be dissolved. By writing her own scripts, or at least repeating the old ones differently,[22] this woman's creativity is unbounded by propriety or polarity: Derrida writes, "Because woman is (her own) writing, ["*Elle (s')ecrit*"] style must return to her" (S 57). She thus upsets an Order which, rooted as it is in anxiety, is characterized by a poverty of difference; binary oppositions are its specific domain: Man and Woman, Truth and Illusion, Real and Simulation, Self and World, Subject and Object, Form and Matter, Culture and Nature, Identity and Difference. In revaluing the latter halves of these dichotomies, those that have been devalued, the artifical woman invalidates the hierarchies themselves.

Since these customarily regulated classifications appraise the pairs according to criteria which, occuring within the Symbolic, are always, already phallogocentric, that is, already circumscribed by masculine meanings which find identity in oppositional difference, the set of former polarities are always already distinguished as the more significant. Split as these dichotomies are into discrete conceptual halves, the meanings which inhere in the one extreme necessarily condition the other, thus allowing the former to derive their worth from the latter: "Man" as a meaning-laden concept accrues his substantive import in relation to a meaning-deprived Other whose lack of significance is determined by Him. His identity is thus tainted or contaminated by that which is in excess of him; yet, her exclusion enables the containment of those meanings, allowing man to limit his identity to that domain of which he believes himself master.

When this Other, 'Woman' (or other woman) claims significance of her own, that she is not-for-man, the system that propagates her degradation can no longer stand up. Derrida writes:

> The question of the woman suspends the decidable opposition of true and non-true and inaugurates the epochal regime of quotation marks which is to be enforced for every concept belonging to the system of philosophical decideability. The hermeneutic project which postulates a true sense of the text is disqualified under this regime. . . Truth in the guise of production, the unveiling/dissimulation of the present product, is dismantled. (S 107)

The masquerade of the woman that is employed in the first kind of play that we have delineated inevitably reproduces phallic power in a dissimulation which recapitulates the masculine fantasy that no matter how many veils there are, reality, "the feminine woman," lurks underneath. Although this woman knows that the phallus isn't there, she acts as if it were; in this way, her play affirms the masculine ego, assuring him that he really is bigger and better, even if she does, as Derrida says, silently "mock" him (S 61). She presents herself as a mystery, yet verifyies his virility; he is convinced that what lies beneath her masks is properly his. The dogmatic conviction that there exists an authenticity to be attained both bestows a specifically narrow meaning on our world and shores up the foundations upon which anxiety can be kept at bay. Men remain unchallenged in their belief that they possess both the phallus and women, whose access the phallus supposedly guarantees.

The play of the artificial woman, in contrast, enacts a different species of dissimulation. Whereas the first kind of dissemblance functions to preserve masculine Identity, and indeed depends upon this Identity for its own effect, the artificial woman acts to dissolve the imperative of femininity, and masculine identity along with it. In so doing, she threatens the patriarchal Order itself. In refusing to submit to its Law, she both creates and substantiates its inefficacy. This second woman operates in the distance between the Symbolic reality of the phallus and its illusory status. She does not prevaricate; instead, she listens for this neglected space, that between the Man embroiled in his sea of projects and 'Woman' who, from his perspective, is sailing amidst the remote parameters of serenity. She does not accept the meaning of these projected visions, but undoes them by moving closer and then further away, though neither to nor from him, belying the stasis of a reified, quantifiable distance or difference which is always imputed to subtend her Being. Nietzsche describes this movement as an indefinite, non-reifiable distance:

> the delight in [dis]simulation, exploding as a power that pushes aside one's so-called "character," flooding it and at times extinguishing it; the inner craving for a role and mask, for *appearance*; an excess of the capacity for all kinds of adaptations that can no longer be satisfied in the service of the most immediate and narrowest utility. (Nietzsche 1974, §361)

The artifical woman is stylish excess, not mere difference. In her dance the meaning of the binary opposition between man and woman collapses, the absolute fixity of its interval disintegrates. This is the work of the artist, without whose art, Nietzsche writes, "we would be nothing but foreground and live entirely in the spell of that perspective which makes what is closest at hand and most vulgar appear as if it were vast, and reality itself" (§78). Feminine style leads us away from facts, and toward interpretation.

Using the veils in a creative fashion, the artifical woman does not recapitulate the illusion that there is either, on one side a primordial world or on the other, an essential self. While the veils she employs retain meaning, it is meaning she derives within a disrupted structure, since in reconfiguring the meaning, she reconfigures the structure: she changes the rules. In generating a myriad of interpretations and never just one she makes less plausible a system which relies upon One True Reality. It might be said that this artificial woman, like the "stylate spur,"

> rips through the veil. [She] rents it in such a way that it not only allows there the vision or production of the very (same) thing, but in fact undoes the sail's self-opposition, the opposition of veiled/unveiled (sailed/unsailed) which has folded over on itself. (S 107)

This woman acts from "no-where" but in so doing she also brings Man closer to his end, closer to the "no-where" where Man is no longer viable. Metaphysical systems have been predicated upon universal man and particularized woman. With the collapse of this assymetrical dualism, we may at last realize both masculine specificity and the "End of Man,"[23] the end, in other words, of man as universal human. The dispersal of gendered meanings might initiate a feminine Imaginary, a feminine desire, unrecuperated by the masculine Symbolic, a space of overflowing sexualities and the fluidity of multifarious identities.

Remember, the figure who defies capture by the dogmatic philosophers is characterized by Nietzsche as a wench. In confounding the notion of essence by refusing to present herself as substantive, the artificial woman, we must conclude, is a wench. Those who attempt to penetrate her depths will be frustrated in their quest to possess the truth of her. They impute to her an essence circumscribed by their own sense of mastery; but her artifice exceeds their method of inquiry. Incommensurate with the established patterns proper to dogmatic discourse, the artificial woman's style defies the grave project of her suitors. Nevertheless she gathers the material for her play from the (dis)continuous spectrum which lies unacknowledged between the two polarities of Man and 'Woman.' As Nietzsche writes,

> perhaps this is the most powerful magic of life: it is covered by a veil interwoven with gold, a veil of beautiful possibilities, sparkling with promise, resistance, bashfulness, mockery, pity, and seduction. Yes, life is a woman. (Nietzsche 1974, §339)

This magic is the feminine (or perhaps feminist) imaginary. The affirmation of the feminine occurs as women recognize that we have no truth, and moreover that truth is not a thing to be possessed or appropriated. If the feminine is the "in-essential," then there is no transparent gender, there is only dissimulation.

Wenches and the Exploitation of 'Woman'

In spite of Derrida's apparent dislocation of the category of 'Woman,' we must question (again) whether the effect of his discourse favors its characterization as a reinscription of identity logic. And, even if not, even if the displacement of 'Woman' does serve to upset the logocentric order, it may still produce no transformation in women's social and political situation. *Spurs* exposes the Imaginary binaries of Western metaphysics, but this exposure may remain Derrida's end, the "end of man," and not one performed for women's ends.

Spurs begins with Derrida's declaration: "it is woman who will be my subject" (S 37). We have already recognized the dual significance of the subject in this context; she is both the locus for displacement of phallogocentrism and the servant to Derrida's interrogation. Up until this point, we have granted Derrida's success in relying upon the former signification to subvert the latter. But she remains *his* subject: "it is woman who will be my subject," he says. This possessive grammatical form which runs throughout the text prevents Derrida's escape from his own complicity in mastery. Elsewhere in *Spurs*, Derrida writes of "the question of the woman" (S 107). In this instance as well, there is an evasion of the distinction between the question of woman, and women's questions. These latter are, predictably enough, forgotten by the text, displaced by Derrida's own questions. Derrida's instrumental use of woman as a critique of masculinity is thus not unproblematic. Caught within a conversation between men—between, on the one hand, Derrida and Nietzsche, and on the other, Derrida and his colleagues, women's distance can only be exacerbated. With "the feminine" at his disposal, Derrida mocks his fellow man and implicitly invites him to forgo his masculinity. Yet, "such might also be the advice of one *man* to another" (S 49, emphasis ours), as Derrida himself recognizes. Derrida too succumbs to this discourse in which one man initiates another man into a finer intercourse with the world, seeming to ignore the ways in which he is implicated in seduction. Anxiously, Derrida solicits men into a revamped ethics of performativity.

Women have always been exchanged in the service of men's subjectivity. Derrida may simply be offering a new twist on an old theme: he exchanges women in the service of the *deconstruction* of men's subjectivity. As a dealer of these goods, his authorial position remains stable, consistent with that structurally accorded to men. Derrida rests easy with the intransigence of a network of masculine privilege and shared pleasure. Recall that he says of woman, "it is impossible to resist looking for her" (S 71), this locution clearly indicating both that he accepts the male gaze, and furthermore assumes masculine, and not feminine, interlocutors. In so positioning himself, Derrida reveals his own investment in the heterosexual contract, in the exchange value of women as objects. As readers of *Spurs*, women are thus illicit interlocutors, voyeurs, or eavesdroppers on a conversation not meant for our ears. The dual meaning of "subject" hence persists in destabilizing *our* authorial position, while his lingers undisturbed in spite of, or perhaps because of, his efforts to the contrary.

What can we make of Derrida's conclusion, toward the end of *Spurs*, that "woman, then, will not have been my subject" (S 121)? By renouncing "his" subject, Derrida seems to simultaneously surrender his possessive prerogative, and therefore also women's servitude. Women may, after all, escape the bondage of the metaphorical function. Nonetheless, it is for Derrida to grant and then rescind our subjectivity: as objects of exchange, he can take us or leave us, and it is in his interest, at this juncture, to leave us, since *Spurs* is an attempt to dislocate subjectivity as such. Derrida's disavowal of mastery only implicates him in its system all the more since such a disruption of subjectivity could only have genuine efficacy and value in relation to those who have always been subjects. Without this limit to the disorientation of the subject, deconstruction can only ever leave women as it found them: as ghosts or shadows.

Spurs makes apparent the always, already masculine character of subjectivity. Equally clear is that women have a stake in dislocating this subjectivity whose categories exclude women and so operate to constitute men's identities. Such an exclusion means that women cannot but assume their identities as objects. Derrida fails to recognize, however, that there is an alternative to this project of dislocation: to make subjects of women. This recreation of feminine identity would radically transform the very category of subjectivity, parasitic as it has been on an 'Other' pushed outside its boundary. Drafted into the service of masculine identity, the feminine 'Other' has been burdened with the task of supporting the structure which positions men as dominant. In this economy of subjectivity, trafficking in women is the means by which identity is established for both genders. Furthermore, feminine identity, determined as 'Other,' is fixed, i.e., consolidated through the ontological barricades of "nature," so that its induction will be able not only to produce but also to reproduce the effects of rigid gender differentiation. The withdrawal of the 'Other' from this commerce which defines subjectivity could therefore undermine the stability and

universality grounding masculine identity. When women refuse to be determined as objects, we raid the bastion of male subjectivity, plundering its
resources by claiming ourselves. Such a pillaging, if done often enough, by
many women, could evacuate the prevailing category of subjectivity, leaving
a vacuum where women could reconstitute the meaning of subjectivity
itself. In these terms, such reconstitution is clearly not about expanding the
existent category so that it may include or accommodate women. It is rather
about deranging this category so that a proliferation of subjectivity is possible.[24] In other words, to say that women are subjects is not to say that
women are invested in the terms of ideal masculine subjectivity, whose traits
are conceived as unitary, closed, and complete. Such assimilation is pre-
vented by putting into motion the fixity of a devalued 'Other' whose role has
been to support the semblance of clearly drawn boundaries marking identity. Without this 'Other,' a deranged subjectivity would perhaps constitute
multiplicitous subjects who refuse closure in favor of becoming.[25]

This additional recognition of the need to make women subjects provides
us with the means to better put deconstructive analysis to work for feminist
ends. By capitalizing on the instabilities which inhere in any concept—in
this case, subjectivity—deconstuction finds it to depend on that which it
excludes—in this case, the feminine. Derrida recognizes that the relation of
dependence is the reverse of what it had always seemed: Western philosophy
takes women to be a deviation from the norm which is man, and in that
sense sees man as self-sufficient, with woman dependent upon him. Deconstruction demonstrates that it is rather man who is dependent on the
deviance it constructs. This conceptual reliance goes unacknowledged since
the subject claims to support himself, to be independent. But if the concept
of man excludes woman, then it must rely on this exclusion in determining
its boundaries. When therefore the tension native to it is exacerbated, the
concept displaces itself, revealing its undecidability. Men's identities are rent.
The political recognition that women need to be made subjects is thus consistent with Derrida's recognition that the category of universal subjectivity,
i.e., man, is coming to an end. Both undertakings seek to do away with man.
But there is a fundamental distinction to be made: Derrida is exploiting
women's position outside of subjectivity, while we propose that women take
subjectivity for ourselves.

We have characterized this feminist project of reconstituting subjectivity
as an alternative to Derrida's project of dislocating subjectivity. As we have
argued above, to introduce women as subjects is to reconstitute the category
by removing the support of its foundation, and thereby necessitating it be
rebuilt on new ground. We might better say, therefore, that reconstitution is
complementary to dislocation, and in fact implies it. When women become

subjects, the category is shaken, dislocated; similarly, when subjectivity is put at issue, fissures arise which women may exploit to become subjects. We therefore find it necessary to think these endeavors together, and yet certainly they are incongruous with one another: dislocation presumes that the category of subjectivity is so thoroughly tainted with universality and masculinity that it could have no meaning with regard to women; reconstitution implies that the category of subjectivity can be reproduced differently, can be made over by being newly articulated. The one would do away with subjectivity, while the other would rework it. A duplicitous position is thus demanded of us if we are to engage in both ventures.

Let us assume that the reconstitution of subjectivity required if women are to be counted as subjects entails Derrida's project of dislocating subjectivity so that it no longer operates as an oppressive category. We can locate this necessity where it arises at the point on which these dual aims converge: the site of masculine identity. Both projects aim at and work toward the destabilization of this identity in order that "the" subject can no longer exist.[26] However, if masculinity is our target, this means that, like Derrida, feminists must exploit women's position outside of subjectivity in order to take subjectivity: 'Woman' is the only resource for this project, since it is that upon which masculinity depends. The dual perspectives of 'Woman' and wench enable us to conceptualize the nature of this exploitation. The scenario of the Trojan horse offered in our first section suggests the possiblility that 'Woman' can be productively exploited by wenches. As we have already suggested, 'Woman' may be useful as a diversionary tactic allowing wenches to sabotage the masculine economy. In this way, wenches exceed containment or identification by masculine categories through use of 'Woman' to vandalize any prefabricated demarcation. Wenches' material bodies are excessive; they bleed beyond the borders of identity.

For women to exploit the image of 'Woman' is therefore to occupy a position previously exclusive to men, and thereby to undermine the very possibility of women's exploitation. Because it is not conducive to masculine ends, this use of 'Woman' throws into doubt the solidity of men's identities. This occupation of the masculine domain by women operates as the reversal which is the necessary counterpart to any displacement.[27] Our seeming complicity in exploitation must then also be understood as a duplicity: we are the apparent representatives of 'Woman,' it is 'Woman' who we are supposed to be, and yet in taking on that mantle, the wench belies its circumscription of her identity. Her art lies precisely in this dance with the veils of 'Woman.' This veiling/unveiling is an affirmation of the potency of feminine duplicity.

Conclusion

We must conclude that, consonant with his signature, Derrida elides the distinction between women-for-Derrida and women-among-ourselves. In the enforced representation of "the feminine" is suggested once again the gendering of women, and the non-gendering of men, i.e., the gender-neutrality that *is* masculinity. Derrida compels women to bear the burden, metaphorically, for specificity, making "the feminine" of use to philosophy.[28] In so doing, he recapitulates the heterosexual contract within whose terms women remain accessible concepts, rather than desiring subjects. This positioning of women repeats the masculine stance of philosophy, thus reinscribing Derrida as a seducer. Just as the critics of metaphysics are always, already embroiled in metaphysics, so the critics of seduction (the flirters) are always, already embroiled in seduction. Moreover, if Derrida is the "stylate spur," he concedes that violence against women is necessary to his project; he "rips through the veil" (S 107). This renting marks Derrida's own inexorable participation in patriarchal categories. With this metaphor of a spur renting the veil, Derrida identifies style with, or appropriates it to, a masculine endeavor: the laying bare of woman. *Spurs* is therefore not, or not only, an abdication of propriation, insofar as it remains a mode of heterosexual violence.

As we have seen already, this violence derives its force from the metaphorical enchantment with 'Woman.' The ambiguity within which metaphor derives its meaning can be dangerously alienating when it is woman herself who is metaphorized: "Supposing truth is a woman—what then?" (Nietzsche 1968, 192). In this formulation, one is viscerally carried to the experience of truth, but away from the experience of *woman* and, more importantly, away from women's experiencing. Nietzsche admits that "the magic and most powerful effect of women is, in philosophical language, action at a distance" (Nietzsche 1974, §60). Philosophical discourse utilizes 'Woman' most effectively when it makes her magically disappear from consideration. To the extent that women are engaged in this society as images and metaphors, we are mythologized, our existence as women obscured by our appearance as 'Woman'—effaced behind a metaphysical veil.

Derrida claims that 'Woman' acts at a distance because, as metaphor, she acts where she is not: "distance is the very element of her power," because "Woman is but one name for that untruth of truth" (S 49–50). But this assignation can be too easily reconfigured: might not women act as metaphors because as distant from ourselves, we can act only where we are not and cannot be? In Derrida's representation of 'Woman,' women are taken to be the shadows that they cast of themselves, rather than embodied actors. Bartered in the commerce of men, this representation of women maintains our status as objects in their exchange. We might then understand Derrida's redemptive category of "the feminine" as no more than an imaging which, in its recapitulation of philosophy's conceptual appropriation of women, causes the erasure of materially, ethically demanding women and rejuvenates the conceptual metaphysics of 'Woman.'

We are left therefore with a recognition of our own ambivalence toward *Spurs*, unable finally to resolve the tensions within Derrida's text. It has enticed us with its declaration that 'there is no such thing as a woman' (S 101), seeming to free us from the reifying terms of substantive identity. But in being so lured, we have found ourselves entangled in the persistent relegation of women's identities to metaphors, shadows, concepts, and bodies. This philosophic strategy effectively maintains women outside the sphere of subjectivity. Nonetheless, Derrida has revealed the power which resides in the exercise of feminine style. It is this style which we have elaborated and affirmed in the practices of the artificial woman. Through this artifice, women's resistance is expressed, even within the grave categories that circumscribe her possibilities. Herein lies one prospect for a feminine subjectivity. *Spurs* is a work of significance for feminists, but as its readers we must be prepared to reckon with its multiple and seductive dangers, and resist its temptations.

Perhaps it is not inappropriate to end with a reflection on our own collaboration, the "conspired plotting . . . betwixt wom[e]n" (S 83). To ask who wrote this text is to presuppose that there must be a unitary productive force, an originary subjectivity behind all interpretations. Our collaboration has undermined this authorial/authoritative positioning by doubling the signature. When asked, we could not trace the foundation of any given thought or expression in this paper. Neither *one* of us wrote it. And yet, we certainly would not want to say that it was written through us, as though we were mere vessels for the stylus; we were not passive receptacles for the word, nor was our writing active in the sense of arising from the agency of an individual. We styled this project together, orchestrating meaning with one another, and thus our text is inter-active, arising from women-among-ourselves.

Notes

We would like to thank Mary Rawlinson and David Allison for their close readings of earlier versions of this paper. We are indebted to them for their valuable comments.

1. In *Of Grammatology*, Derrida defines logocentrism as "the metaphysics of phonetic writing." By this he refers to the centrality of the idea that any system of language can make meaning present (that the word, the signifier, can

make present the signified) and thus the idea that we can reach a kind of metaphysical 'closure.' Logocentrism does not presume that truth is always present but that it can be made present—and this is the work [and pleasure] of philosophy. When Derrida engages in the deconstruction of metaphysics, he does so by showing that logocentrism is always embedded in and with what he calls "differánce," the play of signifiers (of presence and absence) upon which is predicated any discourse. Signifiers are themselves not fully present, because even as they are presented (in writing or discourse), they assume a network of absence which supports them and without which they could not appear at all. Meaning, the signified, is even further removed from presence, mediated by the signifier. In other words, the "presence" of truth is composed of "absences" which condition and subtend its appearance.

With the concept of phallogocentrism, Derrida implicates logocentrism in the Lacanian notion of phallocentrism. For Lacan, the phallus is the transcendental signifier, that which supports all signification as its condition for possibility. The concept of phallogocentrism makes clear the connection between the valuation of presence and the phallicized Symbolic Order. It thus designates that operation by which logocentrism constructs binary, hierarchical categories whose dominant terms are marked as masculine and whose masculine terms are marked as dominant. From a feminist perspective, phallogocentrism can be read as the production of intelligible experience through exclusive categories which privilege the siting of a masculinized perspective. Phallogocentrism makes clear the contrast between the idea of a full, present, apparent phallus and that of the castrated woman, who lacks a phallus, has nothing to be seen, and who therefore represents absence needing to be recuperated.

2. The notion of castration is an important one in psychoanalysis generally, and in Lacan in particular. Since no one can possess the phallus, Lacan understands all subjects, men included, to be castrated. Derrida makes use of this terminology to underscore his use of phallogocentrism—men believe the penis is the phallus, thus marking women as castrated. But this equation itself is founded upon castration anxiety and is formed through the denial of men's own inadequacy to phallic Law; masculinity is thus a presence founded upon lack. We will discuss these ideas more fully in the section on Desire and Dogmatism.

3. Again, this is similar to Lacan's notion that, while to be a man is to be in the position of having the phallus, to be a women is to be in a position of not having the phallus.

4. This notion is clearly informed by Lévi-Strauss, *The Elementary Structures of Kinship* (1969).

5. These monolithic concepts ('Man' and 'Woman') are not necessarily mirrored in reality, but are instead regulatory, determining appropriate representations of the self. In this way, they do real violence by covering over multiplicity and dissonance and demanding unitary forms of subjectivity.

They are hegemonic in that they do successfully maintain the values they set themselves; but they nonetheless fail to realize genuine homogeneity. There is an intractability to empirical heterogeneity which exceeds or eludes the conceptual edicts, but unfortunately not their violence. In the later sections of this essay we will analyze more fully the possibility of formulating strategies to evade the violence perpetuated by these cultural ideals.

6. Cf. de Beauvoir's thesis in *The Second Sex*, that "One is not born, but rather becomes, a woman" (Beauvoir 1989, 267).

7. It follows that masculinity is enjoined upon men in a similar fashion, i.e., that men too must enact their gender.

8. The notion of undecidability refers, somewhat like differánce, to the not fully present character of truth or meaning. The signified of any signifier cannot be decided once and for all, cannot be finally stabilized, since the signifier always returns in new contexts, new networks. But the aim of metaphysics is to solidify, render substantive all aspects of being and it relies on language (which is paradoxically also the enemy of metaphysics) to accomplish this task.

9. Nietzsche indicates, in *The Will to Power*, that modern epistemological pursuits are based not on certainty but on ontological presuppositions which, insofar as they are habitually assumed, undermine the very bases of knowledge. For instance, in §484 and §485 Nietzsche argues that linguistic structures govern assumptions concerning subjectivity and substance, making them intrinsic to the very grammar of our lives. We are obliged to speak in these forms. We are arguing here that gender operates in a similar manner, that it too is intrinsic to the grammar of our lives, and that we all speak through its structures.

10. The "hail" is a formulation of Louis Althusser; it designates the moment of "interpellation," the moment when one is solicited into one's identifications, and thereby constituted in a durable subject-position through the hail of another who wields symbolic power. This is not to be understood as a power limited simply to those with recognized authority, but belongs also to anyone who embodies and enacts cultural norms. It is a generalized and pervasive power.

11. This claim is similar to the one Irigaray makes in "Commodities Among Themselves." She writes, "Woman exists only as an occasion for mediation, transaction, transition, transference, between man and his fellow man, indeed between man and himself" (Irigaray 1985b, 193).

12. Cf. Irigaray's long essay on Freud, "The Blind Spot of an Old Dream of Symmetry" (Irigaray 1985a).

13. It is possible to interpret Kristeva as aligned with this position. For instance, she remarks in "Woman Can Never Be Defined" that "a woman cannot 'be'; it is something which does not even belong in the order of *being*" (Marks and de Courtivron 1980, 137).

14. Wittig speaks eloquently to this point in "The Category of Sex" and "One is Not Born a Woman" (Wittig 1992).

15. Cf. "Commodities Among Themselves" (Irigaray 1985b).

16. But, as Derrida notes in "White Mythology," logocentric discourse relies on the obscuring of metaphor which is its ground. Sedimented metaphors take on a metaphysical effect (WM 1982).

17. The idea that all desire is phallic stems from the Freudian notion of the infantile libido. Freud writes in "Femininity" that "the little girl is a little man" (Freud 1933). The implication is that, prior to the processes of femininization which culminate in her Oedipal Complex, the girl is indistinct from the (normative) boy, and hence shares with him a masculine libido which is then altered by her psychic history. But femininization means for the girl an abdication of desire, a retreat which nonetheless does not disallow pleasure. Note however that where desire is construed as active, pleasure is passive. For an excellent taking to task of Freud, see Irigaray's "The Blind Spot of an Old Dream of Symmetry" (1985a). The Lacanian notion of the phallus will be further explicated in the next section.

18. Cf. Gayle Rubin, "The Traffic in Women: Notes on the 'Political Economy' of Sex" (Rubin 1975).

19. With Baudrillard, we distinguish dissimulation from simulation and understand the latter as the power of patriarchy in which men feign possession of what they do not have, i.e., the phallus (Baudrillard 1983, 5).

20. This observation came out of a conversation with Marcos Bisticas-Cocoves.

21. This often occurs in the instruction of other women in these strategies of survival, especially in that directed toward daughters by mothers. While we have elected to emphasize, in our analysis of these patterns, their positive significance, we do not wish to overlook the ways in which these patterns perpetuate women's subjugation. Nevertheless, the women who engage in such acclimation can not be too easily condemned, since within the given material circumstances, it is the condition for the possibility of women's continuing viability.

22. The femme lesbian constitutes one example of such artistic repetition. Her "femininity" is clearly *assumed*, i.e., marked as an enactment. In this way she undermines the terms of femininity, the supposedly natural emanation of women, by exposing the operation as a put-on. Moreover, since being accessible to men (being heterosexual), is the hallmark of patriarchal femininity, her desire for women belies masculine access.

23. Cf. "The Ends of Man" (EM 1982).

24. The suggestion that feminists should be interested in a proliferation of subjectivity is a somewhat different claim than the one Judith Butler makes (Butler 1989, 260) in calling for a "proliferation of gender." Although they imply one another, they are not equivalent. The proliferation of gender indicates a breaking open of binary categories ("man" and "woman"). In

this way, gender as a necessary *entree* into the symbolic order is eradicated, replaced by a more tenuous gender as the site of desire. The proliferation of subjectivity indicates a critique of the unitary self. A revamping of subjectivity would continue to keep subjectivity as a symbolic matrix, but would continuously displace the Imaginary demand for subjective closure. The intersection of these two projects is precisely what is necessary: to constitute a subectivity within the Symbolic realm that is not founded in gender bifurcation, and therefore that is freed from the tyranny of adequacy to the Law of the Father.

25.   This is similar to Nietzsche's exhortation that we might learn to become what we are not yet. For instance, Nietzsche writes in *The Gay Science*, "Believers and their need to believe": "one could conceive of such a pleasure and power of self-determination, such a *freedom* of the will that the spirit would take leave of all faith and every wish for certainty, being practiced in maintaining himself [sic] on insubstantial ropes and possibilities and dancing even near abysses. Such a spirit would be the *free spirit* par excellance" (Nietzsche 1974, §347).

26.   It is important to remark here that it is the singularity and substantiveness designated by the "the" which is at issue in our critique. Both the definite and indefinite article have always served the aims of men and metaphysics. This is why Derrida insists that "there is no such thing as a woman" (S 101).

27.   Cf. *Positions*, 41–42. Derrida reminds us that opposition is always hierarchical, and that an overturning of this hierarchy is necessary if we are to avoid neutralizing it by simply jumping beyond the opposition (P 1981).

28.   Derrida is of course asserting both feminine and *masculine* specificity, but our point is that the latter is only conceptualized throught the medium of 'Woman.'

Works Cited

Althusser, Louis. 1971. *Lenin and Philosophy and Other Essays*. New York: Monthly Review Press.

Baudrillard, Jean. 1983. *Simulations*. New York: Semiotext(e), Inc.

de Beauvoir, Simone. 1989. *The Second Sex*, trans. H. M. Parshley. New York: Vintage Books.

Butler, Judith. 1989. "Gendering the Body: Beauvoir's Philosophical Contribution." In *Women, Knowledge, and Reality*, eds. Ann Garry and Marilyn Pearsall. Boston: Unwin Hyman.

Derrida, Jacques. 1976. *Of Grammatology*, trans. Gayatri Chakravorty Spivak. Baltimore: The Johns Hopkins University Press. Cited as OG.

———. 1979. *Spurs: Nietzsche's Styles/Eperons: Les Styles de Nietzsche*, trans. Barbara Harlow. Chicago: The University of Chicago Press. Cited as S.

———. 1981. *Positions*, trans. Alan Bass. Chicago: The University of Chicago Press. Cited as P.

————. 1982. "The Ends of Man," in *Margins of Philosophy*, trans. Alan Bass. Chicago: The University of Chicago Press. Cited as EM.

————. 1982. "White Mythology" in *Margins of Philosophy*, trans. Alan Bass. Chicago: The University of Chicago Press. Cited as WM.

Freud, Sigmund. 1933. "Femininity" In *The Standard Edition* Vol. XXII, trans. James Strachey. New York: W.W. Norton & Co.

Irigaray, Luce. 1985a. *Speculum of the Other Woman*, trans. Gillian C. Gill. Ithaca: Cornell University Press.

————. 1985b. *This Sex Which is Not One*, trans. Catherine Porter. Ithaca: Cornell University Press.

Kristeva, Julia. 1980. "Woman Can Never Be Defined." In *New French Feminisms*, eds. Elaine Marks and Isabelle de Courtivron. New York: Schocken Books.

Lacan, Jacques. 1977. *Écrits: A Selection*, trans. Alan Sheridan. New York: W. W. Norton & Co.

Lévi-Strauss, Claude. 1969. *The Elementary Structures of Kinship*. Boston: Beacon Press.

Nietzsche, Friedrich. 1956. *The Birth of Tragedy and The Genealogy of Morals*, trans. Francis Golffing. New York: Anchor Books.

————. 1967. *The Will to Power*, trans. Walter Kaufmann. New York: Vintage Books.

————. 1968. *Basic Writings of Nietzsche*, trans. Walter Kaufmann. New York: The Modern Library.

————. 1974. *The Gay Science*, trans. Walter Kaufmann. New York: Vintage Books.

Rubin, Gayle. 1975. "The Traffic in Women: Notes on the 'Political Economy' of Sex." In *Toward an Anthropology of Women*, ed. Rayna R. Reiter. New York: Monthly Review Press.

Wittig, Monique. 1992. *The Straight Mind and Other Essays*. Boston: Beacon Press.

The Maternal Operation   3

Circumscribing the Alliance

Kelly Oliver

No woman or trace of woman, if I have read correctly—save the mother, that's understood. But this is part of the system. The mother is the faceless figure of a *figurant,* an extra. She gives rise to all the figures by losing herself in the background of the scene like an anonymous persona. Everything comes back to her, beginning with life; everything addresses and destines itself to her. She survives on the condition of remaining at bottom.

—Jacques Derrida, "Otobiographies."

Derrida's autobiographical essay "Circumfession" is written in response to a request from Geoffrey Bennington, author of the accompanying exposition on Derrida's corpus, to disrupt or surprise Bennington's neatly packaged outline of Derrida's work. "Circumfession" runs along the bottom margin of Bennington's text, all the while looking (up) to say something unrecognizable in the terms of that text. Like Saint Augustine, who turns his eyes upward to God after the death of his mother to confess his life, Derrida confesses his life to God, to Geoffrey, and to Georgette (his mother) as she lay dying. "Circumfession" is presented as the (anti-) code, logic, or grammar that defies the logic or grammar of Derrida's corpus as set out by Bennington. Even with its symbols, "G" (God, Geoffrey, Georgette ...), "SA" (Saint Augustine, *Savoir Absolute*)..), "FP" (facial paralysis ...), "Circumfession" confesses something in excess of any symbolic system, any language; it confesses what cannot be confessed and as such it fails. It fails to confess the blood of the living body, the living maternal body.

Just as Bennington sets out Derrida's corpus as a dead corpse, without even a quotation from one of his texts, Derrida can at best present dead bits of himself in his writing, like so many bits of skin ritually removed from his body. Just as Saint Augustine asks how he can confess anything to an omniscient God, Derrida asks how he can confess to "G" who knows everything there is to know about his texts and has, after all, catalogued them nicely and identified their underlying logics and grammars. Bennington's text circumscribes Derrida's corpus and makes it a proper body of work. Derrida compares this ritual of circumscription to the ritual of circumcision which marks the male child's proper entrance into the Judaic culture and reaffirms the community's alliance with God. What remains after the event of circumcision is the mark on the body, the mark of the proper; but what cannot be recuperated through the mark or scar is the blood shed at the time of the ritual. What is always in excess of any text, any symbolic ritualized mark, any culture or language, is warm blood.

Derrida's challenge, then, is to return to the text that which cannot be returned, the blood from the living body as it performs the ritual of writing; he tries to recall the blood that is shed at the circumcision. His autobiograpy is the attempt to graft warm blood to words on a page that are the leftover dead skin from the ritual of circumfession. His challenge is to present an uncircumcised text, "a supposedly idiomatic, unbroachable, unreadable, uncircumcised piece of writing" (CS 194). Insofar as circumcision marks the community's recognition of its proper member, Derrida tries to write an unrecognizable text. The ceremony surrounding the circumcision is also the Hebrew naming-ceremony and the circumcision marks the proper Hebrew name. Thus, he tries to write an unnamed text.

The name is what is at stake in "Circumfession": ". . . in a story of blood, at the point where I am finally this cauterized name, the ultimate, the unique, right up against what, from an improbable circumcision, I have lost by gaining, and when I say that I want to gain my name against G., that does not mean the opposite of losing . . ." (CS 43–44). Derrida is trying to regain his name against "G" (Geoffrey) and for "G" (Georgette). Geoffrey offers up a total recognition of the proper name "Derrida" and in so doing does not recognize his friend Jacques; Georgette, Derrida's mother, no longer recognizes him or remembers his name.

In "Circumfession" both the name and the circumcision, recognition and blood, come back to the mother: "the role of the mother in circumcision for if she who desires, sometimes commits circumcision with the inhibited desire for child-murder, she is indeed in the position of obsequence (G, with its circumcisions, guillotines, incisions, still illegible tattoos), figure without figure, armed extra who is no longer present among us at the operation she now delegates after having previously performed it herself (7–1–77)" (CS 189–190). By and for the mother, circumcision is the ritual renewing the alliance with God and traditionally a prerequisite for the marriage alliance. In his writing, Derrida performs a ritual circumcision by and for his mother, trying to preserve the blood shed from the body:

> ... sucking up the blood through a lightweight cloth, the tight filter of a white dressing around the penis, on the seventh day, when they would put on orange-flower water in Algeria, with the theory, among so many others, that by mingling with the blood right on that wound that I have never seen, seen with my own eyes, this perfumed water attenuates that pain which I suppose to be nil and infinite, and I can still feel it, the phantom Burning, in my belly, irradiating a diffuse zone around the sex, a threat which returns every time the other is in pain, if I identify with him, with her even, with my mother especially, and when they claimed that orange-flower water has an anesthetic virtue, they were believed, anesthetic they said for the wounded baby, of course, not for the mother kept at bay, sometimes in tears, so that she could not see, in the next room, and I spread out here this white cloth all bloodied in consoling a mother in order to console myself without forgetting all the theories according to which circumcision, another word for peritomy, that cutting of the surround, is instituted by the mother, for her, the cruelty basically being hers ... (CS 66–68)

The relation of the mother to the name and the circumcision is all the more dramatic in Derrida's case where his name is lost to his mother who no longer recognizes him. He writes "Circumfession" to his mother; he wants to reclaim his name against Geoffrey in order to give it back to his mother. Insofar as he is unrecognizable to his mother, in order to write a text unrecognizable to Geoffrey, Derrida attempts to confess his mother and his own lost name, his Hebrew name, Elijah. Elijah is the prophet who condemned the Israelites for breaking their alliance with God (see CS 81). As the angel of the covenant, Elijah supposedly attends the circumcision to oversee the renewal of the alliance. He is also one of the only prophets who did not die; he was translated to Heaven in a chariot of fire. And he will return as a forerunner of the messiah.

While Elijah is the heavenly guardian of the alliance between God and Israel, the wife and mother is the earthly guardian of the alliance. The renewal of the alliance is foreshadowed in Exodus 5: 24–6 when Zipporah circumcises her own son in order to save Moses from God's wrath. Images of Zipporah appear in "Circumfession": the mother with the foreskin of her son in her teeth (CS 97), the loved woman circumcising the son in an act of fellatio (CS 218). In Derrida's images in "Circumfession," Zipporah circumcises her son with her teeth by biting off the foreskin: "Zipporah, the one who repaired the failing of Moses incapable of circumcising his own son, before telling him, 'You are a husband of blood to me', she had to eat the still bloody foreskin, I imagine first by sucking it, my first beloved cannibal, initiator at the sublime gate of fellatio" (CS 68–90). In the simulated castration of circumcision the mother wounds her baby to inscribe his name—the name that connects him to his community—on his body, on his sex (see CS 66, 72, 153). She is responsible for this ritual which inscribes the proper name on the body and insures its proper entrance into the social contract. In this text, the mother's tongue is the guarantor of the mother-tongue; the mother's tongue marks the male body, makes it proper, so that the alliance, the social contract, can be renewed.

Zipporah's role in Exodus is not only to renew the alliance of the convenant, but also to renew the marriage alliance, which was also an alliance between the Levites and the Midianites. Zipporah's father Reuel or Jethro was the priest of Midian (Exodus 2:18, 3:1). Moses had been raised as an Egyptian prince after the Pharaoh's daughter had rescued him from the water and from the order that her father had issued which commanded the death of all male children born of the Israelites. Once Moses saw the suffering of his people, he left Egypt and went to Midian. There Reuel gave him his daughter Zipporah after Moses protected Reuel's sheep from some hostile shepherds. Until Exodus 4:25–6 there is no mention of Moses' circumcision (he was raised as an Egyptian), which would symbolize his proper entrance into the people of Israel and renew their alliance with God; nor is there mention of Moses' marriage, which would symbolize his alliance with Zipporah and the alliance between the Levites and the Midianites. In Exodus 4:25–6 the alliance between man and woman, between one tribe and another, and between man and God is reaffirmed through Zipporah's circumcision of her son and her symbolic circumcision of Moses: "Then Zipporah took a flint, and cut off the foreskin of her son, and cast it at his feet; and she said: 'Surely a bridegroom of blood art thou to me.' So he let him alone. Then she said: 'A bridegroom of blood in regard of the circumcision.'"[1] David Rosenberg translates the passage: "On the way, at a night lodging, Yahweh met him—and was ready to kill him. Zipporah took a flinty stone, cutting her son's foreskin; touched it between Moses' legs: 'Because you are my blood bridegroom,' she said, 'marked by this circumcision'"(Rosenberg 1990, 144).[2]

Zipporah not only circumcises her son, but also symbolically circumcises Moses by touching the blood to his legs and proclaiming him a blood bridegroom.[3] With this ritual Zipporah circumscribes her union with Moses and his union with God and the Israelites. By so doing, she saves Moses' life. There have been various speculations on why God suddenly threatened Moses' life. When God calls upon Moses, he protests that he is not the candidate to speak on behalf of the Israelites because he is slow of speech and tongue (Exodus 4:10). Could it be that God means to punish Moses for his hesitance to serve Him? Perhaps Zipporah's ritual circumcision of Moses is also meant to address his uncircumcised lips, his lack of words.[4] Derrida points out that the spoken Hebrew word "*milah*" can mean either word or circumcision (CS 89).

In his "Circumfession," Derrida mentions the notebook for a book on circumcision, "The Book of Elijah," that he had planned to write in 1976. On the cover of this notebook Derrida writes the Hebrew *milah* (CS 89). Possibly it makes no difference that he has not written "The Book of Elijah" since, as he says, circumcision is "all I've ever talked about" (CS 70). Derrida describes writing as a ritual of circumcision. He says that the desire for literature is circumcision (CS 78). He calls the attic where he stores all of his writing "the sublime" that contains all of the "skizzies" of his circumcision (CS 134). The text is the mark of circumcision, the skin cut from the body, from the sex—the skin without blood. Derrida dreams of a pen that could write the living body in warm red blood. He confesses that he has always dreamed "of a pen that would be a syringe" so that he could write himself into a sentence and find himself there (CS 10). But this is something that neither he nor Geoffrey can do. *He* is not the proper name that signs the text, the name that is circumscribed by the circumcision. What is lost in this symbolic ritual is the blood; the blood is shed:

> I have been seeking myself in a sentence, yes, I, and since a circumbygone period at the end of which I would say I and which would, finally, have the form, my language, another . . . I call it circumcision, see the blood but also what comes, cauterization, coagulation or not, strictly contain the outpouring of circumcision, one circumcision, mine, the only one, rather than circumnavigation or circumference, although the unforgettable circumcision has carried me to the place I had to go to, and circumfession if I want to say and do something of an avowal without truth turning around itself . . . the pulsion of the paragraph which never circumpletes itself, as long as the blood, what I call thus and thus call, continues its venue in its vein. (CS 14–15)

How can Derrida write this blood, the blood shed in the ritual circumcision? . . . Especially given the mother's role in, and relation to, circumcision? The blood shed in circumcision is both started and stopped by her (tongue). The mother's tongue is what makes his language possible. He has come to language because she properly marked him for the social. She sacrifices him to the social, which can know nothing of her pain. It is her sacrifice. It is her pain. What mixes prayer and tears with blood is what Derrida must write, but cannot (CS 20). Blood exceeds any writing. Moreover, in "Circumfession" blood, tears, and prayers are always of the mother, for her child. She weeps for her child and his pain. It is what mixes *her* blood with prayers and tears that he must confess but cannot.

Derrida laments that his mother can no longer weep for him. She does not recognize him and therefore she cannot weep for him. He no longer exists for her. Yet, what is most troubling for him is that if he died before her, she could not mourn his death. Forgetting his immortal namesake, Elijah, Derrida is obsessed with his own death. For his mother, he is already dead. He is already absent to her and even his absence is not present. How can he confess this absence that is not even present as an absence? This confession, the confession of his absence to his mother, is the uncircumcised text. He has no name for her. His name has slipped her mind. It is this slipping away of the name for the mother that shakes Derrida. It is the double sense of the slipping of the name *for* the mother that rocks him: her name like the name of God is unpronounceable (CS 58, 264), and his name no longer exists for her—for the rest of her life he has no name (CS 22). At least in the circumcision there is a mark, a trace, of the blood shed from the body. But where is the mark, the trace, of Derrida on the body of his mother? Does her body exist only for the sake of her son? She provides the name and marks the body for it. But where is her body, the maternal body, in his "Circumfession"?

Except in the photographs where his mother's body is young and beautiful, when it makes an appearance in the text of "Circumfession," his mother's body appears as scarred, immodest, already dead (CS 24, 25, 82, 101, 108). In this text, her body is slipping away, already gone: "Now she is becoming—I'm with her this eighteenth of June—what she always was, the impassability of a time out of time, an immortal mortal, too human inhuman, the dumb god the beast, a sleeping water in the henceforth appeased depth of the abyss, this volcano I tell myself I'm well out of . . ." (CS 80). As his mother, "G" is not embodied; she is outside of time, a god, a beast, a volcano, a sleeping water. She is outside of culture, outside of the realm of the name, the guarantor, but not the beneficiary, of both.

This pre-culture mother appears elsewhere in Derrida's texts. In the *Ear of the Other*, and *Glas*, among others, there are signs that the mother is associated with nature that stands outside of culture and language as its silent source and telos. In *Glas* Derrida says that "[t]he breast [*sein*] of this mother steals away from all names, but it also hides them, steals them; it is before all names, as death, the mother fascinates from the absolute of an *already*"

(G 133–134). Here the mother occupies the traditional role as nature, before all names, that makes the name possible. Within this economy, as nature she is necessarily silent and as speaking she is necessarily phallic. The son speaks for/as her.

In *Glas* Derrida says that the mother follows and he suggests that he not only follows his mother, but that he *is* his mother: "I am (following) the mother. The text. The mother is *behind*—all that I follow, am, do, seem—the mother follows" (G 116). The mother is in the background, setting the stage. Like the absent woman in *Given Time*, she stands outside of time setting its tempo: "You will very quickly suspect that, if woman seems to be absent from this narrative, her exclusion could well be organizing the scene and marking its tempo like a clock" (GT 103). She is the nature, the background, out of which time is born. We are born out of mother-earth and when we die we return to her.

In Derrida's *Glas*, man's dialogue with the Other is always a dialogue with himself set against the background of the mother who remains at bottom, speechless. He addresses his text to her, but she calls herself only through him: "I call myself my mother who calls herself (in) me.... I bear my mother's name, I call my mother to myself, I call my mother for myself, I call my mother in myself, recall myself to my mother" (G 117). Where is the mother's call? It is always his own calling to himself. And how does he pay his debt to his mother and settle his account (cf. G 262)? He remembers her by giving birth to himself through his text: " I give birth to myself, and I write myself" (G 193). His text lives and speaks only because the mother barely subsists and is mute. He bears his mother's name, but what is her name?

In *Glas* her name is either "the name of a plant or flower," or the name Genêt (G 34–35). As either nature (a plant or flower) or man (Genêt), she is the all-powerful phallic mother. An identification with her protects against castration only because she is the phallic mother, the masculine mother. But Derrida identifies with her name; by taking on her name Derrida protects himself against the mother's body. Derrida describes the mother with whom Genêt identifies, the mother in Genêt with whom he identifies: "No longer his mother but his mother, no longer the bad mother, the one that cannot be erected, but the phallus ejaculating on the cross, the right mother, that is, normal, square, who shines, she, forever, whose sex glistens upright, trickling sperm" (G 148). As the phallus, the mother protects against castration. As the phallic mother, she makes love possible.

Is this love the love of oneself, the love of one's ability to give birth to oneself? How is it possible to acknowledge, to recognize, to remember, her love? Is his mourning a deadly nostalgia that turns the mother into silent nature?

Or, can he resuscitate his mother, her life, tears, and blood through his identification with her? By giving birth to himself and remembering her birth
pains? Can he can become "fe-male," become mother? Speaking of Blanchot
in "The Law of Genre," Derrida says: "'I', then, can keep alive the chance of
being fe-male or of changing sex. His transsexuality permits him, in a *more
than metaphorical and transferential way*, to engender. He can give birth . . ."
(LG 76; my emphasis). Speaking of Nietzsche's pregnancy in *Spurs*, Derrida
suggests that pregnancy is "no less praiseworthy in a man than it is in a
woman" (S, 65). As Derrida says in *Glas* (speaking of Kant): "Nature is good,
is a good woman, that is in truth, by her reproductive force, her reason, her
profound logos that dominates all the feminine chatterings, her imper-
turbable and always victorious logic, her educative resources, a father. The
good woman is a father; the father is a good woman" (G 128). The mother
is either nature and/or phallic; and in both cases she becomes a good father.
And a bad father is only a cover for a bad or false mother.

In "Otobiographies" Derrida suggests that even the fascist readings of
Nietzsche are readings of the mother. There he asks how Nietzsche's texts
lead to fascism? What is there in the structure of Nietzsche's texts that can
lead to opposite sorts of interpretations of those texts, particularly the fascist interpretation? Derrida indicates that this is not a question of Nietzsche's intentions but it is a question of the texts as they are read. The
signature of Nietzsche, how he becomes what he is, is determined through
the "ear of the other." That ear is always ultimately the ear of the mother, the
mother-tongue. What do we hear in our mother-tongue? Yet, as Nietzsche
reminds us, even asses have ears. And as Derrida makes it out, fascism's ears
mistake the living mother-tongue for the dead paternal system. Implicit in
Derrida's text is the suggestion that the State gains the kind of authority that
it had in the Third Reich when it passes itself off as the mother:

> Not only is the State marked by the sign and the paternal figure of the dead,
> it also wants to pass itself off for the mother—that is, for life, the people, the
> womb of things themselves. (EO 34)

> In fact the mother—the bad or false mother whom the teacher as functionary
> of the State, can only simulate—dictates to you the very thing that passes
> through your ear and travels the length of the cord all the way down to your
> stenography. This writing links you. like a leash in the form of an umbilical
> cord, to the paternal belly of the State . . . all its movements are induced by the
> body of the father figuring as alma mater. How an umbilical cord can create
> a link to this cold monster that is a dead father or the State—this is what is
> uncanny? (EO 36)

... the ear can close itself off and contact can be suspended because the *omphalos* of a disjointed body ties it to a dissociated segment of the father. (EO 36)

What I hear in Derrida's text is the suggestion that fascism is linked to Nietzsche's texts through the umbilical cord of a bad or false mother. The State poses as the mother, natural and living, who demands certain obligations. This charade makes those obligations appear to be natural insofar as they emanate from the mother, language (the mother-tongue) and life itself. If we look behind the charade it becomes obvious that the patriarchal State is not natural nor does it necessarily protect life. Still, the relation between paternal-culture and mother-nature is complicated in Derrida's texts.

Unlike Lacan, who associates the name with the Father, Derrida associates the name with the mother. It seems that we might expect some kind of deconstruction of the opposition father-name/mother-body or paternal-culture/mother-nature. But is this what we receive from the "Circumfession," *Glas*, or *Ear of the Other*? As the mother-*tongue*, language is identified with the body; and it lives only through this identification with the body. But in the end, does the mother, the maternal body, turn out to be the silent background, the faceless figure, an extra, in Derrida's texts? With Derrida's analysis of the eternal return of the name of the mother, we have come full circle back to mother-nature. The name of the mother is always only alive as a trace of her body (tongue) that remains locked into the crypt of nature. Recall the quotation from the *Ear of the Other* with which I began and with which Derrida concludes his text: "No woman or trace of woman ... save the mother ... the faceless figure of a figurant, an extra ... the background of the scene like an anonymous person.... Everything comes back to her, beginning with life. She survives on the condition of remaining at bottom" (EO 38). Life is born out of her and returns to her; she is mother-earth; she is nature. She is the background and the tongue that make language possible and yet she cannot write or speak. There is no trace of woman save the mother and she is mute.

Derrida bases part of his analysis in "Otobiographies" on Nietzsche's *Future of Our Educational Institutions*, in which Nietzsche discusses the living body of language of the mother-tongue to which the student has certain obligations. The lesson that Derrida takes from Nietzsche is that the revitalization of language "must first pass by way of the tongue, that is, by way of the exercise of the tongue or language, the treatment of its body, the mouth and the ear, passing between the *natural*, living mother tongue and the scientific, formal, dead paternal language" (EO 26; my emphasis).

Derrida maintains that if, as Nietzsche's says in *Ecce Homo*, as his mother he lives on and as his father he is already dead, then the name of Nietzsche lives on as the name of the mother (EO 16). In fact, the signature on his writing is the name of the mother since at the point of writing he is dead as the embodied heir of his father; once the text is written it takes on a life of its own that leaves the embodied life of its author behind. Derrida develops this argument by pointing to a connection between the mother and language. Living writing takes place in the mother-tongue. So too, all agreements and contracts, including marriage, take place in the mother-tongue (EO 21). In fact, to speak the mother-tongue is to engage in a contract of sorts, a marriage, that binds one to the rules of that language. The mother-tongue brings with it certain obligations that result from the very laws of grammar within it.[5] Derrida concludes that "[t]he repeated affirmation— like the contract, hymen, and alliance—always belong to language: it comes down and comes back to the signature of the maternal nondegenerate, noble tongue" (EO 21).

In writing for the (m)other, Nietzsche writes for himself and *visa versa*. He writes *Ecce Homo* as a gift to himself; he tells his life to himself. But Derrida suggests that he can address himself in his text only by addressing his own eternal return. He addresses himself for the sake of his own eternal return, the return of his name, "Nietzsche." His name will return over and over again only through generations of future readers. Nietzsche writes in order to give birth to himself through the eternal return, which he figures as a woman. Derrida concludes that "you cannot think the name or names of Friedrich Nietzsche, you cannot *hear* them before the reaffirmation of the hymen, before the alliance or wedding ring of the eternal return" (EO 13).

It makes sense then, strangely enough, that the woman whom Nietzsche weds in order to give birth to himself is his own mother. Derrida interprets Nietzsche's riddle "already dead as my father, while as my mother, I am still living and becoming old" as a clue to the doctrine of eternal return.[6] Following Deleuze, he suggests that the eternal return is a selective principle that guarantees that life returns as the living feminine who says "yes, yes" (EO 14). Life's "yes, yes" turns out to be a double-affirmation of the birth of her son: she says yes to him by giving him birth and she says yes to him after his birth. The author's "yes, yes" is the acceptance of the gift of life and the acknowledgment of the debt from this gift (EO 15). What Derrida does not mention is that the author's double-affirmation is possible only through the living feminine through which he continues to live; she says yes and insofar as he says yes he is living on as her. And the author's "yes, yes" is not a yes to her, but a yes to himself. Derrida describes the debt as a debt to oneself (EO 14). As a result, any debt to the mother is only a debt to oneself; ultimately there is no debt to the mother. The loan is from oneself and repaid to oneself.

The repeated affirmation, the double affirmation, the "yes, yes," the affirmation of the eternal return, belong to the maternal tongue. It is her tongue, her yes, that reaffirms the alliance; she says yes to her son's position in the alliance with God, with culture, and with woman. He enters the alliance because he has the mother tongue with which to speak. Mute without him, the mother tongue reaffirms the hymen.

The hymen occupies a precarious place in Derrida's corpus; it operates both as the sign of the alliance or marriage and the sign of the impossibility of the alliance. Within the economy of Derrida's corpus the hymen is a marriage and an undecidable "concept" that calls any alliance into question. Even while traditionally the circumscription of the hymen in marriage rituals marks the proper entrance of the woman into the marriage alliance and transfers her as unspoiled property from her father to her husband, within Derrida's corpus, "hymen" becomes associated with an economy that operates outside of the economy of the proper.

Circumcision, as simulated castration, marks the economy of the proper, property. The mark or scar of circumcision is a reminder of the threat of castration that, within Freudian psychoanalytic theory, forces the male child to enter language and culture. Circumcision circumscribes the castration threat and writes the paternal prohibitions that secure the social onto the body. In Derrida's description of the ritual of circumcision, the taboo that raises the threat of castration, incest, is also present; the mother simulates the paternal threat of castration in an act of fellatio. The ritual of circumcision simulates both the prohibited act and the punishment for that act. The ritual of circumcision circumscribes both the social alliance and the threat to that alliance. And both its security and its threat come from the mother. She necessarily stands outside the alliance as it guarantor and its impossibility.

Woman occupies a similar position in the burial ritual. In his analysis of Hegel in *Glas*, Derrida diagnoses "the feminine operation of burial" within which the man entrusts his death to the woman and the woman is responsible for his corpse. For Hegel this is an appropriate task for the woman who is accustomed to the night and the subterranean world of the earth. In addition she is a guardian within the family of an ethics of the singular. Through the burial rituals she protects the singular body of man, his proper individuality, from being eaten by the earth. Paradoxically, the burial ritual, as a symbolic system, separates man from the animals and thereby guarantees that even though his body dies, his spirit does not and he is thus protected from the cannibalism of the earth; his singularity will not be eaten by worms. In Derrida's analysis, however, the feminine operation of burial "does not oppose itself to the exteriority of a nonconscious matter; it suppresses an unconscious desire. The family wants to prevent the dead one

from being 'destroyed' and the burial place violated *by this desire*" (G 144).
And although Hegel does not indicate which unconscious desires are to be
guarded against, Derrida does. The dead man is not only subject to the
threat of material cannibalism but also imaginary cannibalism: "The two
functions of (the) burial (place) relieve the dead man of his death, spare
him from being destroyed—eaten—by matter, nature, the spirit's being-
outside-self, but also by the probably cannibal violence of the survivor's
unconscious desires. That is, essentially, the women's, since they, as
guardians of (the) burial (place) and the family, are always in a situation of
survival" (G 146). So at the same time that woman desires to incorporate
the dead husband into her memory or into herself, she protects him against
her own violent cannibalistic (not to mention necrophiliac) desires. She
prevents herself from ingesting, incorporating, his pure singularity which
has already become universal spirit. She prevents him from returning to
nature by remaining within nature and tending to his needs from the outside. She is responsible for the details of maintaining the symbolic rituals
which maintain the symbolic system but only so long as (and in order that)
she remain outside of that system guaranteeing its survival. When she
threatens to move inside, the system seems to collapse and death destroys
both the man and his system. Woman, then, provides both the threat and
the security against the threat.

Like the hymen, the woman/mother circumscribes the alliance by breaking it.[7] The hymen, intact, is a sign that the woman is a virgin and can properly (in the sense of *propre*, clean and proper) become the property of
another man. Traditionally the marriage ritual involved breaking the hymen
to seal the alliance and displaying the resulting blood as proof of the con-
summation. This blood-mark on a sheet, like the circumcised foreskin, can
only serve as a reminder of the blood shed during the ritual, a reminder of
the living body that is *not* property. The broken hymen, a membrane skin,
with its bloodstained sheet, like the circumcised foreskin with its bloodstained cloth, is a dead skin, a dry parchment, upon which the social ritual
is written. These rituals that make the body *propre* leave only traces of life.

Derrida writes: ". . . I began with this fear, with being scared of her bad
blood, with not wanting it, whence the infinite separation, the initial and
instantaneously repeated i.e. indefinitely postponed divorce from [*d'avec*]
the closest cruelty which was not that of my mother but the distance she
enjoined on me from [*d'avec*] my own skin thus torn off, in the very place,
along the crural artery where my books find their inspiration, they are written first in skin . . ." (CS 227–28). But this skin cannot contain the blood of
a living body, especially the maternal body, particularly the mother's "bad

blood." The blood-mark of the broken hymen is also a reminder of the menstrual blood and the blood of childbirth.

Derrida says that "for 59 years I have not known who is weeping my mother or me—i.e. you" (CS 263). He writes the circumfession "for the death agony of my mother, not readable her but the first event to write itself right on my body . . ." (CS 120). The pain of "Circumfession" is the pain that Derrida cannot feel, the pain of his mother, that is written on his body, on his sex. The guilt that he confesses is the guilt of his murderous mother who wounds her own son in the ritual of circumcision. The pain of his mother's guilt serves as a salve for his own guilt, the guilt of killing her in writing her before she has died: "from what wound is it waiting for me, me who, among other remorse with respect to my mother, feel guilty for publishing her end, in exhibiting her last breaths . . ." (CS 36). Yet, he has to write his mother because he would be guiltier if he did not (CS 37). Writing both kills her as the warm-blooded woman whom he called "*maman*," and saves her from herself, from loss of memory, from association with nature, from devouring mother-earth.

Confessing his mother's guilt is a type of revenge against the murderous ritual of circumcision, the ritual that marks the male infant's entrance into the social and simulates the threat that makes him leave his mother behind. He murders her in writing not only because he writes her death before it has happened, but also because through his writing he can only "de-skin" himself; he cannot remember his mother and her warm blood. He can only confess that he is haunted by the image of embalming his mother alive (C 260). The only mother that he can confess is a bloodless mother who is already dead. Still, only through his murderous confession ritual can he try to acknowledge, remember, or recognize her, whose blood gave him life.

The blood in excess of Derrida's confession is maternal blood. The lost memory of the blood shed at his own circumcision is a lost memory of the blood of his birth, his mother's blood. His pain for his mother is his impossible memory of the pain of childbirth. "Circumfession" is the confession of a phantom pain in his sex that is associated with the forgotten pain (a phantom memory) of his own circumcision, a pain that he attributes to his mother. Yet, is this phantom pain in his sex the phantom memory of the pain in his mother's sex? Perhaps even the pain of his birth? With Derrida, we can "follow the traces of blood" in "Circumfession" back to the mother:

> the first I remember having seen with my own eyes, outside, since I was and remain blind to that of my seventh or eighth day, which happens to be the day of my mother's birth, July 23, that first blood that came to me from the sex of

a cousin, Simone 7 or 8 years old, the day when the pedal of a toy scooter penetrated her by accident, *Verfall*, with the first phantom sensation, that algic
sympathy around my sex which leads me to the towels my mother left lying
around, 'marked' from red to brown, in the bidet, when as I understood so
late, she was having her own 'period'. . . . (CS 108)

Here the traces of blood lead Derrida back to the blood of his own circumcision, to which he is blind, which happens to be the day of his mother's
birth (her birthday or perhaps also the day she gives birth). He traces his
first blood to the sex of his cousin accidentally penetrated and this trace
leads to his mother's menstrual blood. All of these traces bring with them
the (sympathetic) phantom memory in his sex of his own circumcision and
his mother's blood. He is blind to the blood of his circumcision, but he sees
the marks of his mother's blood. But what ritual shed this blood whose
trace remains in the mark? How can Derrida trace this maternal blood? He
remembers seeing the marks of his mother's blood on towels; he sees her
blood coagulated in bedsores on her heals, hips, and sacrum, blood that is
not properly contained by skin (CS 82). But can he see the warm blood of
the maternal body? Even if he can sense it and imagine it, he cannot write it.

His autobiography is only a trace of his life and of she who gave him life;
like the marks on a towel or discarded skin, the words on the page are leftovers from the life of the body. While telling the story of a life, an autobiography speaks only death; its violence is murderous. Even in the attempt to
tell the story of dying—the only story left to tell it seems—the autobiography automatically graphs the other of life to its trace. By grafting lifeless
traces of the life and death of the body into its other, the mother tongue
immortalizes man's life. The mother tongue both protects and threatens the
social and the divine alliance.

If the maternal body is a blind spot in Derrida's texts, it is not only
because the life of the body cannot be written, but also because he associates
the maternal body with nature or God. The maternal body becomes the
speechless mother-tongue and the nameless mother's name. Even in his
most intimate text to/on the mother, his own mother Georgette Safar Derrida, "Circumfession," the maternal body disappears behind the name, and
the mother's tongue becomes the basis for the social contract. The association of the mother with nature or God is what distinguishes remembrance
of the mother from nostalgia for the mother. Nostalgia is always for something that is forever lost because it was never present. Nostalgia for the
mother is a longing for an impossible return to the peace of the maternal
womb, the silence of a tongue that does not speak, a return to mother-earth
associated with the death drive (cf. CS 150). Remembering the mother, on

the other hand, is recalling her as a desiring, speaking subject, to whom we are indebted for life. Autobiography attempts to remember, to give birth to life's story, to give words to a silent tongue, to rescue the body from death. Autobiography attempts the impossible. Perhaps, like G. in Derrida's "Circumfession," autobiography only acknowledges without remembering or recognizing.

Derrida's autobiography is the attempt to write an unrecognizable text, a text that is not a remembering because it is not linear like Bennington's text that sits on top of it. His autobiography is the attempt to write the impossibility of writing autobiography by acknowledging that his life is unrecognizable to her who gave him life, his mother, G. Yet, doesn't the acknowledgment of the debt of life always bring with it the danger of making the mother into a god? Of draining her blood and embalming her alive?

Notes

1. Quoted from *The Holy Scriptures* (New York: The Jewish Publication Society of America), 1955.

2. *The Book of J*, trans., David Rosenberg (New York: Grove Weidenfeld Publishers, 1990), 144.

3. Some commentators maintain that Zipporah refers to her son when she says "bridegroom of blood." Bridegroom was a title that women used to refer to their newly circumcised sons, following the earlier tradition of circumcision just prior to marriage. (See, for example, *The Soncino Chumash: The Five Books of Moses with Haphtaroth*, ed. A. Cohen [Hindhead, Surrey: The Sancino Press, 1947].) Dorothy Zeligs points out that when in Exodus Zipporah says a blood bridegroom by virtue of circumcision that circumcision is plural in the Hebrew (Dorothy Zeligs, *Moses: A Psychodynamic Study*, [New York: Human Sciences Press, 1986], 87). If the Hebrew word for circumcision is plural, then this provides more reason for interpreting Zipporah's circumcision as a dual circumcision of her son and Moses. For a more detailed analysis of Zipporah, see my *Family Values: Subjects Between Nature and Culture* (New York: Routledge, 1997).

4. Cf. Harold Bloom's commentary on *The Book of J*, (New York: Grove Weidenfeld Publishers, 1990), 247.

5. It is interesting that here in *Ear of the Other* and in "The Law of Genre" Derrida associates the law with the feminine and maternal, yet in "The Law of Genre" he also claims that "'I' . . . can give birth . . . to law" (LG 76; cf. LG 77, EO 21). In *Of Grammatology* the maternal plays a fundamental role in the development of law and culture. For the development of this thesis, see my *Family Values, Subjects Between Nature and Culture* (New York: Routledge, 1997).

6. See Nietzsche, *Ecce Homo*, "Why I am so Wise," chapter 1, trans. Walter Kaufmann, (New York: Vintage Press, 1989), 222.

7. For a more detailed analysis of Derrida's use of "hymen" and his attempts to undermine the economy of the proper or castration, see my *Womanizing Nietzsche: Philosophy's Relation to 'the Feminine'* (New York: Routledge, 1995). For an expanded version of this essay, "The Maternal Operation: Circumscribing the Alliance," see my *Family Values: Subjects Between Nature and Culture* (New York: Routledge, 1997).

Works Cited

Cohen, A. ed. 1947. *The Soncino Chumash: The Five Books of Moses with Haphtaroth.* Hindead, Surrey: The Sancino Press.

Derrida, Jacques. 1993. "Circumfession." *Jacques Derrida.*, trans. Geoffrey Bennington. Chicago: The University of Chicago Press. Cited as CS.

———. 1985. *The Ear of the Other,* trans. Peggy Kamuf and Avital Ronell. Ed. Christie McDonald and Claude Lévesque. Lincoln: University of Nebraska Press. Cited as EO.

———. 1992. *Given Time: I. Counterfeit Money,* trans. Peggy Kamuf. Chicago: The University of Chicago Press. Cited as GT.

———. 1986. *Glas,* trans. John P. Leavey, Jr. and Richard Rand. Lincoln: University of Nebraska Press. Cited as G.

———. 1980. "The Law of Genre," trans. Avital Ronell. *Critical Inquiry* 17, no. 1: 55–81. Cited as LG.

———. 1979. *Spurs: Nietzsche's Styles,* trans. Barbara Harlow. Chicago: The University of Chicago Press. Cited as S.

The Holy Scriptures. 1955. New York: The Jewish Publication Society of America.

Nietzsche, Friedrich. (1980). *Ecce Homo,* trans. Walter Kauffman. New York: Vintage Press.

Oliver, Kelly. 1997. *Family Values: Subjects Between Nature and Culture.* New York: Routledge.

———. 1995. *Womanizing Nietzsche: Philosophy's Relations to 'the Feminine.'* New York: Routledge.

Rosenberg, David, trans. 1990. *The Book of J,* with a commentary by Harold Bloom. New York: Grove Weidenfeld.

Zeligs, Dorothy. 1986. *Moses: A Psychodynamic Study.* New York: Human Sciences Press.

Levers, Signatures, and Secrets   4

Derrida's Use of Woman

Mary C. Rawlinson

Though Derrida addresses woman or the question of woman directly and frontally in only a few of his many texts, nonetheless the figure of woman reappears throughout his writing.[1] The profound implication of woman in Derrida's style of reading hinges on the fact that the term has never been, perhaps never can be, successfully domesticated by philosophy.[2] Derrida's analyses demonstrate not only the masculine marking of the supposedly generic human subject of philosophy, but also the way in which a certain "sacrifice" of woman is essential to the project of metaphysics. Always other and outside the metaphysical closure, woman provides for Derrida a point of experimentation and risk, a possible "lever of intervention" by which the circulating of the system of metaphysical concepts might be effectively interrupted. Part I of this paper constitutes a report on this experiment, an analysis of the function or value of woman in Derrida's strategic reading of metaphysics, and, in particular, in the text of Hegel.

The position of woman "outside" the closed system of metaphysical concepts raises the question of alterity, of the relation of the other to the same. Certainly, Derrida's employment of woman as a lever of intervention exploits this exteriority, but does it step beyond it? Does it merely repeat an ancient logic in which woman, the other who is not like me, can never say "I"; or, does it take thought beyond the old oppositions of inner/outer, same/other, subject/object? In his analyses of the logic of the signature, as well as mourning and the gift, Derrida attempts to develop the thought of an irreducible and radically singular other, an alterity which would always exceed any attempt at dialectical mastery, which would always already have marked and disrupted the self-sameness of the "I." Part II of this paper tracks the itinerary of woman in the elaboration of this non-dialectical alterity: it addresses the question of why Derrida wants to "write with the hand of a woman."

In recent work Derrida has set this account of alterity within the context of considerations of friendship, on the one hand, and God, on the other.[3] Part III of this essay queries the destiny of woman within these contexts, and raises the question of whether or not the valorization of these sites of intervention does not doom her return to silence, to an alterity that can never speak for itself, to her place as the inactive soil and nourishment of man's active self-positing. Were woman to find a voice—and given that she is explicitly defined as the other in metaphysics "our language," she could speak only in an "unheard of" tongue—would it not expose friendship as fraternity and prayer as the essential speech of patriarchy? For what is Derrida responsible in engaging these discourses as discourses of the other?

Part I. The Critique of the "We"

> "... we, philosophical consciousness ..."
>
> —Hegel, Phenomenology of Spirit

> "qui, nous? nou magis-
> tral, nou du Sa, nous
> les hommes? Et si
> c'etait toujours le
> meme? Et qui-nous-
> assiste ici"
>
> —Derrida, *Glas*

Derrida regularly resists the appropriation of his practice of reading and writing in the concepts of technique or method; rather, Derrida's style constitutes a strategy which is always multiple, both in its deployment and in its effects. This is because Derrida's practice sets for itself an impossible task: "invention"—of "a novel world, another habitat, another person, another desire even." Derrida aims, on the one hand, to suspend or deflect the very effect of univeralization that in Kant and Hegel is the hallmark of language, and, on the other, to offer a place or open site for the inscription of the other's difference. The aim of this writing is not to create that fiction of a co-presence that is articulated in the "we" of Hegelian metaphysics, wherein each is only an instance of the same and substitutible for the other according to law; rather, this writing signs for (the one who has read, who has gone before) and is signed by (the one who will read, who comes after) the other.

> ... deconstruction loses nothing from admitting that it is impossible; also that those who would rush to delight in that admission lose nothing from having to wait. For a deconstructive operation *possibility* would rather be the danger, the danger of becoming an available set of rule-governed procedures, methods, accessible approaches. The interest of deconstruction, of such force and desire as it may have, is a certain experience of the impossible: that is, as I shall insist in my conclusion, of the other—the experience of the other as the invention of the impossible, in other words, as the only possible invention." (PS 209)

Writing exhibits an intersubjectivity not founded on co-presence, contract, or the exchange of the one for the other as the same, and Derrida's writing exploits this feature in novel approaches to alterity, responsibility, and ethics. In Derrida's practice those forces which resist universalization, codification, and normalization appear via the figure of woman (as, e.g., the "living feminine" or "mother-tongue"). Moreover, the analysis of Antigone's role in the argument of Hegel's *Phenomenology* proves more critical to his critique of the "we" of metaphysics than even Derrida admits.

Strategic, Derrida's practice is also risky. Derrida rewrites certain pretexts in order to work their conceptual systems to the "point of exhaustion," "de-limiting" the system of concepts by revealing that what is defined as "outside" or "other" is, in fact, foundational and inscribed in the system's very heart (See D7, also, P6.). The operation of the concept produces and reproduces identity according to the logic of the Same, wherein the other always reappears as the same. And, "... there will be invention only on condition that the invention transgress, in order to be inventive, the status and programs with which it was supposed to comply" (PS 216).

Such a practice cannot avoid "operating according to the lexicon of the system [it] is delimiting ... borrowing the syntaxic and lexical resources of the language of metaphysics, as one must always do ..." (P 7, 10). The risk is that the writer may merely repeat, rather than reinscribe, i.e., that his language will fail to be inventive. Such a succombing to "paleonymy"—the "damping" of the novel or wild by the habitualities of the old conceptual system—has dire consequences, not only for philosophy, but for life itself where the regulatory violence of the Same is deployed.

The Hegelian text—which "must be read"—serves as the exemplar of metaphysics "our language."[4] Hegel's *Phenomenology of Spirit*, a "science of the experience of consciousness," supplies the site of the production of the "we" and weaves together the themes of life/death, language/life, I/other that Derrida is still unraveling. Even woman.

What marks "our" time—the time of the "we"—for Hegel is the material triumph of general forms: the supercession of the particular consciousness by corporate agencies of massive proportions and immense regulatory powers, more or less hostile or indifferent to individual life. (Hegel remarks that the individual's share in the "work of Spirit" is in our time "very small.") And, though he does not see beyond the bureaucracy of the State to the economic forces and forms of communication that will threaten even the hegemony of the state in "our time," Hegel does look forward to a bureaucracy of normalization by which the economy of the Same is reproduced indefinitely in virtually all domains of human life.

Moreover, Hegel identifies this universalization, this power of the general, with the absorption of life by language, the "element of the universal"; and this very absorption is said to constitute the written body of the *Phenomenology of Spirit*. No domains of intimacy remain unduplicated by their representation; everything is (can be) symbolized, and, thus, treated as a mere instance. The discourse of the Same regulates everywhere: on the one hand, all the registers of actual life, the domain of the blood, are subjected to scientific study and to the regulations and regulatory practices inevitably produced by it; on the other, these material registers, as fields of particulars, can be and are replaced by their symbolic representatives, so that the multiplicity of bodies may be grasped as One or the Same for purposes of manipulation and distribution.

By duplicating himself in the register of the universal, the subject, at once, secures a self-confirming reflection and encloses himself in the system of representation. This figure of inversion controls Hegel's *Phenomenology*: natural consciousness, having emptied itself out into history, embodying in its actual practices and productions all the possible forms and shapes of consciousness, on the one hand, and objectivity on the other, turns back on itself or returns to itself by digesting that life, transforming its flesh and blood, its actual particulars, into the universal discourse of philosophical concepts.

The *we*, which articulates natural and philosophical consciousness with each other in the *Phenomenology of Spirit*, assures the proximity to itself of the fixed and central being for which this circular reappropriation is produced. The *we* is the unity of absolute knowledge and anthropology, of God and man, onto-theo-teleology and humanism. "Being" and language-the group of languages—that the we governs or opens: such is the name of that which assures the transition between metaphysics and humanism via the *we*. (EM 121)

Hegel's analysis of the transformation of the particular consciousness of actual life into the universal subject of science takes the form, famously, of the master-slave dialectic. The slave, having lost his freedom by mistakenly clinging to the singularity of his natural life, by being unwilling to risk it fully in the fight for recognition, regains his freedom through the universalizing processes of work, politics, and language. Through his conversion into the citizen or legal person, the particular consciousness rids himself of the contingency of blood and reconstitutes his relation to the other as one of reciprocal or mutual recognition, guaranteed by the formality of contract. Both the rights of the individual and his property are secured through the universal "we," embodied in his various declarations of independence and articles of confederation or constitution. The achievement of citizenship, this universalization of the particular consciousness that insures recognition by the other, depends on his participation in this "we."

Conditioning this liberating universalization of consciousness, then, is a sacrifice of blood and bodies: contract requires the subjection of blood to a man's word, while, what Hegel often calls oxymoronically "the life of the concept," requires a transfusion of the blood of the particular body who pales to the status of an instance. Yet, the many deaths of many selves or shapes of consciousness that will occur along the dialectic's "highway of despair" return a "surplus value": consciousness is reborn or reappears in a new and "more comprehensive" shape which preserves or returns all that was lost with an added value, viz. the revelation of the truth of what is preserved. "... [T]his unlimited surplus value [is] what the metaphysician systematically prefers" (WM. 211). Like a good capitalist, dialectical consciousness always gains more than it spends: every investment is sure to make a profit. Thus, "the *Aufhebung* is the dying away, the amortization, of death. That is the concept of economy in general in speculative dialectics" (G 345). Whatever sacrifice may be required, the "formed thing," man's technical armamentarium, his "acquired property" and his "resources," including his wife, as well as his "concepts" (whereby he authorizes, justifies, and facilitates these processes of universalization) constitute the full, armed, and positive face of his reclaimed freed and discursive duplication.

Between the theoretical language of metaphysics and the universal discourse of citizenship, on the one hand, and, on the other, the domain of practices and institutions where the "human sciences" deploy their regulatory power upon real bodies, there is the family (See, G 328–29). The "we" emerges out of the family, in the substitution of contract for blood-rela-tionship. Only its emergence out of the family prevents transcendental inter-subjectivity from being "abstract and formal" (G 348). If recognition takes place in language, paradigmatically in the contracts and books of men, nevertheless

> . . . the struggle for recognition does not have its element in the tongue. The struggle is played out between bodies, to be sure, but also between economic forces, goods, real possessions, first of all the family's. . . . [T]he linguistic element implies an ideality that can be only the effect of the destruction of empiric singularities, an effect and not a middle of the struggle. In the practical war between singular forces, the injuries must bring about actual expropriations. They must wrest from the other the disposition of its own body, its language, must literally, dislodge the other from ts possessions. the field of the word does not suffice for this. . . . Hence they must injure one another. The fact that each posits itself as exclusive totality in the singularity of its existence must become actual. The violation [Beleidigung: outrage, rape, abuse] is necessary.'" (G 150)

While the centrality of the figure of mastery and slavery and Hegel's empha-sis on the particular coming to see himself as "only a moment" of the uni-versal might lead one to believe that it is a sacrifice of man that is at issue here, it is, in fact, woman who must be sacrificed, or as Hegel remarks "left behind," in the process of universalization.

A radical bifurcation marks Spirit. The two sexes ". . . appear in their eth-ical significance, as diverse beings who share between them the two distinc-tions belonging to the ethical substance" (Hegel 1979, 459). Woman is identified with immediacy and feeling, with the body and its blood, with domesticity and the enclosure of the home (replicating her representation in the womb as enclosure), and above all with death and redemption. The specific act of Antigone, who gives her life to perform those rites necessary to rescue her brother's corpse from its vulnerability and degradation as a mere thing, those rites necessary to respiritualize his body, constitutes the duty of woman in general. The man, on the other hand, achieves the universalization of his particular consciousness by "leaving the family behind," substituting for the bonds of blood, the self-determining associa-tions of contract in the domain of politics and theory in science. Man finds his "actual substantial life in the state, in science [*Wissenschaft*], and other-wise in work and struggle with the external world and with himself" and through this "division" or exteriorization of himself in the formed thing, scientific practice, or symbolic language he achieves "self-conscious being" (Hegel, 1991 §166). His educational transformation into "we, philosophical consciousness" requires that he turn away from the immediacy and singularity of the relation to the mother and turn toward the world of men wherein he will take his father's place.

> Like every formation, every imposition of form, it is on the male's side, here the father's, and since this violent form bears the parent's death, it imposes itself above all against the father. But the death of the father is only the real death of the mother [who is 'simply' abandoned], corresponds to the idealization of the father, in which the father is not simply annihilated. The relieving education interiorizes the father. (G 345)

Thus man is constituted as a speaking subject with the right to recognize and be recognized, and we discover the "most traditional phallocentrism within the Hegelian onto-theo-teleology."

While the man can represent and reflect the private domains of domesticity, feeling, and the blood in the discourses and practices of science, thereby superceding, but preserving them, woman enjoys no correlative opportunity to reflect the public domains of the city, laboratory, and the workplace. Hegel deems her incapable of those "higher" activities—science, art, government—that "require a universal element." She is deprived of that element in which she might go out to the other and come back to herself, viz., language, the "element of the universal." Having no language of her own, she is a material condition for the universal language which is marked masculine. She cannot partake of the specular economy wherein by seeing herself in the other she would be returned to herself in a reflection. She preserves for man the dimension of blood or life from which he has become divided, and, thus, makes it possible for him to preserve or recoup that dimension in a specular reflection. He reflects her self back to her as an object, but she cannot be represented as a subject and cannot represent herself. Thus, she cannot return his reflection so as to complete the circuit of recognition. Moreover, if woman attempts to enter "man's dominion," the domain of language or "scientific universal cognition," she puts the very province itself "in danger" (VPR, III, 525–26.) It is just this danger that Derrida would exploit:

> The concept of the concept, along with the entire system that attends it, belongs to a prescriptive order. It is that order that a problematics of woman and a problematics of difference, as sexual difference, should disrupt along the way. (CH 100)

Hegel's analysis of sexual difference disrupts the logic of the concept precisely insofar as a moment or figure of consciousness—woman—remains external to it. (The concept subverts itself.) In spite of the requirement that the system preserve everything, she is "left behind." Moreover, the non-reciprocity of man and woman is essential to the system, a necessary condition of "we, philosophical consciousness." All this Derrida demonstrates by way of "soliciting" and "delimiting" the Hegelian system, forcing it to "write itself otherwise," and, thereby, shaking and loosening the multiple ligaments by which the discourse of metaphysics is bound to the concrete practices of the human sciences.[5] As an effect of this strategy, through this "inventive" relation to the language of metaphysics, there appears a different dissymmetry, another alterity.

II. The Logic of the Signature

> . . . Once
>
> to everything, only once. Once and no more. And we too,
> once. And never again. But this
> once to have been, if only this once:
> to have been of the earth seems beyond revoking.
>
> —Rilke, *Duino Elegies*

> The "me" or the "us" of which we speak then arise and are delimited in the way that they are only through this experience of the other, and of the other as other who can die, leaving in me or in us this memory of the other. This terrible solitude which is mine or ours at the death of the other constitutes that relation to self which we call "me," "us," "subject," "intersubjectivity" . . .
>
> —Derrida, *Memoires for Paul de Man*

Against the resistance of (Hegelian) metaphysics, Derrida writes out another logic wherein the themes inherited from (transcendental) phenomenology—life and death, sacrifice, language, the other (of sexual difference)—are rewoven. In developing this logic of the signature Derrida remarks that he "wants to write with the hand of a woman," and explicitly female interlocutors appear in his text, appear to write the text (EO 79; see, e.g. AT). Woman is doubly implicated in this logic: on the one hand, in a critique of normalization already anticipated here, woman appears as the vital mother-tongue, acted upon by and resistant to the dead, paternal language of the State; on the other, woman appears more obliquely as the figure of aporicity as such.[6] As such woman marks through displacement—in the impossibility of woman being placed—the holding open of a future toward the other, i.e., a promise. Through the operation of this logic of the signature in which woman is implicated, Derrida reveals at least three movements counter to metaphysics and its ethics: 1) the "me" of the one who speaks can be constituted only on loan from an other who remains other and different from the same, who is not present to "me," who comes before/after in a relation paradigmatically manifested in mourning and in reading; 2) the other is always a *singular* other, just this one and no other, so that my relation to the other cannot be constituted by the homogeneity of contract or duty, rather by the promise, the gift, and the sacrifice; and 3) responsibility arises from human mortality, from the irreplaceability of the subject who will die.

In stepping beyond dialectical (sexual) difference, Derrida does not propose the utopia of an unmarked humanity prior to woman, rather the difference is initially intensified through the appearance of woman as the "mother-tongue." Where the issue is teaching, and specifically the teaching of Nietzsche, Hegel appears again as the "thinker of the State," that institution through which the language of the universal is disseminated in bodies.[7] Resisting these forces and marked by them is the body of the "mother-tongue." Associated with life, "living on," with excess—with the future, in short—the mother-tongue is both a real materiality, an actual marked corpus, and full of "secrets" or "unheard of possibilities."[8] The State, in the guise of the mother, pretending to nurture us and supply our needs, disfigures this body of the mother tongue in its attempts to fix it, to codify and normalize it in the conventionalized language of science. The state, through the university, exercises a policing function with respect to language; it would control and regularize the proliferating body of the mother, reducing it to the common language of the Same. While "my-death" is structurally necessary to pronouncing "I am"—insofar as the actual individual is only a displaceable instance and the meaningfulness of the utterance must be given in my absence—

> There has to be a pact or alliance with the living language and language of the living feminine against death, against the dead. The repeated affirmation—like the hymen and alliance—always belongs to language: it comes down and comes back to the signature of the maternal, nondegenerate, noble tongue. (EO 21)

Back to an "inventive" writing, then, like Derrida's, which in resistance to metaphysics and its concepts casts itself in the role of the mother tongue vis-à-vis the state and its dead language. Thus,

> Our interpretations will not be readings of a hermeneutic or exegetic sort, but rather political interventions in the political rewriting of the text and its destination. (EO 32)

Politics enters into writing through reading the other's text which is then signed in being written about. In contrast to Hegel's confidence that truth only comes at the time that is "ripe to receive it," Nietzsche describes himself as a "posthumous birth," one who will come to be, for better or worse, in the history of the appropriation of the texts circulating under the name "Nietzsche." The proper name and the text detach themselves from the author and circulate without him, after his death. And the text, whose author—as Plato remarks—is no longer there to defend it, to decide to whom it should speak and before whom it should remain silent, is subject to the dangers of misreading and co-optation, of which the fate of Nietzsche's text at the hands of the Nazis would serve as a paradigm example. This will have been a possibility of the text, and one not to be avoided by appeals to truth and error.

The reader, who is always alive, returns or repays in his reading the credit which the (dead) author has extended himself. As Derrida repeatedly remarks, *it is the other who signs the text.* "Nothing returns to the living," rather what the reader/writer spends returns to the text and the (dead) author. There is a play of life and death, then, beyond the resistance to the state: the intertwining of thanatography (the writing of the author who dies but is encrypted in his text) and allography (the writing of the other who signs the text through his reading, thereby taking upon himself the political responsibility for it.) In spite of Hegel's confidence the author and reader are never present to one another, and repayment on investment returns either too late or elsewhere.

In this non-presence of reader and writer that constitutes the intersubjectivity of writing Derrida evokes the alterity of an other who is not to be mastered. An inventive writing, faithful to the "logic of the living feminine," demonstrates that, while in the mode of the present the other can be only an object or a constituted sense, in the modes of before and after—of loss and expectation—the other appears in his difference.

When the other dies, he can no longer be absorbed into the complacency of the "we's" present (M 66). What is lamented in mourning is what happens to us" . . . when everything is entrusted to the sole memory that is 'in me' or 'in us'" (M 33). The dead other who can no longer answer the call of his name, nonetheless, "resists the closure of our interiorizing memory," and it is this resistance that founds both alterity and the "in me."[9] Only in an "impossible" mourning, a mourning without consolation or recovery, would the other be preserved as other, rather than incorporated in the Same. Correlatively,

> The 'within me' and the 'within us' acquire their sense and their bearing only by carrying within themselves the death and the memory of the other; of an other who is greater than them, greater than what they or we can bear, carry, or comprehend, since we then lament being no more than 'memory.' (M See also, PS 203)

This failure of mourning—the difference btween the other and my memory of the other—marks the fact that the other is not just a constituted sense in me. When mourning cannot adequately evoke the "we" of the plural present it reveals in me the impossibility of substituting (for) the other, according to the logic of the same.[10] In inventive writing alterity implies a mortal and singular other, one who is singular because he will die his own death, who is not "only an instance." And, whether he is alive or not, it is (the possibility of) the other's death that marks the difference between him and me—the fact that *there can be no substitutions* (M 33ff.).

In mourning the irreplaceable other appears in his absence as something more than a constituted sense in me or an object for me. In this loss, as in the non-presence of reader and writer, the radical alterity of the other is marked. An inventive writer gives himself—his labor, even, as Proust insists, his life—for the other who will come after, as the reader gives himself— thought, feeling, time, reputation—to the one who has gone before. Similarly, mourning constitutes a "gift," a dedication of the self to the other without thought of return. Whereas the ethics of contract, based upon a logic of exchange, or the ethics of virtue, based upon submission to a common law or discipline, embody a specular economy in which the other returns myself to me as the same, an ethics deriving from the gift and mourning reveals the dependence of the "in me" on the non-return of the other, on his absolute difference and the impossibility of his presentation as a constituted sense or object. Responsibility is evoked by and returns to the other in the singularity of his mortality (D 51).

What is sacrificed here is neither the "me" who speaks, nor the other, but the "others" to whom I do not respond. Responsibility will always involve this guilt and failure to respond.[11] Guilt is intrinsic to responsibility because "one is never responsible enough" (GD 51). The real issue, then, for ethical judgment is not the cultivation of a "beautiful soul"; rather, the task is to develop a strategy of response— a kind of writing, for example— that will hold open the future to the other who is not the same.

To give one's word without thought of return and for the sake of the *other's* future is to make a promise, and Derrida's writing is suffused with a specific promise. According to an aporetic logic which refuses to stabilise itself in the customary binaries of metaphysics, Derrida's writing ". . . trace[s] its path by linking its 'act,' always an act of memory, to the promised future of a text to be signed" (M 135). This non-thetic writing holds open a place for (the response) of the other; it gives the other a place and a future. And the figure of this writing which instead of taking place makes a place for the other is woman. Woman's atopie brings with it ". . . the chance for a risky turbulence in the assigning of places within our small European space," a chance to do away with "maps, topographies . . . sexual identity cards" (CH 94). Eccentric to the logic of dialectical mastery, alien to the dead language of paternity and the state, the living feminine or the mother-tongue intertwined with the mortality of the singular other, woman the affirming promise that seals an alliance with the other, mortal to mortal. In the face of the inexorable workings (and, as we have seen these are far from "merely" linguistic) of paternal language, in an expenditure without profit, the aporia of the unplaceable woman holds open the future of what is to come (See, M 19; EO 13, 88).

Part III. Not God, but Woman

> It is the other who will decide what I am—man or woman.
> —Derrida, *The Ear of the Other*

In risking a discourse on woman Derrida remarks a number of traps lying in wait. One trap is the search for a "new concept" of woman. This essentialising gesture reduces the aporetic status of woman and returns woman to the dialectical logic of identity. (Thus, pallocentrism appears as feminism.) Another trap arises from the practical necessity of preserving certain metaphysical presuppositions as a precondition for practical struggles (economic, ideological, political) (CH 97). Just as Derrida's writing repeats the language of metaphysics in order to subvert it, and, thus, risks *merely* repeating, so too these practical struggles may be reabsorbed by the forces they resist. The attempt to neutralize sexual difference is a third trap in which Derrida finds both Heidegger and Levinas ensnared. (See GE 384ff. and AT 432–33) The attempt to institute behind sexual difference an unmarked generic humanity repeats the "classical gesture" which ". . . gives a masculine sexual marking to what is represented as a neutral originariness or, at least, as prior to or superior to all sexual markings" (CH 102). Woman—figure of singularity, mortality, and the future of the other—

(margin: Mauss)

never appears as the generically human. If Derrida has escaped all these traps, has he not fallen into another?

Derrida emphasizes repeatedly that the selection of a site of intervention is a strategic decision determining the "inventiveness" of writing in relation to metaphysics, "our language." Woman intervenes so as to subvert the logic of the Same and introduce the singular face of the other who will die and to whom the "me" who speaks is responsible. When Derrida's analyses are set, as they frequently are, within the context of friendship and prayer or the invocation of the name of God, however, do not the signature, the gift, and the other not become something wholly other, and very like the logic of the Same? Will not the name of God (even, and perhaps especially, in negative theology) always invoke the logic of paternity and the parricide by which the brothers are bound together? Does not the invocation of God as a figure of alterity remove from the other her singular face? And, is not friendship ineluctably tied to its Aristotlean soil, where it is always determined as fraternity?

> An apostrophe (to God) is turned toward another apostrophe in the
>   direction of him . . .
> —Never of her. . .
> —Not to my knowledge, not in this case (but don't hasten to
>   conclude that the scene is unfolding between men and above all
>   that the one who speaks is a man.)
> (SN 38; N.B.: the interlocutor who interrupts here is explicitly
> marked "female.")

Derrida anticipates the trap; nevertheless, he considers whether or not the gift, the signature, and the logic of alterity that they embody might not exceed the aporicity of woman,

> . . . whether sexual difference, femininity, for example (my italics)—however
> irreducible it may be—does not remain derived from and subordinated to
> either the question of destination or the thought of the gift. . . . Must one
> think "difference" "before" sexual difference or taking off "from" it? (CH 98)

He "dreams" of an opening toward the other "where the code of sexual marks would no longer be discriminating," an opening onto a "multiplicity of sexual marked voices." Just as Descartes insists that the thought of God proves his existence, Derrida urges us to believe that his dream "prove[s] that what is dreamt must be there in order for it to provide the dream." Does this confidence in the origin of his dream not close down the questions of the "we," life and language, life and death that are broached in woman? Does this gesture not interrupt the dream's own itinerary and reinscribe that "neutralization" of sexual difference that returns to a generic marked masculine?

Woman, figure of the aporetic, remains, like the question, suspended, and will return.[12]

Notes

1. The question of woman is explicitly broached in *Spurs* (1978) and "Otobiographies" (1982) in the context of readings of Nietzsche on the themes of truth and education, in *Glas* (1974) in relation to a reading of Hegel's analysis of the family as an ethical form, in the interview CH (1982), in "Le Facteur de la verite" (*Le Carte Postale* 1980) in relation to a reading of Lacan, in GE (1987) and "Geschlecht II" (1987) which consider Heidegger's ontological difference in relation to sexual difference, and in "At This Very Moment in This Work Here I Am" (1987) where, in the context of a reading of Levinas, a female interlocutor is explicitly inscribed in the text. (Of course, I do not pretend that this is an exhaustive list.) For a discussion of obliqueness and frontality in the approach to philosophical problems see, "Passions: 'An Oblique Offering.'" Here in a meditation on responsibility Derrida remarks, ". . . we should not above all approach in a direct, frontal projective, that is, thetic or thematic way. . . . Nothing would seem more violent or naive than to call for more frontality, more thesis or more thematization, to suppose that one can find a standard here" (PA 10–11).

   No doubt the same must be said of woman.

2. Derrida often cautions the reader not to rush to decision. To ask what "woman" means here would be to assume the logic of the concept, viz., that the term expresses or grasps some non-conceptual or pre-conceptual given. To ask about its reference—perhaps to some subset of human beings (a class of ambiguous, unstable borders) or perhaps to a set of institutions, practices, figures, and operations by which actual women are produced— would be to foreclose the question broached here of the intertwining of life and language. Following Derrida, woman is here posed as a path of thought. What will it open? (See, e.g., CH 100.)

3. See, e.g., "*Sauf le nom*" (1992), *The Gift of Death* (1992), *Given Time* (1991). Though these themes are not new to Derrida's writing they do seem to be more frontally presented since *Memoirs for Paul de Man* (1986).

4. See "Diff'rance" 16, 19 on the "privilege" of Hegelianism as an exemplar of philosophy.

5. Or rather, these themes are here demonstrated after Derrida. The engagement of them is, perhaps, more "frontal," i.e., more directly political than Derrida prefers, at least in the philosophical register. Derrida's inability to effectively engage "frontally" with the operations of institutions upon real

bodies has been remarked; and, perhaps, the necessity of a supplementary detour through Foucault could be marked here. Perhaps, however, this is no fault in Derrida's writing, but precisely what gives him the power to intervene "obliquely" via the language of metaphysics. (On "frontality" in relation to the political, see, AP 82.)

6. Prosopopoeia is the general logic of the figure: through the figure an absent, unpresentable other appears, but "obliquely." Woman is not, however, a "determinable identity," not "a figure"; rather, woman, who has no place within the logic of identity and the concept, is a figure of figuration, the mark of an openness to the return of the unmastered other (See, e.g., S 51; on prosopopoeia, see, M 25–26, 38–39).

7. The primary site of this dissemination is, of course, the (State's) university whose practices are here, as in "The Ends of Man," put in question. The institution of the university ". . . institutes above all the transmission of what has been inherited, the conservation and interpretation of the archive . . ." (EO 51). Derrida, after Nietzsche, describes the instructor as a "mouthpiece" of the State, that is of the normalizing language of the universal, and the student as a passive ear which gradually loses its "keenness," i.e., its difference (See EO 27, 35). The "transmission" of the "inheritance," of course, follows a paternal logic.

8. See, e.g., SA 54 where Derrida speaks of the way in which negative theology "imprints a mark" or "leaves some remains on the body of a tongue." On the "secrets" of the mother-tongue, see GD 88.)

9. See EO 59, where this encryption of the other is contrasted with the dialectical mastery of *Erinnerung*.

10. A reading of Husserlian phenomenology, focusing on the problem of transcendental solipsism and the appresentation of the other as a constituted sense, could be joined here. See my "Perspectives and Horizons: Husserl on Seeing the Truth," in *Discursive Vision*, David Levin, ed. (Cambridge: MIT Press, 1997).

11. Derrida offers two concrete examples in *Donner la mort*, one trivial—I feed one cat and not the others and cannot justify my choice—the other profound enough to be worth quoting: ". . . because of the structure of the laws of the market that society has instituted and controls, because of the mechanisms of external debt and other similar inequities, that same 'society' puts to or (but failing to help someone in distress accounts for only a minor difference) allows to die of hunger and disease tens of millions of children (those neighbors or fellow humans that ethics or the discourse of rights of man refer to) without any moral or legal tribunal ever being considered competent to judge such a sacrifice, the sacrifice of others to avoid being sacrificed oneself. Not only is it true that such a society participates in this incalculable sacrifice, it actually organizes it. The smooth functioning of its economic, political, and legal affairs, the smooth functioning of its moral discourse and good conscience presupposes the permanent operation of the

sacrifice. And such a sacrifice is not even invisible, for from time to time television shows us, while keeping them at a distance, a series of intolerable images, and a few voices are raised to bring it all to our attention. But those images and voices are completely powerless to induce the slightest effective changes in the situation, to assign the least responsibility, to furnish anything more than a convenient alibi" (GD 86). Here—in the generality of the unemployed, the poor, the refugees—no other appears, no singular other appears who might evoke a response.

12.   Many thanks to Ellen Feder and Edward S. Casey for their very productive criticisms of an earlier draft of this paper.

Works Cited

Derrida, Jacques. *Memoires for Paul de Man*, trans. Cecile Lindsay, Jonathan Culler, and Eduardo Cadava. New York: Columbia University Press, 1986. Cited as M.

———. *Glas*, vols. I and II, Paris: Editons Denoel/Gonthier, 1981. Cited as G.

———. *The Gift of Death*, trans. David Wills. Chicago: University of Chicago Press, 1995. Cited as GD.

———. "Sauf le nom." In *On the Name*, trans. David Wood, John P. Leavy, Jr., and Ian Mcleod, ed. Thomas Dutoit. Stanford: Stanford University Press, 1995. Cited as SN.

———. "Passions: 'An Oblique Offering.'" in *On the Name*. Cited as PA.

———. "The Almost Nothing of the Unpresentable." In *Points*, trans. Peggy Kamuf, ed., Elisabeth Weber. Stanford: Stanford University Press, 1995. Cited as ANU.

———. "Choreographies." In *Points*, trans. Christie V. MacDonald. Cited as CH.

———. *Psyche: Inventions de l'autre*. Paris: Editions Galilee, 1987. Cited as PS.

———. "At This Very Moment in This Work Here I Am." In *Between the Blinds*, ed. Peggy Kamuf. New York: Columbia Univesity Press, 1991. Cited as AT.

———. "*Geschlecht*: Sexual Difference, Ontological Difference." In *Between the Blinds*. Cited as GE.

———. *Positions*, trans. Alan Bass. Chicago: University of Chicago Press, 1981. Cited as P.

———. *Given Time: I. Counterfeit Money*, trans. Peggy Kamuf. Chicago: University of Chicago Press, 1991. Cited as GT.

———. *Aporias*, trans. Thomas Dutoit. Stanford: Stanford University Press, 1993. Cited as A.

———. "Différance." In *Margins of Philosophy*, trans. Alan Bass. Chicago: University of Chicago Press, 1972. Cited as D.

———. "The Ends of Man." In *Margins*. Cited as EM.

———. "White Mythology." In *Margins of Philosophy*, trans. Alan Bass. Chicago: University of Chicago Press, 1972. Cited as WM.

————. *The Ear of the Other*, trans. Peggy Kamuf and Avital Ronell, ed. Christie V. McDonald. New York: Schocken Books. Cited as EO.

Hegel, G.W.F. . *Phenomenology of Spirit*, trans. A.V. Miller. New York: Oxford University Press, 1979.

————. *Elements of the Philosophy of Right*, trans. H.B. Nesbitt, ed. Allen E. Wood. Cambridge: Cambridge University Press, 1991.

————. *Vorlesungen über Rechtsphilosophie*, K.–H. Ilting, ed. Stuggart: Frommann Verlag, 1974. Cited as VPR.

On Not Reading Derrida's Texts   5

Mistaking Hermeneutics, Misreading Sexual Difference,
and Neutralizing Narration

Tina Chanter

This mistake of hermeneutics, this mistaking of hermeneutics—it is this that the final message [*envoi*] of "I forgot my umbrella" should challenge. But let us leave that. The truth value (that is, Woman as the major allegory of truth in Western discourse) and its correlative, Femininity (the essence or truth of Woman), are there to assuage such hermeneutic anxiety.

—Derrida, "Choreographies"[1]

Humanity is not thinkable on the basis of two entirely different principles

—Levinas, "And God Created Woman"[2]

[T]he afternoon of the last day of her life when she got out of bed, skipped slowly to the door of the keeping room and announced to Sethe and Denver the lesson she had learned from her sixty years a slave and ten years free: that there was no bad luck in the world but whitepeople. "They don't know when to stop," she said, and returned to her bed, pulled up the quilt and left them to hold that thought forever.

—Morrison, *Beloved*[3]

I: Reading without seeing, seeing without reading

Has Derrida's work on the question of sexual difference ever been read?[4] Has it received so much attention that there is nothing left to be written on the subject, or has it, to quote *Spurs: Nietzsche's Styles/Eperons: Les styles de Nietzsche*[5]—a text in which Derrida takes woman as his subject (see S 37)—

*Is this
something
or the
other?*

received countless responses that fail to go beyond that of the "dogmatic philosopher who *believes* in the truth that is woman, who believes in truth just as he believes in woman" and who "has understood nothing" (S 53)? In "Choreographies" Derrida suggests the latter, recalling, but not identifying, some responses to *Spurs* that revert to the "isolation of Nietzsche's violently anti-feminist statements" from the "movement and system" that Derrida tries to "reconstitute," and others that are "unable to see beyond the end of phallic forms projecting into the text" (CH 170). Derrida goes on to comment, "Generally speaking, this cannot be considered reading, and I will go so far as to say that it is *to not read* the syntax and punctuation of a given sentence when one arrests the text in a certain position, thus settling on a thesis, meaning or truth" (CH 170).

In *Spurs/Eperons*, Derrida attempts to "decipher" an "*inscription of the woman*" (S 87) that he finds deposited, but unread, in Heidegger's reading of Nietzsche:

> Nietzsche has underlined ... the words *sie wird Weib*, "it becomes female." Heidegger cites this sequence, even respects its underlining, but in his commentary (as seems to be generally the case) he skirts the woman. ... Heidegger analyzes all the elements of Nietzsche's text with the sole exception of the idea's becoming-female (*sie wird Weib*). In such a way does one permit oneself to see without reading, to read without seeing. (S 85)

Thus Derrida sees *Spurs/Eperons* as having suffered the same fate as woman at the hands of Heidegger—neither of them were read. They were seen but not read, read without being seen.

If Derrida attempted to rectify the situation in the case of Heidegger, *Spurs*—at least on Derrida's account—appears to have succumbed to readings that "settle in a counter-meaning" (CH 170). In opposition to Nietzsche, for whom "There is no such thing as the essence of woman ... no such thing as the truth of woman" (S 51), readers of *Spurs* have allegedly—just like "those women feminists so derided by Nietzsche" (S 65)—laid claim to the truth about women, without reading what *Spurs/Eperons* has to say about such truths, opposing themselves to Derrida's texts without reading what he has to say about women in the context in which it is written. Ignoring the movement of the text—"On the one hand ... But, on the other hand" (S 51–3), they refuse to read the distance with which Derrida infuses his text on woman ("the remote proximity in *Entfernung*") (S 51). "That's right," Derrida assures us in another context, "distanced, which does not forbid, on the contrary, proximity."[6] This other context will not refrain from making itself felt in a gradual movement that will wash over this text incessantly, as waves encroach upon a shore. They do not read the "abyssal" structure of "property" (S 117) that Heidegger imports into Derrida's understanding of Nietzsche; they neglect the "affirmative power" that Nietzsche, on Derrida's reading, acknowledges in women, emphasizing only the "reactive" instances "of negation" in which she is debased (S 97); they leave aside the "Heideggerian landscape" (S 73) that sets the scene for Derrida's discourse on woman—perhaps most notably the difference between regional and fundamental ontology (S 109), a difference that in the end shares the same structure as the abyssal truth that woman is for Nietzsche. In short they take no account of the "scene of writing" or "the effects of invisible framing"[7] that Derrida finds missing in a text by Lacan,[8] and documents in yet another text—"*Le facteur de la vérité*" ("The Purveyor of Truth")—whose association with *Spurs* should not be lost on us, particularly insofar as they both concern the lack or failure that as such is excluded from the symbolic, and yet guarantees representation, namely truth in the form of (a) woman—in a word, castration.[9]

Perhaps we should settle the account, make up for past errors, atone for these readings that do not read, by producing a corrective interpretation—one that is more responsible to Derrida's texts. But what would responsibility mean here? To be responsible for having read certain texts, texts that Derrida draws on in *Spurs/Eperons* (Nietzsche's *The Gay Science, Beyond Good and Evil, Twilight of the Idols*, and Heidegger's lectures on Nietzsche)?[10] To return to Heidegger's *Being and Time* and *The Metaphysical Foundations of Logic* and to Derrida's readings of those texts in "*Geschlecht*: Sexual Difference, Ontological Difference"?[11] To reproduce the litany of Heideggerian gestures that Derrida recites, emphasizing the "order of implication" that Heidegger observes (GE 79; GS 427, and GE 82; GS 430), an order which banishes the question of sexual difference from ontology, thereby relegating it to the arena of ontical questions? As Derrida says, this would remove "sexuality from every originary structure," thereby confirming "the most traditional philosophemes" (GE 79; GS 428), while at the same time preserving the possibility of sexual multiplicity precisely to the extent that sexual difference is not yet designated, is "not yet" or "no longer" divided into male or female, "not sealed by a two" (GE 83; GS 430). And what would it mean to produce readings of such texts that are responsible, that respond to Derrida's questioning of woman? To affirm the validity of Derrida's interpretation of these texts, to corroborate the "undecidability" (S 105) of sexual difference? To respect his word?

If such gestures manage to avoid the risks of superfluous reiteration—parodying the texts they are designed to elucidate, and flirting with the danger of reproducing the religious cults that Derrida warns against

(S 99)—they might succeed in uncovering something new, in providing more grist for the critical mill. But no matter how scholarly and responsible such readings, no matter how carefully they avoided the possibility of unnecessary duplication, even to the point of contributing some "original insight," there is a sense in which these efforts are thwarted in advance. Here, I mean to indicate routes that, as a feminist, I could have taken, but chose not to. Still governed by oppositional thinking, such an approach would sustain itself by producing competing readings which are set in motion by those against which they compete, and which derive their energy from the assumption that they can correct the faulty positions of others, not by challenging the rules of engagement, but by applying the rules of the game all the more rigorously. Having given up the hope of producing any genuine alternative to those allegedly irresponsible readings against which they set themselves up, before they have even begun such gestures are destined to remain counter-readings, designed to combat readings that do not read. No doubt this process is effective in keeping the machinery of critical production well-oiled, and ensuring that arguments run along the well-worn tracks of critique and counter-critique, but the price is a refusal to acknowledge that the positions thereby taken for granted and the truths for which one settles might be unsettled.

My interests do not lie in capitalizing on the effects of paying off some imagined feminist debt to Derrida. Yet equally, I want to begin not by "pulling out" of context or "isolating" certain points, as if these points were unguarded barbs, "phallic forms projecting into the text" (CH 170). I want to try not to begin "with style, the spur or the umbrella," not to forget "the difference between style and writing or the bisexual complication of those and other forms" (CH 170). I want not "*to not read* the syntax and punctuation of a given sentence" by "arrest[ing] the text in a certain position, thus settling on a thesis, a meaning, or truth" (CH 170). To settle on such a thesis, meaning, or truth is to read the position Derrida takes in his discourse on the feminine as if he were simply a female impersonator, an imposter, even a drag queen—like the minister in Poe's "The Purloined Letter," who, according to Lacan, "in playing the part of the one who hides . . . is obliged to don the role of the Queen, and even the attributes of femininity and shadow, so propitious to the act of concealing" (Lacan 1988, 44; 1966, 31). Just as Derrida observes about Lacan's reading of Poe, "There is here a problem of framing, of bordering and delimitation" (PC 431; CP 459). Here too, as in Lacan's "Seminar on 'The Purloined Letter,'" if we are to believe Derrida, we are "missing . . . an elaboration of the problem of the frame, the signature, and the *parergon*" (PC 432; CP 460).[12] I will return to the lack of framing that Derrida locates in Lacan's text on Poe. For now let me say for the record that if we are content to see Derrida's representations of woman as if he were a pillager of the trope of woman as it occurs in the texts he reads, we are in danger of "missing the position of the narrator" (PC 483; CP 511), or of failing to take an interest in the "subject-author" (PC 432; CP 460). When Derrida says "I speak from my place as woman" (AT 44; EM 56), the work[13] that places him in that position must be considered, as much as the fact that he accepts that he is ineluctably "at fault" in taking up that position (AT 12; EM 22; AT 44; EM 56).

In attempting to follow the directives that Derrida himself issues, in the allusions buried in his comments as to how his texts have been read by readers who read without reading, I neither want to remain innocent of the questions he raises (often in relation to Levinas, but also in his relations to others) about the ethics of following such directives, nor do I want to remain captive to unjustifiable, teleological, and utopian desires (be they in the name of feminism or at the service of other ideologies). I do not want to submit to a naive belief in "continuous progress" (CH 167), a belief in a "continuously accelerated 'liberation' at once punctuated by determinable stages and commanded by an ultimately thinkable *telos*, a truth of sexual difference" (CH 165), where "everything would collapse, flow, founder in this same homogenized, sterilized river of history" that "carries along with it the age-old dream of reappropriation, 'liberation,' autonomy, mastery, in short the *cortège* of metaphysics and the *tekhnè*" (CH 166). If, in taking Derrida seriously, I appear to situate myself on one side of the polemical and ideological divide that constitute readings according to the apparently bipolar opposites "feminist" or "deconstructive," I want to disrupt the ease with which such oppositions become entrenched. I want to suggest that to read Derrida in a way that does not read without seeing, or see without reading need neither subordinate "feminism" to "deconstruction," accepting unquestioningly the master's authority, nor subordinate "deconstruction" to "feminism," defensively protecting our rights to a reclaimed territory by warding off prospectors, and punishing trespassers. In another context, one whose importance to the present text should emerge in due course, bell hooks warns against behaving "as though feminism is a turf we have conquered, a field of power where we can maintain authority and presence, and reap rewards only if there are a few of us present, if we are always a rare commodity."[14] I want to suggest that we read otherwise—to refuse to be captivated either by feminism or by deconstruction, although the most vigilant attempts to read succumb to the attendant risks and aporias of hermeneutics, even as such gestures strive to register these risks, these aporias. What it means to read "*otherwise*" (AT 25; EM 37)[15] here, in this context—and "the border of a context is less narrow, less strictly determining than one is accustomed to believe" (AT 12; EM 22)—is to acknowledge that readings, while they may not always succeed in escaping blind alleys, can "interrupt themselves" (AT 27; EM 39).

But here, with this word "otherwise," thought interrupts itself. To read this word "otherwise" is to recall, in this context, an interruption in a text by Derrida that invites us to re-read another text, one that has not, by and large, been read by those who claim to know what is at stake in questions of sexual difference.[16] The invitation, in the form of "Choreographies," asks us to return to *Spurs*, and the interruption—which does not so much "arrest" as intervene—occurs in the form of a footnote invoking Levinas. In other words, we are invited, by Derrida's interviewer, Christie McDonald, to turn back to *Spurs* by turning away from it, to turn to other texts—neither by Heidegger nor by Nietzsche, but by Levinas—in order to re-read a text that questions the truth of woman through a reading of Heidegger's interpretation of Nietzsche. Taking up this invitation to re-read Levinas, I also want to turn away from it, or perhaps, still turning within it, turn it back on itself, doubling back to listen for echoes that are suppressed, and yet whose register surpasses the textual maneuvers that recognize woman as a trope for the abyssal truth of metaphysics.

What, then—and I will ask my question again, this time with an altered emphasis—would it take to do justice to Derrida's reading of sexual difference? Would this be the right question, and if being responsible to a text is a question of justice, how are we to understand justice? Is there a prior question, a question that has always already been set in motion before we can speak of doing justice in any straightforward sense, a question that Derrida knows better than most—the question of respecting alterity, otherness, other ways of reading?[17] Does Derrida's reading of woman, like Heidegger's reading of Nietzsche, "open on to still another reading which for its part refuses to be contained there" (S 115)? Perhaps, then, this attempt to remain "faithful" (CH 168)—to repeat another gesture that Derrida makes—can do so only by going beyond the text we are asked to re-read, only by going beyond *Spurs/Eperons*, which might still not have been read. This other way of reading will proceed according to "a completely other history" (CH 167).[18] It will go beyond mere reiteration, not simply allowing the continuous flow of history to repeat itself, nor slavishly mimicking, by way of "parody" or "simulacrum" (S 99), nor yet by re-enacting the silences and blindness that characterize its own previous history. Of course, there are parallels between different histories, which does not mean that these parallels circumscribe those histories completely.

I want to follow the logic of certain texts—the "movement and system" Derrida tries to "reconstitute" (CH 170)—by taking them to their extreme, by moving beyond them, by exceeding these texts in a gesture that points toward other texts of heterogeneous kinds—by doing so according to a law that Derrida nonetheless articulates, within the limits of his own text (see S 109–11). Designating the limits of his own texts, knowing how to draw the boundaries around a text, is something Derrida practices well—the "numerous analyses" of woman in Nietzsche's texts are said to be "impossible to elaborate here"—but they are nonetheless judged as taking shape "according to an already formalized law" (S 109);[19] Heidegger's "development . . . of the *es gibt Sein*" is similarly attenuated—it "cannot be reconstructed here" (S 121). "I must limit myself to merely naming: ontological difference and sexual difference" (CH 180); or again, in a gesture that includes what it excludes, incorporating what it acknowledges at the same time cannot be contained, "In another conference it would have been necessary to explore these experiences of the edge or of the borderline under the names of what one calls the body proper and sexual difference;"[20] once more,

> . . . Without being able to review here the itinerary of a reading in *Spurs/ Eperons* clearly divided into two moments, I must limit myself to a piece of information, or rather to an open question. The question proceeds, so to speak from the end; it proceeds from the point where the thought of the gift [*le don*] and that of "propriation" disturbs without simply reversing the order of ontology, the authority of the question "what is it," the subordination of regional ontologies to one fundamental ontology. I am moving much too rapidly. (CH 172)[21]

I want to take account of the logic of the gift that Derrida invokes, a logic by which woman is both giver and taker, both appropriated and appropriator, both mistress and master—she both "gives" herself, and "in giving, she is in fact *giving herself for*" (S 109). Woman appears in disguise, standing in for herself while dissimulating herself, playing a role, representing herself, adopting a pose—in short, women act "at a distance."[22] It is with this thought of giving oneself out as other, with the thought of the gift, of "propriation," both as a "sexual operation" and as that which organizes the "symbolic exchange in general" (S 111)—and therefore as not yet sexual—that Levinas's name must be brought to bear. Invoking Levinas's name is a way of remaining loyal to the inspiration that marks the steps taken in Derrida's "Choreographies," steps delimited by a footnote. This sense of loyalty is to be understood in the excessive sense of going beyond any responsibility I might have, to the point of overturning every expectation of what my responsibility could amount to. By following out the implications of this footnote—which constitutes an interruption of Derrida's text—I will have opened a space for another reading that is not implied directly by the interruption Derrida allows Levinas to perform in his text. In this sense it will constitute yet another reading of Derrida's texts that does not read his texts, but it nonetheless reads them otherwise—according to the radical ingratitude that turns away from Derrida in one sense, while turning toward the otherness that he asks us to think in a Levinasian gesture that goes beyond Levinas's intentions.

The long footnote, by Christie McDonald, that interrupts "Choreographies" refers us to a text that Derrida devotes (with all the complications that such devotion entails, given the themes that dominate the text—restitution and debt, ingratitude and responsibility) to Levinas. The text, to which Derrida refers without naming—a reference which McDonald makes explicit by naming and quoting this text—is "At This Very Moment in This Work Here I Am." The quotation from that essay which Christie McDonald provides includes two further quotations from two further texts, by Levinas, "And God Created Woman" and "Judaism and the Feminine Element."[23]

In "At This Very Moment" Derrida quotes a passage by Levinas that motivates his reading of Levinas, and which serves at the same time as a directive (again with all the complications to which such a concept gives rise here) for the current essay:

> Suppose that in giving to you—it little matters what—I wanted to give to him, him Emmanuel Levinas. Not render him anything, homage for example, not even render myself to him, but to give him something which escapes from the circle of restitution or of the "rendez-vous." ("Proximity," he writes, "doesn't enter into that common time of clocks that makes the rendez-vous possible. It is derangement.") I would like to do it faultlessly (*sans faute*), with a "faultlessness" ("*sans-faute*") that no longer belongs to the time or logic of the rendez-vous. Beyond any possible restitution, there would be need for my gesture to operate without debt, in absolute ingratitude. The trap[24] is that I then pay homage, the only possible homage, to his work (*oeuvre*), to what his work says of the Work (*Oeuvre*): "The Work thought to the end requires a radical generosity of the movement in which the Same goes toward the Other. Consequently, it requires an *ingratitude* from the other. (AT 13; EM 24)[25]

This thought of a radical generosity that demands ingratitude will have been one of the thoughts orchestrating what has been said here, and what still, always, remains to be said. I am going to call attention to a final passage in "Women in the Beehive," a passage that cautions against assuming Derrida's position on the question of woman lacks complication. In "Choreographies," Derrida had emphasized the need for "re-sexualizing a philosophical or theoretical discourse, which has been too 'neutralizing'" (CH 181), but in

"Women in the Beehive" his understanding of neutrality has changed, under-going a bifurcation. It is Heidegger's name that Derrida invokes to mark the change. He says, referring to his discussion in "*Geschlecht*,"

> Heidegger's discourse is not simple, nor simply beyond classical thought on this subject; certainly this motif on neutralization in his discourse could also reconstruct phallocentrism. There is a certain neutralization which can reconstruct the phallocentric privilege. But there is another neutralization which can simply neutralize the sexual opposition, and not sexual difference, liberating the field of sexuality for a very *different* sexuality, a more multiple one. At that point there would be no more sexes . . . there would be one sex for each time. One sex for each gift. A sexual difference for each gift. (WB 199)

The concept of neutrality plays a strange but important role for Derrida. Not only does it play the organizing role in his discussion of Heidegger and sexual difference in "*Geschlecht*," it is also a recurrent motif in his response to Lacan's reading of Poe's "The Purloined Letter." Furthermore, it is Levinas's alleged neutrality that provokes comment in Derrida's remarks about "And God Created Woman" in "At this Very Moment." But in each of these texts, the word "*neutralité*" functions differently.

In the case of Lacan, Derrida finds the "neutralizing exclusion" (PC 428; CP 456) that Lacan performs on the scene of narration to have negative effects. The "curious place of the narrator," an old friend of Dupin's, is "glimpsed" (PC 428; CP 456), but then excluded, read without being seen. Derrida says,

> As for the narration, at the very moment when it is invoked, we find it reduced to a "commentary" that "doubles" the drama, something that stages and makes visible, with no specific intervention of its own, like a transparent element, a general diaphanousness. Later on, the issue will be one of the "general narrator" . . .
>
> . . . the specific status of [the narrator's] discourse—which is not neutral, or whose effect of neutrality is not neutral, his interventions, and even his psychoanalytic position will never be questioned . . .
>
> . . . . he is like the neutral, homogeneous, transparent element of narration. He "adds nothing" says Lacan (S 48).[26] As if one had to add something to a relation in order to intervene in a scene. Especially in a scene of narration. And as if his questions and remarks and exclamations—these are the forms of the so-called general narrator's interventions in what Lacan demarcates as the "first dialogue"—added nothing.
>
> . . . the narrator who is onstage in what he places onstage is in turn placed onstage in a text more ample than the so-called general narration. A supple-

mentary reason not to consider him as a neutral place of passage. The "Seminar" gives no specific attention to this overflowing text: rather, it isolates, as its essential object, the two "narrated" triangular scenes, the two "real dramas," neutralizing simultaneously the fourth character who is the general narrator, his narrating operation, and the text which puts onstage the narration and the narrator. (PC 428–29; CP 456–57)

Not only does "this neutralization of the narrator commit" Lacan to the exclusion of the "invisible, but structurally irreducible, frame around the narration" (PC 431; CP 459), but "By framing in this violent way, by cutting the narrated figure itself from a fourth side in order to see only triangles, one evades perhaps a certain complication, perhaps of the Oedipal structure, which is announced in the scene of writing" (PC 433; CP 461). Lacan sees that "the minister begins to identify himself with the Queen" (PC 439; CP 468); he even sees that Dupin "reproduces the process called feminization: he subjects himself to the (desire of the) minister, whose place he occupies as soon as he possesses the letter—the place of the signifier—and conforms to the Queen's desire" (PC 452: CP 480). What eludes Lacan's grasp, what he does not see because he cannot see it—having excluded the place of the narrator, and the operation of his narrative in advance—is the narrator's narration of his "progressive identification with Dupin" (PC 489; CP 518). In other words, the feminization of the narrator is excluded, perhaps because it might jeopardize the triad.

By excluding the frame of the narrated-narrator, Lacan then appears to veil the sense in which the narrator doubles Dupin's feminization, and, through his identification with Dupin, becomes identified with a queen. The double valence of this last phrase speaks for itself. For Dupin, in discovering where the letter is, identifies himself with the minister, who in his turn is a substitute for the one from whom he stole the letter in the first place, namely the Queen. This exclusion of the role played by the narrator, this neutralization of the narrative frame, in its refusal to see the feminine identification of the narrator, seems to close down, rather than open up new possibilities, different positions, other sexualities—unlike the neutralization that *Dasein* undergoes at the hands of Heidegger.

Of Heidegger, Derrida says,

Whether a matter of neutrality or asexuality (*Neutralität, Geschlechtslosigkeit*) the words accentuate strongly a negativity which manifestly runs counter to what Heidegger thereby wishes to mark out. . . . By means of such manifestly negative predicates there should become legible what Heidegger doesn't hesitate to call a "positivity" (*Positivität*), a richness, and, in a heavily charged code, even a power (*Mächtigkeit*). Such precision suggests that the a-sexual neutrality does not desexualize, on the contrary; its *ontological* negativity is not unfolded with respect to *sexuality itself* (which it would liberate), but on its differential marks, or more strictly on *sexual duality*. (GE 71; GS 423)

Thus, far from writing sexual difference out of the picture, Heidegger's insistence upon the neutrality of *Dasein* would be read here as a sign of expanding the possibilities of sexual identity beyond the conventional binary couple. If *Dasein*'s neutrality is in some respects negative, this negation of sexuality finds a respite in the "positivity" also harbored in Dasein's *Geschlechtslosigkeit*, "which would not be more negative than *aletheia*" (GE 72; GS 423). The "negative signs attached to the word 'neutrality'" are effaced, says Derrida: "neutrality rather leads back to the 'power of the origin' which bears within itself the internal possibility of humanity in its concrete factuality" (GE 73; GS 424).

While Heidegger's *Dasein* is said to be both a sign of the disappearance of sexuality, and a sign of its incorporation, the neutrality that Derrida detects in Levinas's position is found to be an impossible neutrality—impossible because the neutrality Levinas wants to maintain in claiming the status of commentator proves untenable. In "And God Created Woman" Levinas uses the status of his formal role as commentator to exempt himself from the responsibility of deciding whether to agree with the text on which he comments. He maintains, or claims to maintain—for there is surely a sense in which he has always already decided in favor of the text in question—a stance of neutrality. Despite his disclaimer, his claim to be a dispassionate, impartial commentator, as Derrida says "the distance on the commentary is not neutral" (AT 42; EM 54). There is certainly, in Levinas' alleged refusal to take sides, in his apparent neutrality, more than a hint of the necessity of women's roles. Levinas says,

> I think of the last chapter of Proverbs, of the woman praised there; she makes possible the life of men; she is the home of men. But the husband has a life outside the home: He sits on the Council of the city; he has a public life; he is at the service of the universal; he does not limit himself to interiority, to intimacy, to the home, although without them he could do nothing. (Levinas 1990, 169; 1977, 135)

Woman is praised in Proverbs to be sure. She is praised as the one who should stay home and make sure everything is comfortable for her husband when he returns from his business in the public realm. What is Levinas actually saying about this? He says, "I think of the last chapter of Proverbs." Does he approve of the last chapter of Proverbs? Does he disapprove? He refuses to come down on either side. He says, "I am not taking sides; today, I am commenting" (Levinas 1990, 170; 1977, 137). It could go either way. If we take care to notice what he acknowledges, we will see that he claims both that man does not "limit himself to interiority, to intimacy" (implying that woman does) and that he could do nothing without the interiority and intimacy woman provides. Explicitly then, what we have is both an affirmation of woman's limitations, and an affirmation of the necessity of her role. If she did not ensure that the home functions smoothly, man would not be able to fulfil his all-important public obligations. We find no outright condemnation of this situation, nor any clear celebration of it. What we find in Levinas's text is a refusal to "take sides." Is this possible? In refusing to take sides, is Levinas not very clearly situating himself on the side of the men who go about their business, supported by women?

We can see why Derrida describes Levinas's work as having the dubious virtue of being "one of the first and rare ones, in the history of philosophy to which it does not simply belong, not to feign effacing the sexual mark of his signature" (AT 44; EC 56). There is a sense in which the very audacity of Levinas's work in this respect—and this insistent sexualization of his texts is a characteristic that Levinas shares with Lacan—is what allows Derrida to make use of Levinas—and Lacan. By taking to extremes their positioning as men, albeit in very different ways, both allow the question of sexual difference to emerge more clearly. Let me merely signal the overt sexualization of Lacan's discourse by quoting from the passage in "Seminar on 'The Purloined Letter'" where it is most evident:

> Just so does the purloined letter, like an immense female body, stretch out across the Minister's office when Dupin enters. But just so does he already expect to find it, and has only, with his eyes veiled by green lenses, to undress that huge body. . . . Look! between the cheeks of the fireplace, there's the object already in reach of a hand the ravisher has but to extend . . . Lacan 1988, 48; 1966, 36).

In returning the theme of sexuality, graphic in Lacan, and more than evident in Levinas, to a place where one might least expect to find it—to Heidegger's *Sein and Zeit*—Derrida finds in the neutrality that covers over the sexual difference of *Dasein* a decisive positivity, prior to the specification of sex as binary. Strangely enough then, Heidegger, who at first glance would appear not to treat sexual difference at all, in the end provides more fruitful resources for Derrida in thinking through this question than either Lacan or Levinas—although one suspects that without the impetus of the Lacanian and Levinasian discourses, the difficulty of reading back into Heidegger's corpus new possibilities for sexual difference, via the word "*Geschlecht*," would be considerably augmented. Indeed in the absence of such sexually marked discourses, such a reading might even be impossible. At the very least the contours of this reading would be significantly changed.

It hardly needs to be added that without the impetus of feminism, Derrida would not be able to retrieve Heidegger's "*Geschlecht*" in the way that he does. And this debt is, perhaps, one that Derrida might acknowledge more than he does. There is, after all, a certain irony in the fact that, of all the available resources for rethinking sexual difference, it is Dasein's neutrality that harbors the most radical possibilities for Derrida. To remark upon this irony here need not be read in terms of the oppositional motif that I have suggested we need to move beyond. The same can be said of my implied criticism of feminists who insist on holding Derrida at fault. Both gestures, of course, remain vulnerable to recuperation by an oppositional reading— a possibility I am willing to risk.

The fact that the word "*Geschlecht*" includes among its connotations not only "sex" but also "race" is not incidental to my reflections.[27] There is a background against which mainstream feminist theory has been played out, one that has too often been silenced in the history of feminism, rendered invisible—seen but not read, read without being seen—by feminists themselves. Another history, other histories. Derrida, as is well known, has made significant interventions into the question of race, as have many feminists.[28] We seem certain, in the arrogance of our postmodernity, that now we see the importance of race, and other such "factors" of diversity; we understand how feminist theory has itself unthinkingly imbibed the racial biases of our patriarchal society, and we can congratulate ourselves on having become aware of the need for "multiculturalism" and ethnic identity. I want to suggest that we need to hesitate before confidently asserting our belief in difference, multiplicity, and otherness, and ask ourselves if we have really understood what it is we are calling for.

In situating the debate between Derrida and feminism against this background, I mean to ask what it takes for feminists to think seriously about the other, a question that is pivotal for Derrida, and one that Teresa De Lauretis focuses upon in her paper "Eccentric Subjects."[29] De Lauretis suggests that feminism first gained its identity or "came into its own . . . became possible as such . . . in a postcolonial mode" (De Lauretis 1990, 131). By this she means that in a sense feminism was forced to confront its own authority when "certain writings by women of color and lesbians explicitly constituted themselves as a feminist critique of feminism," thereby revealing themselves as the "other" of feminism. Feminism was forced to look in the mirror that feminists who were being marginalized held up to it—and it didn't like what it saw—a group of white, middle-class, heterosexual, privileged women who were dictating the terms of feminism.

De Lauretis, having characterized the feminism of the 1970s and 1980s in terms of two prior moments of feminism, describes the 1990s as a third moment:

> (1) a reconceptualization of the subject as shifting and multiply organized across variable axes of difference; (2) a rethinking of the relations between forms of oppression and modes of formal understanding—doing theory; (3) an emerging redefinition of marginality as location, of identity as dis-identi-fication; and (4) the hypothesis of self-displacement as the term of a move-ment that is concurrently social and subjective, internal and external, indeed personal and political. (De Lauretis 1990, 116)

I want to retain, above all, from De Lauretis's description of this third moment of feminism an emphasis on the need for white feminists to dislo-cate and displace ourselves from the center of our feminist narratives. To mark this need for dislocation I turn now to Toni Morrison's *Beloved*, a novel which attends to what Mae Henderson calls "The complex situated-ness of the black woman as not only the 'Other' of the Same, but also as the 'other' of the other(s)" which "implies . . . a relationship of difference and identification with the 'other(s).'"[30] In exploring Sethe's relationship not only to white slaveowners, but also to Paul D and Sethe's own community, Morrison confronts the manifold difficulty of Sethe's positioning as a black slave woman. Morrison also underlines the incommensurability between the lives of white women, and those of black women.

Morrison asks her readers not to allow the past to become simply a bur-den, whose weight forbids escape, a past destined to repeat itself.

"Lay em down, Sethe. Sword and shield. . . . Don't study war no more. Lay all that mess down. Sword and shield. Don't study war no more. Lay all that mess down. Sword and shield." Sethe thought "Do like Baby said: Think on it then lay it down—for good" (Morrison 1987, 86 and 182).

At the same time, she asks us not to forget—not to facilitate the "beating back the past" (Morrison 1987, 73), that forces Paul D to keep his memories locked "in that tobacco tin buried in his chest where a red heart used to be" (Morrison 1987, 72–73).

Nothing is quite what it seems in *Beloved*.[31] Sweet Home, where Sethe and Paul D were enslaved, in the words of Paul D, "wasn't sweet and it sure wasn't home" (Morrison 1987, 14). When Paul D, worried about Denver's health and well-being, tries to persuade Sethe to move from 124, Sethe's response appears to be direct enough: "I got a tree on my back and a haint in my house, and nothing in between but the daughter I am holding in my arms" (Morrison 1987, 15). But the reality of each of her claims will be contested. For Paul D, Sethe's tree was "Not a tree, as she said. Maybe shaped like one, but nothing like any tree he knew because trees were inviting; things you could trust and be near" (Morrison 1987, 21). The tree that Paul D trusted and wanted to be near most, he called "Brother." About Sixo—the best of the Sweet Home men, the one for whom Paul D had the most respect—and Brother, Paul D thinks "Now *there* was a man, and *that* was a tree. Himself lying in the bed and the tree lying next to him didn't compare" (Morrison 1987, 22). It thus becomes clear that the reason Paul does not yet see in Sethe someone he can trust and be near is intricately bound up with the fact that he does not yet see himself as a proper man. Paul D's manhood is in question throughout the novel.

About the baby ghost, we are told that "It took a man, Paul D, to shout it off, beat it off and take its place for himself" (Morrison 1987, 104). But of course Paul D cannot beat off *Beloved*. Far from beating her off, he succumbs to her, he touches her "inside part" and calls her by her name, "Beloved," as she asks him to do, even though he knows that if he does, "he too would be lost" (Morrison 1987, 117). He loses himself in his failure to beat off a ghost—whose ghostliness is as much in question as is Paul D's ability to see himself as a man. Beloved's uncertain identity is not a question that is easily resolved. That she haunts the house is certain—but we are unsure whether it is as a ghost, or as a stranger who happens upon the house, brought over on the slave ships from Africa.[32] In either case, she is the embodiment of, a figure of, slave history, and a channel for the "rememory-ing" of that history.

"I am not a man" (Morrison 1987, 128)—these are words that Paul D cannot say to Sethe. "Since he could not say what he planned to," since he could not tell Sethe of his seduction at the hands of Beloved (see Morrison 1987, 116–17), "he said something he didn't know was on his mind. 'I want you pregnant, Sethe'" (Morrison 1987, 128). He cannot say the words "I am not a man," but instead he tells Sethe, that he wants her to have his child, as if—should she have his baby—he might begin to know that he was a man. But it is Beloved, and not Sethe, who becomes pregnant. Paul D does not know where manhood lies. His quest for this knowledge, and his confused attempts to assure himself of his manhood is a structuring theme of *Beloved*, one that reflects Sethe's search for her humanity as a woman and mother.[33] Paul D reflects:

Garner called and announced them men—but only on Sweet Home, and by his leave. Was he naming what he saw or creating what he did not? . . . Oh, he [Paul D] did manly things, but was that Garner's gift or his own will? What would he have been anyway—before Sweet Home—without Garner? . . . Did a whiteman saying it make it so? Suppose Garner woke up one morning and changed his mind? Took the word away. (Morrison 1987, 220)

Was that it? Is that where the manhood lay? In the naming done by a white-man who was supposed to know? . . . Because he was a man and a man could do what he would: be still for six hours in a dry well while night dropped; fight raccoon with his hands and win; watch another man, whom he loved better than his brothers, roast without a tear just so the roasters would know what a man was like. (Morrison 1987, 125–26)

If Paul D is preoccupied with naming, it is significant that he lacks a proper name, especially in a novel written by an author who so often, following the model of Greek tragedy in this as in so many other tropes, uses names as symbols. Garner, for example, gathers more than just the fruits of Paul D's labor: he grants—or removes, should the mood take him—Paul D's very manhood.

Just as Paul D puts in question Sethe's humanity by asking if she has two feet or four, so he doubts the reality of Sethe's tree—a tree which becomes a symbol for her womanhood. When Sethe's back is covered Paul D cannot see the tree:

What tree on your back? Something growing on your back? I don't see nothing growing on your back.
It's there all the same.
Who told you that?
Whitegirl. That's what she called it. . . . A Chokecherry tree. Trunk, branches, and even leaves. Tiny little chokecherry leaves. But that was eighteen years ago. (Morrison 1987, 15–16)

Sethe's answer to Paul D's question about who told Sethe she had a tree on her back parallels his own question about his manhood, and the ability of a whiteman to designate him a man—or not. If Paul D cannot see the tree when she is dressed, he becomes blind to it again when she is undressed, even after he has "touched every ridge and leaf of it with his mouth" (Morrison 1987, 18). For "the wrought-iron maze he had explored in the kitchen like a gold miner pawing through pay dirt was in fact a revolting clump of scars" (Morrison 1987, 21).

Inscribed on Sethe's body were the years of slavery that drove her to kill her own child. And Paul D's look cannot sustain what it sees. Sethe tells Paul D about her escape from slavery: "I did it. I got us all out. . . . It felt good. Good and right. I was big, Paul D, and deep and wide and when I stretched out my arms all my children could get in between. I was *that* wide" (Morrison 1987, 162). The image recalls the span of tree branches.[34] Paul D understands, but what he does not understand is that Sethe loves with "her too-thick love" (Morrison 1987, 165), a passion that leads her to murder her child. Paul D thinks that, "For a used-to-be-slave woman to love anything that much was dangerous, especially if it was her children she had settled on to love. The best thing, he knew, was to love just a little bit; everything, just a little bit, so when they broke its back, or shoved it in a croaker sack, well, maybe you'd have a little love left over for the next one" (Morrison 1987, 45). Paul D "protected" himself against the "men who had the guns" and "loved small" (Morrison 1987, 162). "On nights when the sky was personal, weak with the weight of its own stars, he made himself not love it. . . . Anything could stir him and he tried hard not to love it" (Morrison 1987, 268). Sethe "moved him" too (Morrison 1987, 114), so he tried hard not to love her. "Loving small and in secret" was all he could allow himself (Morrison 1987, 221).

A Cherokee tells Paul D how to get to the North—and freedom. "'That way,'" he said, pointing. 'Follow the tree flowers. As they go, you go. You will be where you want to be when they are gone.' So he raced from dogwood to blossoming peach. When they thinned out he headed for the cherry blossoms, then magnolia, chinaberry, pecan, walnut and prickly pear. At last he reached a field of apple trees whose flowers were just becoming tiny knots of fruit" (Morrison 1987, 112).

The trees compose a map for Paul D, a map drawn by a Cherokee. At the same time his journey to freedom is tracked by another journey, a psychological one, which is mapped out for him on Sethe's back. Sethe's back has chokecherry tree flowers on it, and there is a sense in which Paul D's search for himself is also a search for her, one that allows him to finally come to terms with Sethe's taking an axe to her child. The connection between the history that is branded (as if she were an animal) on Sethe's back, and the signs that the tree blossoms become for Paul D is emphasized by the fact that the "Cherokee" who points to the trees to mark out the way that will take Paul D north almost forms a homophone to Sethe's "cherry tree." When Sethe feels hands around her neck (Beloved's), choking her, once again the image of the choke-cherry tree that grows on her back is invoked. The history that she has survived, but which nearly choked her, is enacted on her body once more.

As Susan Bowers says about Sethe and Paul D, "The past that was too painful for either to remember alone can be recovered together: 'Her story was bearable because it was his as well.'"[35] Paul D makes peace with himself and his own past partly through accepting Sethe and her past, by learning that her murderous act was performed out of love, and that it was her capacity to love that helps her bear her memories, while he must beat back his (see Morrison 1987, 73). Despite the fact that Sethe's love killed her child, which is the hardest thing for her to bear, she has not lost the capacity to love. Her beaten back—yet another reversal or mirroring of Paul D, who has to "beat back" the past—tells the story of the memories of slavery, a history which drove her to murder her child rather than allow her to become a slave.

If it appears to take a long time for Paul D to come to terms with Sethe's having killed her own child in order to protect her from slavery, this time is nothing compared to the years of slavery both have endured and survived—and by the end of the novel Paul D understands Sethe's strength, a strength that allows her to overlook his humiliating bit. "How she never mentioned or looked at it, so he did not have to feel the shame of being collared like a beast. Only this woman Sethe could have left him his manhood like that. He wants to put his story next to hers" (Morrison 1987, 273). When Paul D, out of incomprehension, asks Sethe if she has two feet or four, he gives voice both to the theme of counting[36] that dominates the novel, and to the animal imagery that infuses its prose. Is Sethe, who kills her own child, who is "Down in the grass" like a "snake" (Morrison 1987, 32), an animal or a human? Is Paul, who suffers Mister's smile, "less than a chicken sitting in the sun on a tub" (Morrison 1987, 72)? And who is Denver, the child to whom Sethe manages to give birth as a runaway slave? Morrison describes her as a "little antelope" who "rammed" Sethe "with horns and pawed the ground of her womb with impatient hooves. While she was walking, it seemed to graze quietly—so she walked, on two feet meant, in this sixth month of pregnancy, for standing still" (Morrison 1987, 30). The question of what constitutes humanity is one which haunts *Beloved*. What counts as animality, what belongs to the realm of spirit, and how humans situate themselves in relation to those ambiguous domains are issues that dominate Morrison's work.

If the status of the tree on Sethe's back is brought into question, and Beloved's identity as a spirit or a stranger is at issue, so too is Sethe's claim that the one thing she can be certain of is her daughter. It is Paul D who calls attention to the fact that Denver, who never leaves the house, and has no friends, is "half out of her mind" (Morrison 1987, 15). As Budick points out, there is a mirroring of Denver's birth in Beloved's "re-incarnation," and the close bond between them is enacted through the mothering role that Denver takes on in relation to Beloved.[37] Denver becomes Beloved's protector, and in doing so it is as if she usurps Sethe's mothering function, putting into doubt her own relation to Sethe—how can she be the daughter of Sethe if she also mothers Sethe's daughter? Sethe in turn, towards the end of the novel, becomes like a sister to Beloved, playing together with Denver and Beloved (see Morrison 1987, 240). But soon "it was Beloved who made demands" (Morrison 1987, 240), and Sethe who satisfied them, so that "it was difficult for Denver to tell who was who" (Morrison 1987, 241).

Morrison says in an interview,

> A large part of the satisfaction I have always received from reading Greek
> tragedy, for example, is in its similarity to Afro-American communal struc-
> ture (the function of song and chorus, the heroic struggle between claims of
> the community and individual hubris) and African religion and philosophy.[38]

The excessive complication of family roles in *Beloved* recalls the incestu-
ous relationship that orchestrates Sophocles' Oedipal trilogy, fleshing out a
parallel that is made explicit as Morrison describes Sethe's swollen feet
(Morrison 1987, 29–30), and as she describes the hubris of Baby Suggs, who
overstepped some invisible line by indulging in the excesses of feasting. As
if she no longer knew her station, as if it were not her place to display such
riches, her neighbors have Sethe and her children atone for this excess by
failing to warn them of the slavecatchers' arrival.

> Sethe was walking on two feet meant for standing still.... [T]hey were so
> swollen she could not see her arch or feel her ankles. ...
>   Baby Suggs' three (maybe four) pies grew to ten (maybe twelve). Sethe's
> two hens became five turkeys. The one block of ice brought all the way from
> Cincinnati—over which they poured mashed watermelon mixed with sugar
> and mint to make a punch—became a wagonload of ice cakes for a washtub
> full of strawberry shrug. 124, rocking with laughter, goodwill and food for
> ninety, made them angry. Too much, they thought. Where does she get it all,
> Baby Suggs, holy?.... It made them furious. They swallowed baking soda, the
> morning after, to calm the stomach violence caused by the bounty, the reck-
> less generosity on display at 124. Whispered to each other in the yards about
> fat rats, doom and uncalled-for pride ... (Morrison 1987, 29–30; 137)

Her friends and neighbors were angry at her because she had overstepped, given too much, offended them by excess. "Sethe walked past them
in their silence and hers. ... Was her head a bit too high? Her back a little too
straight? Probably" (Morrison 1987, 152).

The tree on Sethe's back is not a tree, the haint that embodies the spirit
of Beloved is not merely—if at all—a ghost, but also the incarnation of the
cruelty visited upon slaves, and Denver is not Sethe's daughter. She cannot
compete with Beloved for Sethe's attention, is caught up in mourning for
the daughter she has lost, and whose spirit governs 124. Paul D does not
believe in his manhood, and Sethe is denied her humanity by both the slaveowners, and her own community, who cannot understand a love that would
allow a mother to murder her child.

I have dwelt on the deceptive appearances that structure Morrison's *Beloved* in order to point to another false appearance: a feminism that takes no account of the history of slavery is not feminist for the victims of that slavery whose legacy lives on, nor it is feminist for those of us who have benefitted from a legacy of white oppression. The history of slavery is a burden we too must learn to take on. And, in taking it on, we must be prepared to think about the oppression of men as well as women, as Morrison's eloquent depiction of Paul D's search for his manhood encourages us to do.

If the question of "my position" remains, let me do no more than reiterate what I hope to have made clear. I do not want to be constrained by the choice: either Derrida or feminism. I want to use Derrida for feminist purposes—accepting that these may not necessarily be purposes which he himself would sanction, while also insisting that I find nothing in his work to outlaw a version of feminism that learns from him, among others. One way I have tried to use not only Derrida, but also Lacan, Levinas, Heidegger, and Morrison is by emphasizing the urgency of taking seriously not only sexual difference, but also race.

Morrison's novels are peopled by very few "whitepeople," but when she does include them they serve a specific function. Let me focus, finally, on one of the few white figures portrayed in *Beloved*. Morrison highlights the incommensurability between the lives of Amy, a young, poor whitegirl, and Sethe, a pregnant runaway slave woman. Amy helps Sethe. She even saves her life. At the biological level, that is. But one of the points Morrison makes poignantly throughout the novel is that Sethe needs to find a way of saving her life beyond the physical level. It is the psychological level that poses more difficulty both for Sethe and for Paul D. Two levels of freedom are at stake here—first the escape from slavery, and secondly the escape from the escape. Retelling the story of slavery Morrison adds a second dimension to what Bowers, following Willis, calls the "typical format of the slave narrative [which] is to trace the story of the individual's life in slavery, escape, and the journey to freedom. What Morrison reveals is that the process must be repeated twice: first to leave physical enslavement by whites and the second time to escape the psychological trauma created by their brutality."[39]

At issue is how to remember, how to live the history of slavery. This slavery—and many other forms of subordination—still structures our thinking, and remains to be thought, over and over again. Amy's starry-eyed vision of Boston, where she will get herself carmine velvet is not something that is within Sethe's horizon. The incommensurability of Sethe's life, and the whitegirl's, is underlined by the imagined life that stretches out before Amy, in comparison to the darkness that envelops pregnant Sethe, carrying her antelope-child. A quilt with a patch of orange will cover Sethe, not a velvet dress.[40]

When Amy says of Sethe's swollen feet, "Anything dead coming back to life hurts," Denver—hearing the story—thinks "A truth for all times" (Morrison 1987, 35)—a thought that responds to the "unspeakably horrific experiences" upon which Morrison, in the words of Bowers, asks us to dwell.[41] It is not enough to reflect on why some women are more advantaged than others, why race might be an important "element" or "factor" within the question of how to advance the feminist project. It is not even enough to concede that sexual orientation or ethnicity, or class might be "more of an issue" for some women than it is for others. It is a question of re-visioning the idea of feminism from the ground up, of uprooting feminism as a movement, of not merely recultivating the "fem" that is "in" the "ism," but relocating it, rehabilitating it, re-forming it, reshaping it. It is a matter of dislocating ourselves from the safety of the environments in which we can play the ones who are put upon, and asking ourselves what we are putting on others when we gather our strength and stand up for ourselves. On whose shoulders are we standing, whose oppression are we sanctioning, when we speak for ourselves "as women" or when we allow ourselves to be spoken for by a feminism that defines itself by what Judith Butler has called the "embarrassed 'etc.,' " of the infinite others we could never fully enumerate in terms of "color, sexuality, ethnicity, class, and able-bodiedness" or any number of other qualifiers?[42] Teresa de Lauretis refers to the "various axes of difference" which "are usually seen as parallel or coequal, although with varying 'priorities' for particular women." She goes on,

> For some women, the racial may have priority over the sexual in defining subjectivity and ground identity; for others still it may be the ethnic/cultural that has priority at a given moment—hence the phrase one hears so often now in feminist contexts: "gender, race, and class," or its local variant, "gender, race, and class, and sexual preference." But what this string of seemingly coequal terms, conveying the notion of layers of oppression along parallel axes of "difference," does not grasp is their constant intersection and mutual implication or how each one may affect the others—for example, how gender affects racial oppression in its subjective effects. (DeLauretis 1990, 133–34)

African-American feminist theorists have been saying for years—but the point is only just beginning to be understood—that we cannot afford to separate the sexual and the racial dynamic from one another because they are not just intrinsically connected to one another as axes of oppression: they are constitutive of one another.[43] Unless we refuse the model of feminism as a uniform project, constituted by more or less identical subjects—whatever lip service we may pay to our differences—and based on an irreversible linear history that marches on in the name of progress, we blind ourselves to our own complicity in the successes and failures of feminism.

By taking up a posture of radical ingratitude, Derrida's questions open up another site of enquiry for us: is it ungrateful to arrest his path of thought, to force a confrontation which may seem to do violence to the logic of these particular texts, to introduce the question of slavery—or rather to re-introduce it as a question, by way of "rememory"? In offering a commentary on Morrison's *Beloved*, I am well aware, as a white feminist, of the charges of "appropriation" to which I open myself.[44] I prefer to take this risk, rather than dwell in a complacency that allows me to rest more easily in the assumption that I am addressing the issue of race by vaguely embracing talk of "difference." I have purposely located myself in a discourse that takes account of the oppression that occurs, despite our best intentions, in the very "progress" of feminism.

I have been concerned here with the question of neutrality, the question of invisible framing, of positioning oneself in relation to the texts one writes, with the exclusions perpetrated in the name of feminism, as much as with the oppression of women, with the idea of excess in relation to the question of responsibility, with the question of fictions in truth and truths in fiction, with questions of ownership, property, and the gift, with questions about how to read, and with Derrida's questioning of woman as veiled truth, as castration. But most of all I have tried to think through, following Derrida's cue, what it might mean for the radical generosity that Levinas proposes to demand an absolute ingratitude. Derrida says,

> what I "want" to "do" here is to accept the gift, to affirm and reaffirm it as what I have received. Not from someone who would himself have had the initiative for it, but from someone who would have had the force to receive it and reaffirm it. And if it is thus that (in my turn) I give to you, it will no longer form a chain of restitutions, but another gift, the gift of the other. Is this possible? (AT 14; EM 25)

I too have presumed to occupy a place that is not my own. I have taken a gift meant for another. I have re-read Derrida's texts on sexual difference by turning, through Derrida's own texts, to Levinas, but I have also turned away from Levinas, to another text—to the text of Morrison, and to the history of race. I have asked what it means for a thought to be guided by that which exceeds it, by its other, knowing all the while that it cannot possibly be adequate to that for which it tries to account—for its exclusions—and knowing also that this thought bears the imprint of what nonetheless exceeds its grasp.

Has Derrida ever been read on the question of sexual difference? What would a responsible reading amount to? Would it be a reading that took up the gift of Levinas's text, a gift that derives not from Levinas's own initiative, but from elsewhere? Could it be a reading which turned Levinas's gift, his text, toward a wholly other history? In the background of Levinas's questioning of the reciprocal economy of sameness lies the destruction of the Jews in World War II. By taking up the excesses committed in the name of slavery that Morrison's *Beloved* makes present, this ungrateful reading has not so much opened up the question of Derrida, feminism, and sexual difference to a history that is extraneous to this question, as it has sought to highlight the logic of exclusion. If the texts of Derrida, Heidegger, Lacan, and Levinas risk neutralizing the question of sexual difference in various ways, there is equally a danger of feminist texts duplicating this neutrality by eradicating racial difference—or any other difference. If feminism contents itself with the task of dogmatically reasserting counter-claims in the face of exclusionary gestures, then it will prohibit itself from thinking through the logic of exclusion that it presupposes. Feminism will blind itself to the ways in which it proliferates the exclusion of others in its attempt to secure its own inclusion.

Notes

1. Jacques Derrida, "Choreographies," Interview with Christie V. McDonald, *The Ear of the Other: Otobiography, Transference, Translation,* reedition, ed. Christie McDonald (Lincoln: University of Nebraska Press, 1988), 163–85, see esp. 170. Originally published in *Diacritics* 12: 1982, 66–76. Henceforth cited as CH, followed by page numbers.

2. Emmanuel Levinas, "And God Created Woman," in *Nine Talmudic Readings,* trans. Annette Aronowicz (Bloomington, Indiana: Indiana University Press, 1990), 161–77, see esp. 173; *"Et Dieu créa la femme"* in *Du sacré au saint, cinq nouvelles lectures talmudiques* (Paris: Minuit, 1977), 122–48, see esp. 128.

3. Toni Morrison, *Beloved* (New York: New American Library, 1987), 104.

4. I want to thank Tamsin Lorraine, Robert Bernasconi, and the editors of this volume for helpful critical feedback on this paper.

5. Jacques Derrida, *Spurs: Nietzsche's Styles,* trans. Barbara Harlow (Chicago: University of Chicago Press, 1979); *Eperons: Les Styles de Nietzsche* (Paris: Flammarion, 1978). Since the 1979 edition is bilingual I have simply referred to the translation, leaving the reader to consult the French on the facing page. Henceforth citations will be to S followed by the English pagination.

6. Derrida, "At This Very Moment In This Work Here I Am," trans. R. Berezdevin, in *Re-Reading Levinas,* ed. R. Bernasconi and Simon Critchley

(Bloomington, Indiana: Indiana University Press, 1991), 11–48, see esp. 12; *"En ce moment même dans cet ouvrage me voici"* in *Textes pour Emmanuel Levinas*, ed. Françoise Laruelle (Paris: Jean-Michel Place, 1980), 21–60, see esp. 22. Henceforth cited as AT; EM, followed by page numbers.

7. Derrida, *"Le facteur de la vérité,"* The Post Card: From Socrates to Freud and Beyond, trans. Alan Bass (Chicago: Chicago University Press, 1987), 413–96, see esp. 483; *La Carte postale: de Socrate à Freud et au-delà* (Paris: Aubier-Flammarion, 1980), 441–524, see esp. 511. First published in *Poétique* 21: 1975. An abbreviated version of Bass's translation can be found under the title of "The Purveyor of Truth," in *The Purloined Poe*, ed. John P. Muller and William J. Richardson (Baltimore: The Johns Hopkins University Press, 1988), 173–212. References are to *The Post Card*, henceforth cited as PC; CP, followed by page numbers.

8. Jacques Lacan, "Seminar on 'The Purloined Letter,'" trans. Jeffrey Mehlman, in *The Purloined Poe*, ed. John P. Muller and William J. Richardson (Baltimore: The Johns Hopkins University Press, 1988), 28–54; "Le séminaire sur 'La lettre volée'" in *Écrits* (Paris: Seuil, 1966), 11–41.

9. See particularly S: 59, 61, 73, 89–93, and PC: 439–44; CP: 467–73.

10. Nietzsche, *The Gay Science*, tr. Walter Kaufmann (New York: Vintage Books, 1974); *Beyond Good and Evil*, trans. R. Hollingdale (Harmondsworth, Middlesex: Penguin, 1987); *Twilight of the Idols*, trans. R. Hollingdale, Harmondsworth, Middlesex: Penguin, 1972; Heidegger, Martin (1981) *Nietzsche, vol. 1: The Will to Power As Art*, trans. David Farrell Krell (London: Routledge & Kegan Paul) 1981.

11. Martin Heidegger, *Being and Time*, trans. John Macquarrie & Edward Robinson (Oxford: Basil Blackwell), 1980; *Sein und Zeit* (Tübingen: Max Niemeyer, 1984). Heidegger, *The Metaphysical Foundations of Logic*, trans. M. Heim (Bloomington: Indiana University Press, 1984); *Metaphysische Anfangsgrunde der Logik im Ausgang von Leibniz* (Frankfurt: Vittorio Klostermann, 1978). Derrida *"Geschlecht:* Sexual difference, ontological difference," *Research in Phenomenology* 13 (1983): 65–83; *"Geschlecht:* différence sexuelle, différence ontologique," *Martin Heidegger*, ed. Michel Haar, (Paris, L'Herne, 1983), 419–30, henceforth cited as GE; GS, followed by page numbers.

12. Derrida also addresses the problem of enframing in *The Truth in Painting*, trans. G. Bennington and I. McLeod (Chicago: University of Chicago Press, 1987); *La Vérité en peinture*, (Paris: Flammarion, 1978). See in particular his discussion of sexual difference in relation to Heidegger in the essay "Restitutions."

13. The work in this case is Levinas's, but as Derrida points out, Levinas "withdraws" his "signature" from his work, (AT: 33; EM: 44–45) and does not claim the "initiative for it" (AT 14; EM 25).

14. bell hooks, "Third World Diva Girls," in *Yearning: Race, Gender, Cultural Politics* (Boston: South End Press, 1990), 100–101.

15. See also AT 12; EM 23, and AT 33; EM 45.

16. Drucilla Cornell has a useful discussion of what Derrida says about the secondariness of sexual difference, but does not address the text by Levinas that Derrida is commenting on, *Beyond Accommodation: Ethical Feminism, Deconstruction and the Law* (New York: Routledge, 1991), see esp. 97.

17. In thinking about the question of the other I have in mind, Derrida says of the other in the following passage: "property" or the proper (*propre*), "Even as it is carried away of itself by its desire, it founders there in the waters of this its own desire, unencounterable—of itself. It passes into the other. . . . But—if the form of opposition and the oppositional structure are themselves metaphysical, then the relation of metaphysics to its other can no longer be one of opposition" (S 117–19).

18. See Derrida, "Force of Law: The 'Mystical Foundation of Authority," *Deconstruction and the Possibility of Justice*, ed, Drucilla Cornell, Michel Rosenfeld, and David Gray Carlson (New York: Routledge, 1992), 27–28.

19. Also see Derrida's observation:

    rather than examine here the large number of propositions which treat of the woman, it is instead their principle, which might be resumed in a finite number of typical and matrical propositions, that I shall attempt to formalize . . . Three types of such a statement are to be found. Furthermore, these three fundamental propositions represent three positions of value which themselves derive from three different situations. And according to a particular sort of investigation which can be no more than indicated here these positions of value might in fact be read in the terms (for example) of the psychoanalytic meaning of the word "position." (S: 95)

20. Derrida, *Aporias,* trans. Thomas Dutoit (Stanford: Stanford University Press, 1993), 21.

21. See also Derrida's comments on Levinas's exclusion of what exceeds his texts, in a gesture that nonetheless includes, or marks this excess within the text (AT 31; EM 43).

22. Nietzsche, *The Gay Science,* trans. Walter Kaufmann (New York: Random House, 1974), 124.

23. Levinas, "Judaism and the feminine element," trans. E. Wyschogrod, *Judaism*, 18, 1 (1969): 30–38, originally published as "*Le judaïsme et le féminin*" in *L'Age Nouveau*, 107–108 (1960), reprinted in Levinas, *Difficile liberté: essais sur le Judaïsme* (Paris: Albin Michel, 1963), pp. 51–62.

24. Derrida will later take back what he says here: "I spoke, *wrongly,* of a trap just now. It is only felt as a trap from the moment when one would pretend to escape from absolute disymmetry through a will to mastery or coherence. It would be a way to acknowledge the gifts in order to refuse it. Nothing is more difficult than to accept a gift" (AT 14; EM 25).

25. The quotation is from Levinas's "On the Trail of the Other," trans. Daniel Hoy, *Philosophy Today* 10 (1966): 34–47, see esp. 37; "Le trace de l'autre,"

Tijdschrift voor Filosofie 25 (3) (1963): 605–23. Reprinted and integrated into "Signification et le sens" *Humanisme de l'autre homme* (Montpellier, Fata Morgana, 1972), 17–63. Also reprinted in *En découvrant l'existence avec Husserl et Heidegger* (Paris: J. Vrin, 1967), 187–202, see esp. 191.

26. "Women in the Beehive: A Seminar with Jacques Derrida" in *Men in Feminism*, eds. Alice Jardine and Paul Smith (New York: Methuen, 1987), pp. 189–203. Originally published in *Subjects/Objects* (Spring 1984).

27. *Geschlecht* also means family, generation, lineage, species, genre.

28. See, for example, Derrida, "The Laws of Reflection: Nelson Mandela, In Admiration," *For Nelson Mandela*, ed., Jacques Derrida and Mustapha Tlili (New York: Seaver Books/Henry Holt, 1987), 11–42. "Racism's Last Word," *Critical Inquiry* 12 (1985), 290–99.

29. Teresa De Lauretis, "Eccentric Subjects: Feminist Theory and Historical Consciousness," *Feminist Studies* 1 (1990): 115–50.

30. Mae Henderson, "Speaking in Tongues: Dialogics, Dialectics, and the Black Woman Writer's Literary Tradition," *Reading Black, Reading Feminist*, ed. Henry Louis Gates (New York: N. A. L., 1990), 116–41, see esp. 118.

31. Among the articles I found most useful on Morrison's *Beloved* are the following: Susan Bowers, "*Beloved* and the New Apocalypse," *The Journal of Ethnic Studies* 18, 1 (1990): 59–77; Mae G. Henderson, "Toni Morrison's *Beloved*: Re-Membering the Body as Historical Text," in *Comparative American Identities: Race, Sex, and Nationality in the Modern Text*, ed. Hortense J. Spillers (New York: Routledge, 1991), 62–86; Charles Scruggs, "The Invisible City in Toni Morrison's *Beloved*," *Arizona Quarterly: A Journal of American Literature, Culture, and Theory* 48, 3 (Autumn 1992): 95–132.

32. Elizabeth B. House suggests, in contrast to those who assume Beloved to be "the ghostly reincarnation of Sethe's murdered baby," that there is evidence to suggest that the girl is "simply a young woman who has herself suffered the horrors of slavery." "Toni Morrison's Ghost: The Beloved who Is not Beloved," *Studies in American Fiction* 18, 1 (Spring 1990): 17–26, esp. 17.

33. On Paul D's manhood see Emily Miller Budick, "Absence, Loss, and the Space of History in Toni Morrison's *Beloved*," *American Quarterly* 48, 2 (Summer 1992): 117–38, esp. 123–27.

34. For further discussion of tree imagery in *Beloved* see Jacqueline Trace, Dark Goddesses: Black Feminist Theology in Morrison's *Beloved*," *Obsidian II: Black Literature in Review* 6, 3 (Winter 1991): 14–30, esp. pp. 19–23.

35. Bowers, "*Beloved* and the New Apocalypse," *The Journal of Ethnic Studies* 18, 1 (1990): 59–77, see esp. 63. The quotation is from *Beloved*, 99.

36. On the theme of counting and numbers in *Beloved* see Budick, "Absence, Loss, and the Space of History in Toni Morrison's *Beloved*," *American Quarterly* 48, 2 (Summer 1992): 117–38, esp. 129–36, and Scruggs, "The Invisible City in Toni Morrison's *Beloved*," *Arizona Quarterly: A Journal of American Literature, Culture, and Theory* 48, 3 (Autumn 1992): 95–132, esp. 110.

37. Budick, "Absence, Loss, and the Space of History in Toni Morrison's

Beloved" *American Quarterly* 48, 2 (Summer 1992): 117–38, see esp. 121.

38. Morrison, "Unspeakable Things Unspoken: The Afro-American Presence in American Literature," *Michigan Quarterly Review* 28, 1 (Winter 1989): 1–34, see esp. 2.

39. Bowers, "*Beloved* and the New Apocalypse," *The Journal of Ethnic Studies* 18, 1 (1990): 59–77, see esp. 64. Bowers refers to Susan Willis, "Black Women Writers: Taking a Critical Perspective," *Making a Difference: Feminist Literary Criticism*, ed. Gayle Greene and Copelia Kahn, (New York: Methuen, 1985).

40. My point is not to romanticize Amy's life, but to underline, in Scrugg's words, "their different cultural histories," "The Invisible City in Toni Morrison's *Beloved*," *Arizona Quarterly: A Journal of American Literature, Culture, and Theory* 48, 3 (Autumn 1992): 95–132, esp. 118. As Scruggs goes on to point out,

> The likely fate of women like Amy in the late nineteenth century was to end as drudges in the company towns of New England textile mills. Behind this episode [the meeting between Sethe and Amy] are not only the historical origins of the modern consumer culture, but also the debate between Richard Wright and James Baldwin on the value of Afro-American culture as a means of resistance. Sethe, it seems, will retain a more authentic culture than Amy—she learned her lineage from Nan, and practical things from Sixo that she never forgets, and the cloth by which she is defined is not a luxury good like velvet, but hand-made quilt. (118–19)

41. Bowers, "*Beloved* and the New Apocalypse," *The Journal of Ethnic Studies*, 18, 1 (1990): 59–77, see esp. 62.

42. Judith Butler, *Gender Trouble: Feminism and the Subversion of Identity* (New York: Routledge, 1990) 143.

43. See, for example, Tracey A. Gardner, "Racism in Pornography and the Women's Movement," *Take Back the night*, ed. Laura Lederer (New York: William Morrow & Company, 1980), 105–114.

44. Katherine J. Mayberry, "White Feminists Who Study Black Writers," *The Chronicle of Higher Education*, October 12, 1994. Also see Drucilla Cornell, "What takes Place in the Dark," *Differences: A Journal of Feminist Cultural Studies* 4, 2 (1992): 45–71; Susan E. Babbit, "Identity, Knowledge, and Toni Morrison's *Beloved*: Questions about Understanding Racism," *Hypatia* 9, 3 (1994): 1–17.

From Euthanasia to the Other of Reason 6

Performativity and the Deconstruction of Sexual Difference

Ewa Plonowska Ziarek

The relation between deconstruction and feminism, even if we assume that these terms imply uniform and coherent positions, cannot be limited to the analysis/contestation of Derrida's appropriation of or indifference to sexual difference in his reading of specific philosophical or literary texts, although, no doubt, such an analysis is both much needed and still useful. Nor can it be supposed that the alliance between feminism and deconstruction follows in any obvious way from the general poststructuralist project, which, by undoing all binary oppositions, destabilizes sexual difference as well. Rather, the relation between feminism and deconstruction is still very much open to invention if it is to be capable of producing new critical interventions. I risk the word "invention" here deliberately to stress the open-ended future of this alliance rather than the predictable outcome assured by the application of a method.

In this article I discuss the powerful instance of such an invention, namely, the recent debates of the performative character of sex. The category of the performative, in particular the way it is deployed in Judith Butler's work, has a rather rich and convoluted intellectual genealogy—this genealogy brings together Derrida's critique of speech act theory (a critique, let us recall, that is meant to dislodge the opposition between empiricism and Husserlian transcendental phenomenology) and the Foucauldian analysis of the productive character of power. The disregard for this intellectual tradition has produced some of the most outlandish misreadings of Butler's work in particular, and poststructuralism in general, ranging from the charges of voluntarism to those of linguistic determinism. In order to avoid some of the common misconceptions of the poststructuralist uses of performativity, I start first with a rigorous objection, raised frequently by Lacanian psychoanalysis and perhaps most eloquently by Joan Copjec, that the deconstruction of sexual difference leads to the "euthanasia of reason." As an alternative to the feminist alliance with deconstruction, Copjec refers to Lacan's formulation of sex in terms of a radical failure of signification. Yet, by interpreting this failure according to the Kantian antinomies of reason, Copjec reads failure in a determinate way—that is, she contains the impasses of signification within the structural stability of sexual difference. This exclusive emphasis on the *epistemological* impasses of signification not only limits the explanations of the compulsory character of sex to the structural necessity of failure but also assimilates an ethics of sex to the question of knowledge (or its impossibility).

I argue that Copjec's rigorous critique of feminist deconstruction gives us the opportunity to develop crucial, yet frequently overlooked, implications of the performativity of sex, in particular, the relation between sex, force, and the failure of signification. First, since the performative is inseparable from the pragmatics of speech, and thus emphasizes the internal relation between force and signification, it enables us to account for the compulsory character of sex and the formation of sexual norms. Second, since the performative equally strongly exposes the unavoidable failure of signification, it not only prevents the assimilation of sex to cultural determinations but also opens the possibility of intervention into sexual norms. And, finally, we have to stress that for Derrida the failure of signification does not mark an unfortunate epistemological impasse but, on the contrary, discloses the possibility of an ethics of sexual difference. To negotiate between the politics and ethics of sexual difference, I stress the inescapable "co-implication" between the two modes of performativity in Derrida's work—between the iteration of the law and the ethical relation to alterity.

I.

Deconstruction of Sexual Difference and the Lethal Confusion of Reason

Let us start our considerations about the alliance of feminism with deconstruction with the assumption that the project of deconstructing sexual difference cannot succeed. Referring specifically to Judith Butler's work, but extending her conclusions to deconstruction at large, Joan Copjec blames deconstruction for critical impasse within feminism:

> This is to say, among other things, that *sex, sexual difference, cannot be deconstructed*, since deconstruction is an operation that can be applied only to

culture, to the signifier, and has no purchase on this other realm. To speak of the deconstruction of sex makes about as much sense as speaking about fore-closing a door; action and object do not belong to the same discursive space. (Copjec, 1994, 210)

So uncharacteristic of the overall analytic sobriety of Copjec's text, this dramatic but hasty proclamation concludes that the deconstruction of sexual difference simply does not make sense. Not concerned with the usual wor-ries about the apolitical character of deconstruction, Copjec argues instead that the "deadly" combination of deconstruction and feminism will lead to the "euthanasia of reason." The immediate argument articulated in this pas-sage is that deconstruction "can be applied only to culture," as if Copjec were forgetting that already in "Structure, Sign, and Play," one of his early essays, Derrida announces deconstructive project by contesting the nature/culture distinction.[2] In his later work, Derrida locates a similar impasse of the na-ture/convention difference in the conception of law in general.[3] One cannot thus limit deconstructive operation to culture without inquiring first how the very opposition between culture and nature, or culture and "this other realm" (the Real of sex in the case of Copjec's argument), is first affirmed, and then contested in Derrida's texts. Not surprisingly, it is the opposition between culture and nature that Butler makes problematic through her revi-sion of the constructivist argument—the argument that aligns construction with the force of culture and treats nature or the body as the mute substra-tum of cultural inscription. To ignore this contestation and the reinscription of both sides of nature/culture dichotomy, is, after all, to miss the "founding gesture" of deconstruction itself.

With this caution in mind, we can attend to other objections raised in Copjec's text. Her argument starts with an elaboration of the central con-tradiction of language—with the observation that the nature of differential signification both demands the totality of signifiers and, at the same time, precludes such a totalization.[4] Following Lacan, Copjec links this linguistic contradiction—this impossibility of totalization which is nonetheless demanded by the very nature of discourse—with sex itself: "when we speak of language's failure with respect to sex, we speak not of its falling short of a prediscursive object but of its falling into contradiction with itself. Sex coincides with this *failure*, this inevitable contradiction" (Copjec 1994, 206). Although not a prediscursive object, sex nonetheless raises the question of the outside of language—of the unsayable created by the very impasse of language. Escaping the nature/culture dichotomy, sexual difference belongs to the Real, and as such, it cannot be inscribed in language, only the effects of the failure of its inscription can be marked.

By linking sex to the failure of signification, Copjec claims that psycho-analysis performs the most radical desubstantialization of sex—it is not just an incomplete entity, but a totally empty one, without any positive predicate (Copjec 1994, 207). Consequently, one of Copjec's main objections advanced against feminist deconstruction is that it treats sex as an incomplete entity, or as an entity subverted by the collisions of the external differences of class and race, and not as the very failure of signification: "Sex is, then, the impossibil-ity of completing meaning, not (as Butler's historicist/deconstructionist would have it) a meaning that is incomplete, unstable" (Copjec 1994, 206). Thus, the deconstruction of sexual difference is not radical enough because it disregards this more fundamental failure, or default, of language, which pro-duces the experience of the unsayable. Incapable of acknowledging the Real, deconstruction does not distinguish *two* modalities of failure and, therefore, it does not recognize the compulsory character of sex: "Deconstruction falls into this confusion only by disregarding the difference between the ways in which this failure takes place. Regarding failure as uniform, deconstruction ends up collapsing sexual difference into sexual indistinctness" (Copjec 1994, 216). This brings us to the central question: how is failure to be read?

Yet, the radicality of psychoanalysis proclaimed by Copjec is perhaps a source of gender trouble of a different sort. Paradoxically, the failure of sig-nification does not increase the "plasticity" of sex but reinforces its "com-pulsory dimension," its "inescapability"—despite the fact that sexual difference cannot be inscribed in language, or perhaps because of it, "*sex does not budge*" (Copjec 1994, 210). As these formulations suggest, Copjec limits the compulsory character of sex exclusively to the structural necessity of failure without discussing the relation between this compulsion and the other kind of necessity associated with the normative force of law. As But-ler remarks, sex in this formulation is "condemned to the pathos of perpet-ual failure" (Butler 1993, 3). The assumption that "sex does not budge" is fortuitous in ways more than one—it assures both the permanence of sex-ual difference and the eventual failure of all historical determinations of sexual norms. Copjec argues that the inevitable failure of signification asso-ciated with sex resists the appropriation of sexual difference by the *external* forces of "compulsory heterosexuality." Yet, this formulation of failure, sex, and necessity disregards the *internal* relation between force and significa-tion thematized by the notion of performativity. That is one of the reasons why the passage from the impasses of signification to the contestation of sexual norms remains rather vague in Copjec's book.

Copjec does not pursue the internal relations of power and sexuality because, as she argues at the beginning of her book, this apparently leads to the rejection of the linguistic model of the social for the sake of the

Foucauldian "battle-based" model—a rejection, which amounts to social immanence and 'bad' historicism (Copjec 1994, 6–9). Yet, as the work of such diverse theorists as Laclau, Mouffe, Lyotard, Derrida (and I would argue Foucault as well) shows, this is simply a wrong assumption. In particular, Derrida's notion of performativity uncovers the necessary co-implication between these two types of analysis—between language and the polemos, force and signification.

Another difficulty confronting Copjec's analysis is the negotiation between the failure of signification and the structural stability of sexual difference—a difference, let us recall, "that founds psychoanalysis's division of all subjects into two mutually exclusive classes" (Copjec 1994, 213) How can a totally empty entity—"to which no predicate can be attached"—an entity disjoined from the signifier, produce two (no less and no more) modalities of failure? If sex is "disjoined from the signifier" in two permanent ways, what does guarantee the fixity of this "disjointment"? In order to bypass the impasse generated by the clash between failure and the structural stability of difference, Copjec goes through an elaborate detour of the Kantian antinomies: "language and reason may fail in one of two different ways. The distinction between these modalities of misfire ... was first made by Kant in *the Critique of Pure Reason* and was employed again in *The Critique of Judgement*" (Copjec 1994, 213).[5] Although the analogy between the antinomies of pure reason and the Lacanian formulas of sexuation is meant to distinguish clearly the two modalities of failure and then link them to sexual difference, the Kantian sub-text reinforces primarily the epistemological effects of sexual difference and limits the asymmetry of sexual relations to the model of epistemological contradiction.

Let us look at this analogy between the Kantian antinomies of reason and the Lacanian formulas of sexuation a bit more carefully in order to see whether the effort to contain the failure of signification within two invariable modalities can succeed, and at what cost.[6] Copjec proposes an analogy between sexual difference, which demarcates the "enunciative positions" of the subject, and even more, on which "the very sovereignty of the subject depends" (Copjec 1994, 208), and the Kantian distinction between the mathematical and dynamical antinomies, that is, the distinction between quantity and causality. This analogy is based primarily on a formal similarity: reduplicating the structure of the antinomies of reason, Lacan in the section of Seminar XX: *Encore*, entitled "A Love Letter," defines each side of sexual difference in terms of two aporetic statements, that is, in terms of "an affirmation and a negation of the phallic function, an inclusion and exclusion of absolute (nonphallic) *jouissance*" (Copjec 1994, 215). Because of this antinomic structure, each side of sexual difference reveals a different impasse or failure of language. According to Copjec, Lacanian formula for femininity corresponds to the Kantian mathematical antinomy (concerning the totality or the incompleteness of the world) whereas the formula for masculinity corresponds to the dynamical antinomy (concerning the dilemma of compulsion and freedom). Yet, this formal similarity notwithstanding, we have to ask whether the Kantian antinomies could correspond directly to the differences between the subjects' "enunciative positions." Kant is very clear that this is not the case: antinomies refer to different modes of "the objective synthesis of appearances," (Kant 1965, 385) and not to "the subjective conditions of all presentation" (Kant 1965, 384).[7] To put it in a different way, we can say that the antinomies describe the contradictions within theoretical judgements but say nothing about the enunciative positions from which these judgements are made.

With his conception of antinomies, Kant makes the transition from the enunciative positions of the subject to the synthesis of the phenomena in the world. This transition is possible because he has already dealt with the transcendental illusion pertaining to the enunciative positions of the subject—namely, with the way we erroneously treat the unity of consciousness as an object and then apply the category of substance to it—in his discussion of the paralogisms of pure reason, the section which precedes the treatment of antinomies. Yet, Copjec completely disregards Kant's discussion of paralogisms, and with it, the Kantian discussion of the impasses of reason pertaining directly to the position of enunciation. By pursuing the analogy between sexual difference and the antinomies, she in fact displaces the problematic of sex from enunciation to cosmology, from the transcendental illusions accruing to the subject to the contradictions accruing to the synthesis of phenomena. Thus, in attempting to move from the sexed subject of psychoanalysis to the neutral subject of philosophy, she misses the (philosophical) subject and ends up drawing the analogy between the subject of psychoanalysis and the Kantian "world concepts." If we were to pursue rigorously the consequences of this displacement, then sexual difference could no longer be said to divide the subjects into two mutually exclusive groups, but merely to show the difference between the mathematical and dynamic syntheses of appearances.

Copjec bases her argument on the formal similarity (or even on "reduplication") between the Kantian solution to the mathematical antinomy, which claims that the world does not exist, and the Lacanian well-know formulation that the woman is constituted as "not all":

> when any being whatever lines up under the banner of women it is by being constituted as not all that they are placed within the phallic function....

There is no such thing as *The* woman, where the definite article stands for the universal. There is no such thing as *The* woman since of her essence—having already risked the term, why think twice about it?—of her essence, she is not all. (Lacan 1982, 144)

According to Copjec, both the idea of the world (as a totality) and the woman (as a whole) should be read as contradictions of reason.

For Kant, let us recall, the mathematical antinomy arises when reason attempts to embrace the totality of all phenomena and produces two contradictory claims: a) the world has a beginning in space and time, therefore it is finite; and b) the world has no beginning in time and no limit in space, therefore it is infinite. Instead of choosing between these two theses, Kant demonstrates that they are both false, because the very choice presupposes that the world exists as a thing in itself apart from our appearances, that it is an unconditioned whole. By arguing that the idea of absolute totality is incompatible with the conditions of experience, Kant claims that "the world can be met with only in the empirical regress of the series of appearances." The series of appearances are never given as a totality, and therefore "the world is not an unconditioned whole, and does not exist as such a whole, neither of an infinite or of finite magnitude" (Kant 1965, 448). Kant thus solves this antinomy by pointing to the erroneous application of the idea of totality to appearances.

Since the concept of the world implies "the mathematical sum-total of all appearances and the totality of their synthesis" (Kant 1965, 392), it does indeed create a possibility of the misplaced application of the concept of the absolute totality to the conditions of experience. Yet, does the term "woman," like the term "world," produce in us the expectation of "the mathematical whole of all appearances and the totality their synthesis"? Can the idea of the woman (the subject) be substituted for the concept of the "world" (the totality of objects) without leaving a remainder? And, since any notion of quantity presupposes a subject performing the synthesis of phenomena, who does, then, occupy the position of such a subject? What needs to be explained in Copjec's reading of Lacan is not the fact that the woman, like the world, does not exist as a whole, but the problem of why and how the categories of the *quantity of objects*, like totality and the mathematical synthesis of all phenomena, become attached, albeit in negative fashion, to the concept of the woman in the first place. Why, indeed should we risk all these terms, without "thinking twice" about them? Otherwise we seem to be condemned to a circular movement in which we start with the improper premise of the woman as the totality of objects and then show that this premise is precisely improper—the woman cannot be a whole because she lacks a limit, or, in psychoanalytic terms, because she does not submit to a threat of castration.

Copjec's interpretation of the sexuation of men in terms of the dynamic antinomy is even more difficult to sustain. In order to pursue this similarity at all, Copjec has to limit herself only to the formal analogy between the Kantian antinomies and the Lacanian formulas, while disregarding the philosophical aftermath of these analogies, namely, the association of femininity exclusively with the notion of the mathematical quantity of objects and of masculinity with the ethical dilemmas of causality and freedom. As Kant explicitly claims, the practical freedom of human action, and therefore the very project of ethics and the ethical subject, depends on the transcendental freedom affirmed in the solution to the dynamical antinomy. Thus, Copjec's alignment of sexual difference with antinomies opens the questions of subjectivity and morality (and, by extension, the ethics of psychoanalysis) on the masculine side whereas simultaneously foreclosing it on the feminine side. The alliance between philosophy and psychoanalysis produces in this case a surprisingly stereotypical outcome, which only reinforces the familiar conclusions about the absence of the feminine superego—the claim Copjec herself would like to modify. Copjec attends only to the psychoanalytical part of this difficulty, namely to the analogy between the dynamical antinomy and the formation of the super ego. Yet, by "making explicit. . . [Lacan's] debt to critical philosophy," Copjec has also to deal with the philosophical impasse created by this debt as well—an impasse, which might undercut her intention to develop "an ethics proper to the woman" (Copjec 1994, 236).

My other observation refers to Copjec's interpretation of the dynamical antinomy. If we recall, this antinomy is also produced by two contradictory claims: a) the laws of nature are not the only causality operating in the world, we also have to accept the causality of freedom to account for the phenomena; and b) there is no such thing as freedom, but everything in the world happens solely according to the laws of nature. In order to draw a parallel between the dynamical antinomy and the Lacanian formulation of the masculine position, Copjec argues that by accepting both the thesis and the antithesis as true, Kant confirms "the existence of the all, the universal, just as Lacan confirms the existence of the universe of men" (Copjec 1994, 229). By disregarding Kant's arguments about freedom, Copjec claims that "suddenly the world, which was prohibited from forming in the mathematical antinomies, comes into being on the dynamical side" (Copjec 1994, 230) just as the universe of subjects, impossible on the feminine side, appears on the masculine side. Yet, to draw such a conclusion amounts to reading the dynamical antinomy in a mathematical way (indeed, in Copjec's case, literally, in terms of additions and subtractions[8]), as if Kant were still concerned with the judgment of quantity (with the question of all). Kant explicitly argues, however, that the dynamical antinomy does not advance any judgments about the mathematical issues of quantity; it considers exclusively the question of causality: "in the dynamical regress, on the other hand, we are concerned *not with the possibility of an unconditional whole of given parts. . .* but with *the derivation of a state from its cause*" (Kant 1965, 480). Consequently, the mere formulation of "everything in the world" in the antithesis does not deny the solution of the mathematical antinomy and therefore does not affirm the existence of the world as a whole. On the contrary, by arguing that his solution of the mathematical antinomy— "the world can be met with only in the empirical regress of the series of appearances"—is true for all antinomies, Kant proceeds to a different issue altogether, namely, to the issue of causality. It seems to me that it would make much more sense to raise the issue of dynamical antinomy in the context of Copjec's fascinating discussion of causality operating in psychoanalytical explications of the social and the psychic.

By reading the dynamical antinomy in a mathematical way, Copjec not only disregards what truly "matters" in the second antinomy ("we will not be concerned in what follows with the specifics of Kant's arguments about the cosmological idea of freedom"(Copjec 1994, 229)), but, more important, erases the *very distinction between the mathematical and the dynamical antinomy*: "In Lacan's formulas, the parallels between two sides are more visible, since *the same symbols* are used throughout" (Copjec 1994, 231).[9] If we recall that the turn to the Kantian antinomies in the first place was supposed to demonstrate the two different modes of the failure as the basis for sexual difference, then the instability of the very distinction between the antinomies in Copjec's argument undercuts the possibility of an "invariable" sexual difference. It is not only the case that Copjec performs the series of subtractions in the Kantian argument in order to establish this double modality of failure—we end up with the number "two" only when we disregard paralogisms of pure reason and reduce the four antinomies to two despite Kant's demonstration of the fact that antinomies are necessarily fourfold because they are derived from the four categories of the synthesis of understanding—but, in the end, even these two kinds of failure can be collapsed into one.

This simultaneous multiplication and reduction of difference from four to one in Copjec's reading of Kant points to the limits of reading failure as the basis of the structural stability of sexual difference. The deadlock of language can hardly serve as the basis of any "invariant" difference, unless, of course, the permanence of this difference receives an unacknowledged support from some immovable ground—the ground that is not submitted to contestation. It is not difficult to guess that this tacit support of the permanence of sexual difference comes from the unsymbolizable Real. Copjec herself argues as much when she claims that sexual difference is not deconstructible because it belongs to the Real—and, as we have already heard, the Real "does not budge."

II.
"Real" Objections / Performative Effects

Not mindful of the "immovable rock" of psychoanalysis, Butler, in the process of deconstructing sexual difference, contests nothing less than the Real itself. Because she is not able to accept the presupposition of the Real in her own analysis, Butler focuses on the second best substitute—on Žižek's reading of the effects of the Real in social formations. The Lacanian Real, central to Copjec's and Žižek's reading of sexual difference, is the realm of being that is radically unsymbolizable, that remains foreclosed from the symbolic order. In this formulation, the Real constitutes a necessary outside of any symbolization—a limit to the totalization of the social or discursive field. Like Copjec, Žižek suggests that any attempt to define the Real leads to paradoxical formulations (witness Copjec's antinomies). As *coincidentia oppositorum*, or as "immediate coincidence of opposite or even contradictory determinations" (Žižek 1989, 171), the Real is the starting point, the "impossible kernel" of symbolization and, at the same time, an effect of the symbolic order, an excess, or left-over of symbolization.[10] In the first formulation, it is a "fullness of inert presence," whereas in the second, it is the void created by the symbolic, opening the possibility of the annihilation of the symbolic universe. An effect of the symbolic, the Real is nonetheless a 'retroactive' cause exercising structural causality.[11] It cannot be inscribed into the symbolic order, but it can be reconstructed backwards from the series of its effects (failures): "the Real cannot be inscribed, but we can inscribe this impossibility itself, we can locate its place: a traumatic place which causes a series of failures" (Žižek 1989, 173). Although totally unknowable, the Real nonetheless remains the same in its symbolic and historical manifestations—and, by such a "manifestation," Žižek means "the inscription of the impossibility of inscription."

At stake in the argument about the Real is, on the one hand, a renegotiation of the relations between contingency and compulsion in social and discursive formations, and, on the other, the status of the concept of the outside of history and symbolization. On the basis of the conceptualization of the Real as the necessary outside of the symbolic order, Žižek condemns both the universalization of the symbolic and its obverse side, its "rapid historicization," which treats the subject merely as the effect or the actualization of its historical conditions.[12] Both of these gestures, he argues, ignore that which is foreclosed from historicization. In order to take into account the incompleteness and contingency of the historical process, the critical accounts of history, Žižek argues, have to presuppose an empty place, an non-historical kernel, that which cannot be symbolized and yet is produced by symbolization itself (Žižek 1989, 135). Yet, Žižek's presuppositions do not end here; they lead to the assumption that the foreclosed Real remains the same in all historical formations even though its sameness cannot be grasped in positive terms: "The Real is the rock upon which every attempt at symbolization stumbles, the hard core which remains the same in all possible worlds . . .; but at the same time its status is thoroughly precarious; it persists only as failed, missed, . . . and it dissolves itself as soon as we try to grasp it in its positive nature" (Žižek 1989, 169).[13]

Butler's argument with the Real neither disputes the contingency of social formations nor denies the constitutive outside to symbolization. On the contrary, through her reading of Laclau and Mouffe, she links such contingency and incompleteness to the promise of radical democracy: "The incompleteness of every ideological formulation is central to the radical democratic project's notion of political futurity. The subjection of every ideological formation to *re*articulation . . . constitutes the temporal order of democracy as an incalculable future, leaving open the production of new subject-positions, new political signifiers . . ."(Butler 1993, 193). What she does contest, however, is the fixity of the Real (or rather, to articulate it more cautiously, the invariable failure of its inscription) and the permanent structure of its exclusion. Even though the foreclosure of the Real "guarantees" contingency and incompleteness of all social relations, the process of this foreclosure is not marked by the contingency or historicity, and therefore is not open to redescription. We are confronted here, Butler argues, with the unchangeable production of the outside, even though the "production" in question is marked by the instability of cause and effect. As Butler points out, "if we concur that every discursive formation proceeds through constituting an 'outside,' we are not thereby committed to the *invariant* production of that outside as the trauma of castration (nor to the generalization of castration as the model for all historical trauma)" (Butler 1993, 205).[14]

The argument about the Real is not just a theoretical hairsplitting, what is at stake here are the ideological consequences of theory. As Butler asks, "what is the ideological status of a theory that identifies the contingency in all ideological formulations as 'the lack' produced by the threat of castration, where the threat and the sexual differential that it institutes are not subject to the discursive rearticulation. . .?" (Butler 1993, 196). According to Butler, it is the "invariable production of the outside" that makes it possible for the unsymbolizable Real to acquire nonetheless social and historical "contents"—which means that the "effects" of historical exclusions are read retroactively as the ahistorical causality. This is especially the case when the exclusion of the Real is linked to the threat of castration, which, as we have seen in Copjec's argument, institutes the invariable and compulsory character of sex. In a gesture that resembles Derrida's critique of Levinasian alterity, Butler points to the contradiction in the formulation of the unsymbolizable which nonetheless "grounds" sexual difference and makes it immovable.

If neither Butler nor Derrida presuppose a permanent structure of exclusion, or a fixed outside to symbolization, how do they account for the social and historical contingency of sexual norms on the one hand, and for their compulsory character on the other? Does the process of historicity that takes into account its own incompleteness and contingency have to imply necessarily the ahistorical "empty kernel"? Does the contestation of such a permanently excluded "rock" suggest automatically, as Žižek charges, an ideological trap of the "rapid historicization" of sex? To answer these questions, we have to examine the relation between the norm and the failure of signification first in Derrida's critique of speech act theory, and second, in Butler's deployment of this critique for her reformulation of the constructivist argument regarding sex.

Derrida's radicalization of the performative starts with an observation about the aporia of the totality and incompleteness of language—that is, with an argument very similar to the one advanced by Copjec. Although Derrida also analyzes the double predicament of the totalization and structural incompleteness of language, he considers this contradiction no longer from the stand-point of structuralist linguistics but from the perspective of the speech act pragmatics. There are several consequences of this shift—a subsumption of the theory of meaning under a more general theory of action, a displacement of the authority of truth for the value of force (which, as Derrida points out, is a Nietzschean gesture), and an emphasis on the internal relation between signification and power. In order to analyze the performative capacity of an utterance, Derrida argues, we have to take into account not only the fact that it can be submitted to the interests of the external political forces but also that it itself communicates a force—that it transforms a situation or produces an effect.[15]

By emphasizing the aporia between the requirement of totality and incompleteness of language, Derrida exposes the failure of signification not as an accidental attribute but as the very law of the performative.[16] Because of this possibility of failure, the performative act cannot be simply reduced to a "real tight," to use Copjec's phrase, realization of the prior historical conditions; on the contrary, it implies discontinuity and rupture from these conditions. Although the performative always founds itself on regulatory conventions and prior performatives, "it always maintains within itself some interruptive violence, it no longer responds to the demands of theoretical rationality."[17] Eschewing any reference to a permanently foreclosed "outside," Derrida explains the instability of language by focusing on the force of interruption separating the utterance from its historical production and on its obverse side, on the structural non-saturation of the context. For Derrida, the performative effect depends as much on the citation of the norm as on the force of rupture separating the utterance not only from the moment of its original production (a cause) but also from all subsequent contextualizations: "a written sign carries with it a force of breaking with its context, that is, the set of presences which organize the moment of its inscription. This force of breaking is not an accidental predicate, but the very structure of the written" (V 1982, 317). The force of separation does not permanently cut language from the ahistorical and non-symbolizable Real, but constitutes the possibility of a repeatable break from the specific historical contexts and causes.

The essential failure of the performative, which is not only an unfortunate predicament but also a positive condition of its possibility, leads Derrida to rethink the very opposition between the singularity of the event and the infelicitous repetition of the norm. As Derrida argues in a more familiar part of his argument, any repetition/re-enactment is linked to alterity, to the inventions of difference, and to the unpredictability of the singular event. Yet, he also adds, the pure singularity of the event is at the same time submitted to redoubling and repetition: "would a performative statement be possible if a citational doubling did not eventually split, dissociate from itself the pure singularity of the event?" (MP 326). The performative is always open to the happening of the event, whose occurrence cannot be derived from the protocol of its code; while the singularity of the event gives itself to repetition and passes through the generality of the code. Derrida's reading of the structural instability of language links this instability not to the permanent exclusion of the Real, but to the possibility of the event, and thus, as Judith Butler argues, to the possibility of an open "future for the signifier." Indeed, in Derrida's later work, this interconnection between performativity and event becomes the condition of justice: 'there is no justice except to the degree that some event is possible which, as event, exceeds calculation, rules, programs, anticipations and so forth" (FL 27).

By bringing together the insights of the Derridian rewriting of speech act theory and the Foucauldian theory of power, Butler reformulates the question of sex as a performative category—that is, a category which, as Derrida suggests, belongs more appropriately to a general theory of force rather than to hermeneutics (MP 321). As we have seen, however, the stress on the performativity of sex does not mean that the linguistic level of analysis is abandoned in favor of the discussion of the power regime, but that signification and force are mutually constitutive. Since it attempts to account for the necessary relation between contingency and norm, Butler's theory of performativity has been called many contradictory things: it has been disclaimed as both voluntaristic and deterministic, idealist and materialist, endowing the subject with too much agency or not enough of it.[18] This confusion stems from the fact that Butler's argument not only seeks to reformulate the category of sex but also to revise the premise of the historicist argument—the argument, which, as Copjec rightly observes, all too often conceives of the subject as simply a fulfillment of the historical demand: "the social system of representation is conceived as lawful, regulatory, and on this account the cause of the subject. . .The subject is assumed to be already virtually there in the social and to come into being by actually wanting what social laws want it to want" (Copjec 1994, 41). Rejecting both the assumption that the subject comes into being "by wanting what social laws want it to want" and the presupposition that the social regime of power/knowledge is "lawful and regulatory," Butler proposes to rethink subjective identifications with the symbolic law as performative acts. As we have already seen in Derrida's argument, this emphasis on the performative dimension of sex precludes any simplistic discussion of the subject as a realization of social conditions because the paradoxical law of the performative posits the rupture between conditions and effects as essential to very success of speech act.

What is the nature of such a performative identification? Performativity for Butler, as for Derrida, consist neither in voluntary decisions of the self nor in involuntary acts governed by the law that is external to them. To avoid impasses of social constructivism that sees the subject as merely an effect of social conditions, Butler stresses the fact that the reiteration of the norm (code) constitutes not only the subject but also the meaning of the symbolic law. Not a simple cause of the subject, the law itself is produced by the repetition of subjective approximations in time. Because it does not have a fixed form apart from its approximations through subjective acts, the law, despite its compulsory force, is marked by the "infelicities" and the infidelities characteristic of performative utterances. The repetition of acts understood as the citation of the law stabilizes the form of the law, and, at the same time, produces a "dissonance" and inconsistency within it. Indissociable from "irruptive violence," reiteration sustains and undercuts both the permanence of the law and the identity of the subject: "the law is no longer given in a fixed form ... but is produced through citation as that which precedes and exceeds the mortal approximations enacted by the subject" (Butler 1993, 14). For Butler, like for Derrida, the possibility of failure and impurity afflicting the repetition of sexual norms is not only an unfortunate predicament or "trauma", but also a positive condition of possibility. By opening the possibility of intervention and redescription of sexual norms, reiteration not only stresses the historicity of the law but also opens an "incalculable" future, no longer submitted to its jurisdiction.

If Butler draws on the Derridian theory of performativity in order to underscore the historicity and impurity of the law, she also supplements this theory in order to stress the compulsory character of heterosexuality. According to Butler, the normative power of heterosexuality requires not only the force effecting subjective identifications with its norms but also the force of dis-identifications, the force of exclusions, in particular, the exclusion of homosexuality: "the normative force of performativity—its power to establish what qualifies as 'being'—works not only through reiteration, but through exclusion as well" (Butler 1993, 188). Thus, the compulsory force of heterosexuality depends on the exclusion of at least two "inarticulate" or "spectral" figures of abject homosexuality: "the feminized fag and the phallicized dyke" (Butler 1993, 96). It is precisely because iterability fails to perpetuate the identical and pure form of the law that any identity claims have to be reinforced by exclusions—they require "a constitutive outside." In other words, Butler, like Žižek, concedes that the normativity of the law works by producing a certain outside to the symbolic universe. Yet, to avoid the ahistorical production of the Real, Butler proposes to rethink "the constitutive outside" as a social abject, the exclusion of which secures the domain of social intelligibility. In this formulation, the process of exclusion is never neutral but performs a normative and normalizing social function:

> the abject designates here precisely those "unlivable" and "uninhabitable" zones of social life which are nevertheless densely populated by those who do not enjoy the status of the subject. ... This zone of uninhabitability will constitute the defining limit of the subject's domain; it will constitute that site of dreaded identification against which—and by virtue of which—the domain of the subject will circumscribe its own claim to autonomy and to life. (Butler 1993, 3)

In Butler's interpretation, what is thus foreclosed from the symbolic is not the prediscursive "empty" kernel but those possibilities of signification that threaten the purity and permanence of the law instituting sexual difference. With such a concept of the outside, Butler articulates the main task of her inquiry in a very different way from Žižek's. She does not intend to affirm the exclusion of the Real as a guarantee of social contingency but questions the stability and ahistorical character of this exclusion: "How might those ostensibly constitutive exclusions be rendered less permanent, more dynamic? How might the excluded return, not as psychosis or the figure of the psychotic within politics, but as that which has been rendered mute, foreclosed from the domain of political signification?" (Butler 1993, 189). By rethinking the historicity and contingency of the law as the sedimentation of subjective approximations through time, Butler can argue that the mechanisms of exclusion are also, "however inevitable—still and always the historical workings of specific modalities of discourse and power" (Butler 1993, 205). As the last chapter, "Critically Queer," demonstrates so well, the "constitutive outside" is an inevitable effect of any identity claims, including the claims of queer identities, but the forms of these exclusions are neither invariant nor ahistorical. Undercutting the political neutrality and ahistorical permanence of "the constitutive outside," Butler's emphasis on the historicity of exclusion removes the threat of psychosis associated with it and opens the borders of intelligibility to political contestation.

III.
Reading Femininity with Style: the Question of the Other

The obvious difference between Derrida's and Butler's use of the performative lies in the seeming sexual neutrality of Derrida's analysis. Yet, if the deconstruction of speech act theory does not engage sexual difference, Butler's rethinking of the performative in the context of sexual difference only follows the Derridian strategy (articulated elsewhere) of the explicit resexualization of the theoretical and philosophical discourse: "the emphasis that I have put on resexualizing a philosophical or theoretical discourse, which has been too "neutralizing" in this respect, was dictated by those very reservations . . . concerning the strategy of neutralization" (CH 181). As Derrida writes in reference to both Heidegger and Levinas, this strategic neutralization "gives a masculine sexual marking to what is presented as a neutral originariness or, at least, as prior and superior to all sexual markings" (CH 178). Derrida's reservations here are precisely against "a surreptitious operation that . . . insures phallocentric mastery under the cover of neutralization every time" (CH 175).

Derrida's resexualization of language enables a *sortie* of sorts, a step beyond the double bind, the double solicitation of femininity in the discourse of philosophy, that is, beyond the topos of "Woman as the major allegory of truth in Western discourse" and its negative correlative, Woman as the name for the absence of truth or the truth of castration. In his polemics with Nietzsche and Lacan, Derrida is at pains to argue that both of these invocations provide a certain 'anchoring' of phallogocentrism, and assure "the complicity of Western metaphysics with a notion of male firstness" (CH 171).[19] If the first invocation of the feminine assuages hermeneutical anxiety by erasing the question of style, the second has the dubious privilege of provoking it by the chic masquerade of femininity conceived merely as style.[20]

Yet, this resexualization of language reaches a certain limit in Derrida's own emphasis on the ethical respect of alterity. What we have considered thus far, through the juxtaposition of Derrida's and Butler's work, is the performative dimension of the sexed subject before the law of "compulsory heterosexuality"—a dimension which not only envelops the subjective identifications with the law but also constitutes the impure form of the law itself, opening it thus to political contestation. What is frequently ignored, however, is that Derrida's later work, influenced by Levinas's conception of ethics, develops yet another modality of performativity—it rethinks iteration, which already links repetition to alterity, in the context of the ethical obligation to other and a call for justice. Obligation is not a voluntary act, commitment, or initiative of the subject, but, rather, an originary exposure to the other, preceding the formation of consciousness. If in "Signature Event Context" the performative force of language is intertwined with the failure of signification, in Derrida's later work, it is no longer discussed exclusively in epistemological terms but is rearticulated more explicitly as the strange condition of ethics. Irreducible to yet another concept, structure, or sign, the ethical relation to the other is linked to the disturbance in the order of representation, to the "diachrony refractory to thematization," and, finally, to the non-coincidence of language with itself. By afflicting the subject with an obligation of response, the ethical encounter with the other interrupts the process of identification and creates a permanent dislocation in the position of the self.

Ungraspable in positive terms, and yet irreducible to epistemological contradiction, the signification of alterity confronts us, once again, with the limit, or the outside to the symbolic order. This limit differs, however, from both the psychoanalytic concept of the Real and Butler's notion of the "constitutive outside." Unlike the radical non-coincidence, both temporal and spatial, that the signification of the other generates, Copjec's and Žižek's discussion of the Real emphasizes the immediate coincidence of opposites. Even more important is the difference between Levinas's and Derrida's insistence that the alterity in the ethical sense has to be thought "otherwise than being" (which does not mean that the other belongs, therefore, to the order of meaning) and the psychoanalytic conception of the Real as the missing kernel of being: "for Lacan it is the being beyond, not the being within language, that is perceived as immutable, as the inert pound of flesh, the 'inch of nature,' which the blank of memory...signals as missing from our own self-image" (Copjec 1994, 52).

However, the ethical import of the other is also irreducible to the abject, even though both of these significations are intertwined with a call for justice. For Butler, the abject— designating the excluded possibilities of signification threatening the purity of the law—functions as the constitutive outside to the symbolic order. The exclusion of the abject is thus an act of violence that ensures heterosexual hegemony. The task of critical intervention, then, is to question the seeming neutrality of this exclusion, and to recover the foreclosed possibilities of signification, even though this recovery will produce different exclusions in its wake. For Derrida, however, the persistence of alterity as a certain beyond or excess of the social and conceptual totality is not a sign of violent exclusion, but the condition of the very possibility of ethics. The other does not belong to the order of the "production" of the constitutive outside—as radically other, the signification of alterity exceeds both the notion of production and constitution. No longer thought in terms of the dialectical opposite, the other, quite literally, constitutes nothing. More originary and more "exterior" than the notion of the "constitutive outside," the ethical signification of the other confronts us with another form of violence—this time, with the violence of inclusion, with the obliteration of alterity in the very process of its recovery. Thus, as Drucilla Cornell argues, "the recovery of the excess, the remain(s) [of the other] is both impossible and necessary; impossible, and yet necessary—for to pay tribute to the remains would be another violation of the *haters*" (Cornell 1992, 71–72).[21] Exposing the obliteration of alterity in the process of its symbolic recuperation, Derrida emphasizes the responsibility imposed by the non-thematizable exposure to the other and the paradoxical inscription of this event in the social typography of language.

Can we afford to supplement Butler's discussion of sex as a performative category with Derrida's subsequent elaboration of the performative force of the address to the other? Are not these two notions—sexual difference and ethical alterity—mutually exclusive? Would not saving the possibility of ethics prescribe a certain sexual neutrality to the other—an operation, let us recall, "that...insures phallocentric mastery under the cover of neutralization every time" (CH 175)? Derrida himself alerts us to the repressive force of this neutralization in Levinas's ethics: "the possibility of ethics could be saved, if one takes ethics to mean that relationship to the other which accounts for no other determination or sexual characteristic in particular"

(CH 178). How, then, can ethics bear on the deconstruction of sexual difference?

What makes the negotiation between ethics and sexual difference possible is Derrida's insistence on the "co-implication" between two mutually exclusive performative forces—between the subject's relation to the norm and the subject's obligation to the other. Rather than resolving this aporia by subordinating one notion of the performative to the other, Derrida embraces it as the very possibility of deconstruction and its "commitment" to justice. The relation to other—to what is singular and heterogenous—interrupts the circle of identification with the law, the coincidence of the subject with itself, and its reciprocity with others. Yet, this singular encounter with the other also has to pass through the generality of the law, it has to move toward the third party, "who suspends the unilaterality or singularity" (FL 17) of the ethical relation. Derrida repeats here Levinas's argument that the context of the third party—that is, sociality—marks a transition from ethics to politics, from the singular ethical relation of responsibility to the question of justice which concerns "all the others."[22] The passage between the generality of the norm and singularity of the other does not entail, however, the subordination of alterity to the rule but an inscription of the dissymmetry within the structure of the law. Only when it occurs within both ethical and political dimension, the relation to the other can preserve, what Derrida calls, "asymmetrical and heteronomical curvature of the social space." As Derrida argues, this co-implication of the law and the affirmation of the radical alterity irreducible to the law does not lead to a higher mode of synthesis or to a communal reciprocity but preserves the aporia between generality and singularity as the possibility of justice: "But this co-implication, far from dissolving the antagonism and breaking through the aporia, aggravates them instead—at the very heart of friendship" (PF 641).

Let us look more explicitly at how this experience of this co-implication is inscribed within the subjective identification with the law. By enveloping the subject's position before the law, the ethical relation to the other produces, what Derrida calls, "the asymmetrical torsion" within the process of identification. Thus, subjective approximations of the law are undercut not only by the force of iteration but also by the non-thematizable ethical relation with the other. In his reading of *Ulysses*, for instance, Derrida gives us an example of a "torsion" within identification by focusing on the most minimal performative utterance, implied in the response "yes." As a performative condition of identification, such an utterance, on the one hand, enables the positioning of the subject in language. Each time the subject dreams of self-appropriation or identifies with the social representations, it addresses itself through a "yes, I will." But on the other hand, the affirmation of "yes, I" is already caught in a response to the other: it illustrates "the het-ero-tautology of the *yes* implied in all *cogito* as thought, the position of the self, and the will of the position of the self." Disrupting the circle of identi-fication, "responding always supposes the Other in relation to oneself; it preserves the sense of this asymmetrical 'anteriority' even within the seem-ingly most inward and solitary autonomy" (PF 639). Since it does not have any specific semantic content, the response of a "yes" functions as a purely performative force: "as a pre-performative force which, for example, in the form of 'I' marks that 'I' as addressing itself to the Other, however undeter-mined he or she is: 'Yes-I,' or 'Yes-I-am- speaking-to-the-other,' even if *I* is saying *no* and even if *I* is addressing itself without speaking" (UG 62–63). By supplementing the notion of iteration with the address to the other, Derrida brings the performative force of the law/norm back to the context of the "intersubjective" exchange and, at the same time, he demonstrates how the protocols of such an exchange are broken by the irreducible asymmetry of the ethical relation.

Although the asymmetrical ethical relation interrupts the rule of the law, Derrida equally strongly insists that this relation passes through the gener-ality of the law. It is this strange passage [*partage*] between the singularity of the other and the generality of the law that preserves for Derrida a non-coincidence at the very core of sexual difference. Instead of reciprocity or complementarity, sexual difference inscribes the asymmetry between the law and alterity, generality and singularity, reciprocity and heterogeneity, on both sides of the divide:

> A certain dissymmetry is no doubt the law both of sexual difference and the relationship to the other in general. . ., yet the dissymmetry to which I refer is still let us not say symmetrical in turn. . .but doubly, unilaterally inordinate, like a kind of reciprocal, respective and respectful excessiveness. This double dissymmetry to which I refer perhaps goes beyond the known or coded marks, beyond the grammar and spelling, shall we say (metaphorically), of sexuality. This indeed revives the following question: what if we were to reach, what if we were to approach here. . .the area of a relationship to the other where the code of sexual marks would no longer be discriminating? The rela-tionship would not be a-sexual, far from it, but be sexual otherwise: beyond the binary difference that governs the decorum of all the codes. (CH 184)

In thinking the asymmetry of sexual difference, Derrida follows here the steps of certain maverick feminists: he mocks the sexual neutrality of alter-ity while at the same time preserving the relationship to an other beyond the predictable branding of sexual marks. Let us note in passing that Derrida's insistence on the asymmetry of sexual difference both recalls and yet differs from the lack of complementarity in sexual relations stressed by Copjec. In Copjec's reading, the lack of complementarity is articulated according to the logical model of antinomy, a model, which implies the simultaneous presence of the two contrary statements. As a radical diachrony eluding the order of the present, the ethical asymmetry Derrida wants to inscribe within sexual relations points to the impossibility of placing the two sexual positions side by side, even in terms of contradiction. By contesting the difference between *two* synchronized terms as the model for sexual relations, Derrida does not intend to collapse "sexual difference into sexual indistinctness"(Copjec 1994, 216) but reads the lack of complementarity between the sexes not only in terms of epistemological failure but also as an ethical non-coincidence.

Derrida's departure from the exclusively epistemological and logical interpretation of the absence of sexual relation does not lead, as Copjec presumes, to skepticism regarding sex or to the "euthanasia of reason." Rather, as I have argued elsewhere, Derrida consistently rewrites the skeptical argument, in this case, the argument regarding sex, as the affirmation of the other of reason and the possibility of ethics without a law (Ziarek, 1995). In a somewhat similar gesture, Copjec cannot finish her book with a mere indictment of the skepticism of deconstruction, but also makes an appeal to a different ethics, "an ethics proper to the woman." Could these two very different calls for a new ethics of sexual difference open a more productive encounter between feminist deconstruction and feminist psychoanalysis? Although beyond the scope of this paper, the answer to this question is a matter of an altogether different invention—the invention of new alliances, new modes of reading, and, finally, of ethics itself.

In the end I would like to reiterate my claim that the emphasis on the double modality of performativity—on the force of the law and the ethical relation to the other—enables us to intervene into the specific historical determinations of sexual norms without succumbing to the trap of historicism. Contrary to Žižek's and Copjec's criticisms of deconstruction, Derrida's notion of asymmetry contests the value of homology and reciprocity in the sexual and social relations and reminds us instead that "we are already caught up in a kind of asymmetrical and heteronomical curvature of the social space." As Simon Critchley suggests, for deconstruction "the space of *polis* is not an enclosed or immanent structure, but rather. . . a structure of repeated interruptions, in which the social totality is breached by the force of ethical transcendence" (Critchley 1992, 238). Inseparable from concrete political struggles, this force of ethical transcendence nonetheless exceeds the political contestation of sexual norms and thus creates the risk of a permanent interruption of the politico-theoretical programs. By assuming this risk, feminism would not weaken its commitment to the political contestation of gender hierarchies but would add to it the urgency of an infinite and excessive demand for justice.[23] Always in excess of the historically determined conditions and possibilities, justice requires the immediacy of action without the assurance of fulfillment for its non-satisfiable demands.

Notes

1. The debate between feminism and deconstruction has generated rich and varied responses. For an insightful discussion of the this debate, see, for instance, Diane Elam (1994, 1–26) and Mary Poovey (1988, 51–65).

2. Let us then recall this early deconstructive argument. In order to illustrate the double gesture of deconstructive intervention "which borrows from a heritage the resources necessary for the deconstruction of that heritage itself," Derrida focuses on the impasse of the nature/culture opposition—one of the founding distinctions of the Western metaphysics—vis-a-vis the "scandalous" status of the incest prohibition in Lévi-Strauss's discourse:

   > Once the limit of the nature/culture opposition makes itself felt, one might want to question systematically and rigorously the history of these concepts. This is a first action.... The other choice (which I believe corresponds more closely to Lévi-Strauss's manner)... consists in conserving all these old concepts within the domain of empirical discovery while here and there denouncing their limits, treating them as tools which still can be used.... Their relative efficacy is exploited, and they are deployed to destroy the old machinery to which they belong... (SSP 284).

3. As Derrida writes in "Force of Law," it is perhaps because law (droit)...is constructible, in a sense that goes beyond the opposition between convention and culture... that it makes deconstruction possible" (FL 15).

4. Yet, I should add, this contradiction between totalization and incompleteness is characteristic only of the theories of language that still struggle (while attempting to move beyond it) with the structuralist emphasis on language as a system. Wittgenstein and, after him, Lyotard dispense with the requirement of totalization altogether by focusing instead on pragmatics of the heterogenous language games.

5. For a lucid commentary on Kant's antinomies, see, for instance, Kemp (1968).

6. Copjec points to one possible difficulty of such a comparison: the subject of critical philosophy is neutral whereas the subject of psychoanalysis is fundamentally sexed. But, she adds, the philosophical subject is considered as unsexed only because sex itself is assumed to be a positive attribute. Since

psychoanalysis does not treat sex as a positive characteristic of the subject, it does not encounter any further difficulty with comparing the failure of signification with the internal contradiction of reason. Yet, the neutrality of the philosophical subject is not the only obstacle here; another difficulty concerns the place where Copjec inscribes the sexual difference in the Kantian text.

7. That is why the antinomies of reason are not treated under the rubric of rational psychology but belong to the critique of rational cosmology: "the ideas with which we are now dealing here have been entitled cosmological ideas, partly because by the term 'world' we mean the sum of all *appearances*, . . . partly also because the term 'world', in the transcendental sense, signifies the absolute *totality* of all existing things" (1965, 393).

8. Copjec explicitly argues that "what is involved in the shift from the female to the male side is a *subtraction*. . .it is this subtraction that installs the limit" (Copjec 1994, 230, emphasis added).

9. And conversely, we can say, that in order to establish the parallel between the woman and the world, Copjec is reading the mathematical antinomy in a dynamical way, since the ultimate explanation of the position of the woman as "not all" is in terms of the castration: "Lacan answers that the woman is not all because she lacks a limit, by which he means she is not susceptible to the threat of castration; the "no" embodied by this threat does not function for her" (Copjec 1994, 226). The prohibition embodied by the threat of castration brings us back to the dilemmas of freedom and compulsion.

10. As Lacan writes in *The Ethics of Psychoanalysis*, deploying the famous Heideggerian example of a vase in order to "represent the emptiness at the center of the real," "the fashioning of the signifier and the introduction of a gap or a hole in the real is identical" (Lacan 1992, 121).

11. For an excellent discussion of the causality associated with the Real, see Joan Copjec, "Cutting Up," (Copjec 1994, 39–63).

12. This "rapid historicization" is in contrast to the psychoanalytic conception of the subject, which "is nothing but the failure point of the process of his symbolic representation" (Žižek 1989, 173).

13. Copjec's formulation of the sameness of the Real is far more nuanced: "For Lacan it is the being beyond, not the being within language, that is perceived as immutable" (Copjec 1994, 52).

14. Butler's critique is particularly directed to Žižek's indifference to the specificity of historical catastrophes, and in particular, to the singularity of the Holocaust. This indifference is especially disturbing in the following argument: "all the different attempts to attach this phenomenon [concentration camps] to a concrete image ('Holocaust,' 'Gulag'. . .) . . . —what are they if not so many attempts to elude the fact that we dealing here with the 'real' of our civilization which returns as the *same traumatic* kernel in *all social systems*?" (Žižek 1989, 50). This seems to be a rather obtuse deployment of

the Lacanian statement that "the real is that which is always in the same place" (Lacan 1992, 70), as if Žižek were forgetting the other part of Lacan's argument that "nothing in that reality that we have learned to disrupt so admirably responds to the call for the security of a return" (Lacan 1992, 75).

15. As Derrida writes in "Force of Law," the performativity implies a relation to power "not in the sense of law in the service of force, its docile instrument, servile and thus exterior to the dominant power, but rather in the sense of law that would maintain a more internal, more complex relation with what one calls force, power, or violence" (FL 1992, 13).

16. Derrida's emphasis on the failure of the performative is remarkably similar at this point to Copjec's discussion of Lacan's notion of causality "that connect[s] cause not to law but to failure" (Copjec 1994, 62). It is only by disregarding this similarity that Copjec can claim that Derrida's performative is "dangerously close" to evolutionary philosophy (Copjec 1994, 58).

17. As Derrida explains, every utterance is governed by the code and normative constraints (and therefore refers to a certain totality) that assure its intelligibility even when its origin is lost. We have to add, as Judith Butler does, that the relative stability of the code is itself an effect of the sedimentation of the past performative acts. However, the possibility of the loss of origin points to the structural non-saturation of the context, which, in the last resort, bankrupts the very idea of the code.

18. We can see this contradiction in Copjec's criticism as well: Butler is simultaneously accused of "confident voluntarism" (Copjec 1994, 202, 210) and of not being able to acknowledge "subject's sovereignty": "Freedom, 'agency' are inconceivable in a schema such as this" (Copjec 1994, 208). Much of this criticism responds to the initial formulations of performativity of gender in *Gender Trouble* (Butler, 1990).

19. The notion of male firstness, Derrida argues in "White Mythology," underwrites even the philosophical concept of metaphor, which remains entrenched within both philosophy and politics of the subject. Defined as the proper human capacity, metaphor allows the Western rational man to claim the essence of humanity by silencing the claims of others and to cover over this violence by maintaining the neutrality of discourse (MP 266–271).

20. Although feminism shares with Derrida this contestation of the neutrality of philosophical language, it does not necessarily embrace his particular strategy. In his reading of Nietzsche, Derrida disrupts the neutrality of discourse by relying on a choreography of femininity, style, and rhetoric. When the significance of rhetoric is reduced to "referential aberration" and the notion of style reduced to literary ornament, such a choreography seems to confirm the frequent criticism that deconstruction is merely a literary and philosophical "school" of interpretation, and as such, it has nothing to offer to feminism, which cannot afford to relinquish its political activism. In order to counter this familiar objection, we need to inquire into

the significance of rhetoric in deconstructive enterprise. Such an inquiry is all the more important because the question of rhetoric exacerbates a widespread confusion between two divergent articulations of "the other of reason" in deconstructive project—between the more textual emphasis on the instability of language and the more socio-ethical emphasis on claims of alterity in linguistic community. Irreducible to mere the manifestation of linguistic undecidability, or to the failure of representation, the function of rhetoric, as I have argued elsewhere, is inseparable from the signification of alterity as an irreparable discord in the grammar of language games. For my discussion of the ethical significance of rhetoric in Derrida's work, see Ziarek (1995).

21. For an excellent discussion of the relevance of the deconstructive ethics to feminist project, see Drucilla Cornell (1993).

22. Levinas argues that "the extraordinary commitment of the other to the third party calls for control, a search for justice, society and the State...But come out of signification, a modality of proximity, justice, society, and the truth itself which they require, must not be taken for an anonymous law of the 'human forces' governing an impersonal totality" (Levinas 1981, 161).

23. As Derrida frequently reminds us, the fact that "justice exceeds law and calculation . . . cannot and should not serve as an alibi for staying out of juridico-political battles, within an institution or a state" (FL 28).

Works Cited

Butler, Judith. 1990. *Gender Trouble: Feminism and the Subversion of Identity.* New York: Routledge.

———. 1993. *Bodies That Matter: On the Discursive Limits of Sex.* New York: Routledge.

Copjec, Joan. 1994. *Read My Desire: Lacan against Historicists.* Cambridge: MIT Press.

Cornell, Drucilla. 1992. *The Philosophy of the Limit.* New York: Routledge.

———. 1993. *Transformations: Recollective Imagination and Sexual Difference.* New York: Routledge.

Critchley, Simon. 1992. *The Ethics of Deconstruction: Derrida and Levinas.* Oxford: Blackwell.

Derrida, Jacques. 1978. "Structure, Sign, and Play in the Discourse of the Human Sciences" in *Writing and Difference.* Trans. Alan Bass. Chicago: The University of Chicago Press. Cited as SSP.

———. 1982. *Margins of Philosophy.* Trans. Alan Bass. Chicago: The University of Chicago Press. Cited as MP.

———. 1984. "Ulysses Gramophone: Hear Say Yes in Joyce" in *James Joyce: The Augmented Ninth.* Ed. Bernard Benstock. Syracuse: Syracuse University Press. Cited as UG.

———. 1985. "Choreographies" in *The Ear of the Other*. Ed. Christie McDonald. Lincoln: University of Nebraska Press. Cited as CH.

———. 1988. "The Politics of Friendship." Trans. Gabriel Motzkin. *The Journal of Philosophy*, 85: 632–644. Cited as PF.

———. 1992. "Force of Law: The 'Mystical Foundation of Authority.'" *Deconstruction and the Possibility of Justice*, ed. Drucilla Cornell, et al. New York: Routledge. Cited as FL.

Elam, Diane. 1994. *Feminism and Deconstruction: Ms en Abyme*. London: Routledge.

Kant, Immanuel. 1965. *Critique of Pure Reason*. Trans. Norman Kemp Smith. New York: St. Martin Press.

Kemp, John. 1968. *The Philosophy of Kant*. Oxford: Oxford University Press.

Lacan, Jacques. 1982. *Feminine Sexuality: Jacques Lacan and the Ecole Freudienne*. Ed. Juliet Mitchell and Jacqueline Rose. Trans. Jacqueline Rose. New York: Norton.

———. 1992. *The Ethics of Psychoanalysis* 1959–1960. Trans. Dennis Porter.

Emmanuel Levinas. 1981. *Otherwise than Being or Beyond Essence*. Trans. Alphonso Lingis. The Hague: Martinus Nijhoff.

Poovey, Mary. 1988. "Feminism and Deconstruction" *Feminist Studies*, 14: 51–65.

Ziarek, Plonowska Ewa. 1995. *The Rhetoric of Failure: Deconstruction of Skepticism, Reinvention of Modernism*. Albany: SUNY Press (forthcoming).

Žižek, Slavoj. 1989. *The Sublime Object of Ideology*. London: Verso.

Dreaming of the Innumerable 7

Derrida, Drucilla Cornell, and the Dance Of Gender

John D. Caputo

Of course, it is not impossible that desire for a sexuality without number can still protect us, like a dream, from an implacable destiny which immures everything for life in the figure 2. And should this merciless closure arrest desire at the wall of opposition, we would struggle in vain: there will never be but two sexes, neither one more nor one less. Tragedy would leave this strange sense, a contingent one finally, that we must affirm and learn to love, instead of dreaming of the innumerable. (Derrida, "Choreographies" 194)

Derrida sometimes disconcerts feminists because he lets "woman" and even "feminism" disseminate or deconstruct, letting them slip into undecidability, letting it seem that he, or at least deconstruction, can do no good for feminism. But, for Derrida, dissemination and undecidability are the conditions, the "quasi-transcendental"[1] conditions, of justice—for women, for men (for animals, for everybody)—conditions of the dream of justice, which is also, when it comes to sexual difference, a dream of the innumerable.

Derrida's relationship to feminism has usually been examined in terms of his earlier, somewhat more Nietzschean writings, in particular *Spurs*. I am interested here in balancing this Nietzschean strain in Derrida with his later, more Levinasian preoccupations with "justice." Hence, after an initial look at the undecidability of "woman," I will take up the work of Drucilla Cornell, who puts deconstruction to work in the service of a feminist legal theory. Cornell employs a strikingly Levinasian and utopian reading of Derrida with which I am deeply sympathetic, and which I regard as crucially important for correcting an overly Nietzschean reading of Derrida, for understanding the ethico-political implications of deconstruction, and for understanding in particular what Cornell calls the "alliance" of feminism and deconstruction. From there I will turn to the "dance" of gender discussed by Derrida in "Choreographies," by which Derrida means the dissemination of the "opposing" genders. This I will interpret as not only a Nietzschean dance of differences (which seems to Derrida's critics to play lightly with the suffering of women), but also a dance of justice, as a utopic, or atopic, dream of a justice to come, and most certainly a justice for women to come. I will argue that in "Choreographies" the dream of the innumerable is a dream of justice, which is, I hold, the final upshot of a Derridean approach to gender—and the good deconstruction can do for feminism.

Undecidability

Woman. The name "woman." In the name of woman. In the names of women, all women, everywhere.

(Of wo/man. Of wo/men everywhere. S/he.)

Is "woman" a proper name? Does it have its own proper truth and identity, an identifiable property and a specific difference? If not, would that not constitute a loss of identity, a fracturing and breakdown of the sense of what or who a woman is, so that women would be disoriented, robbed of a sense of who they are and what they want, disappropriated:[2]

> But was that not what patriarchy always rested on, women's non-identity? Deconstruction, in this reading, is just a disguise of the worst aspects of patriarchy. Who wants to fight for the non-identity we have had imposed upon us? Feminists, on the other hand, assert *our* identity at last. (Cornell 1991, 101–102)

Would that not represent a violence, an injustice against women? But if there is a truth of woman, if woman is a proper, identifiable name, would that not constitute another violence, the violence of classification, categorization, constriction, and even caricature, of typing and stereotyping, the violence of an essentialism that binds, not merely the feet but the very being of women, that prevents movement and becoming and the step of the dance, precluding the possibility of becoming something different, something "sexual[ly] otherwise" (CH 184), otherwise than a feminine essence, otherwise than the essence of the feminine?

Who is authorized to speak or write, properly, of this name, in this name? Can a man write about women? Would that not make woman his "subject"?[3] Can a man write like a woman?[4] Would that not be more masculine mastery, one more masculine usurpation or co-optation of what is properly feminine, one more move men make against women? Were a man to adopt a feminine pseudonym and were he to write in a feminine voice, and even to do so quite well, would that amount, not to the invention of a new voice, but rather to stealing women's voice, and so once again to more injustice? But if a man could not write of or in the name of women, or like a woman, or if there were no room for men in feminism, or among women, or for a womanly side of man, if all that would be reducible to more injustice, then has not woman become something powerfully proprietary and appropriative, a way of silencing new voices, with all the exclusionary, excommunicative violence that appropriation implies?

These questions are not puzzles waiting to be solved or resolved, definitively, one way or the other, by some skillful and clever theoretician, but more or less permanent aporias that block our way, that divert and detour us, that cost us time, even as they give us the time of sexual difference. These aporias are not temporary roadblocks to be cleared away but undecidables that hover over and constitute the space within which the question of woman takes place, the space of "woman"—and of men, of wo/men, of the relationships of men and women. These aporias describe the aporetics or conflictual axiomatics of sexual difference, the more or less permanent tensions within which feminist theory and practice take place. It is not so much a question of settling these questions and then setting them aside, of deciding these undecidables, as it is of living with the permanent menace that they pose, of learning to operate within their lines of force. It is a question of acquiring a heightened sensitivity to the complexity and undecidability that haunt and disturb our reflections and our choices, of maintaining a vigilance about the peculiar dangers that threaten us.

For there are many women, too many to count or contain, in many places, advantaged and disadvantaged, educated and uneducated, Western and third world, women of wealth and impoverished women of color, nameless women and women with old, honorable names, different women with many different needs, in many different situations, in many different places. The question of woman, of sexual difference, is many questions about many women, about many differences.

Nothing in itself, standing by itself, is sexist or non-sexist or anti-sexist, for or against women. Everything said of the name of woman, or in the name of woman, or like a woman, belongs to a context, has a local purpose, serves a certain strategy, and can be turned around, turned against itself, can be made to work for or against women.[5] Identifying what is proper to women, separating women, defending a feminine difference, locating something distinctively feminine, something maternal or sisterly, establishing an identity and a place for women, can be made to work for or against women, depending on how it is used. "Making a place" for women can easily be turned into identifying "a woman's place." For the signifier "woman," like every signifier, functions contextually, in a fluctuating, shifting environment, bent by the winds of undecidability.

For Derrida, "woman" even functions as the very name of or for this undecidability, not indeed as a master name but as a name that undoes all mastery, as a certain quasi-transcendental name—like "hymen" or "invagination"—for the inside/outside, as a way to expose the shifting grounds upon which the powerful, masterful, dogmatic columns of phallogocentrism and *Identitätsphilosophie* are "erected." "Woman" is a name for "undecidability," but not, as Spivak concludes, for "absence." "Woman" is the name not of a lack but of a "more" (*mère/mehr*), always already more than any categorization can identify or more than any gender-role assigned her. So Derrida's anti-essentialism is a function not of skepticism or despair but of a respect for irrepressibility and excess.[6]

What Derrida has written of and about, in the name of and on behalf of woman, is organized by the thought—if it is a thought—of undecidability. Does it still need to be said, now, after so many years of reading Derrida, that undecidability does not mean indecision or inaction, that undecidability is the condition that not only surrounds and besets decision, but also calls for decision, the condition that antedates, provokes, permeates, and follows upon decision?

The View from Cornell: Difference, The Future, and Justice

> Perhaps it is my own autopoiesis as a woman that demands that I begin with difference, the future, and Justice, because the "present" of this social system and legal system is profoundly threatening to women. (Cornell 1992, 144)[7]

Drucilla Cornell lays to rest in the most decisive way this misunderstanding about undecidability, the popular nonsense, repeated unfortunately by well-known philosophers, that deconstruction is some sort of enervating skepticism or even pernicious nihilism. For her, Derrida is the author of a utopian ethics, an ethics of the "beyond," of unimagined possibilities, of "difference, the future, and Justice," and hence of the radical transformation of the present. Her "Derrida"—and his "undecidability"—do not witness to "paralysis" or leave us "helpless":

> Instead, Derrida makes us think differently about the beyond. Iteration "is" as possibility because a system of representation given to us in language cannot

be identical to itself and therefore truly a totality. This possibility is an "opening" to the beyond as a threshold we are invited to cross. As a "science" of the "threshold," deconstruction dares us to commit to "cross over" and perhaps, by doing so, to avoid the horror of having the door of the Law of Law finally shut in our faces. (Cornell 1992, 110)

Because the word "deconstruction" has become too liable to this sort of misunderstanding, Cornell redescribes deconstruction as "a philosophy of the limit." By this she means a philosophy of de-limitation, of delimiting wholes which tend to close over, of showing relentlessly that systems—in particular, legal codes—do not reach closure without violence. This is also what Derrida means by "parergonality," locating the marginal, borderline phenomena that expose the main body of the work (*ergon*)—for her, the body of law—to its other, to what it misses, erases, silences, excludes—for her, the parergonal bodies of women and homosexuals.

The unique effect of Cornell's formulations is to cast deconstruction as a philosophy of the "beyond," of the possible, of the threshold, of what is otherwise than the present—as an (important) dream. In this view of deconstruction, as Derrida himself says in a piece written by him for the conference organized by Cornell at Cardozo Law School on "deconstruction and the possibility of justice," nothing could be less old-fashioned than the classical project of emancipation (FL 28). That is also why Derrida is happy to describe deconstruction elsewhere as a "new enlightenment." Not the old Enlightenment, with its sclerotic eyes frozen open in unrelenting *Aufklärung*—that would be a quite monstrous beast, the monster[8] of a panoptical law—but an Enlightenment of the *Augenblick*, of a blink of the eye, a certain postmodern Enlightenment or enlightened postmodernity (PR 19–20). Cornell's work instantiates this Enlightenment of the *Augenblick*, in a theory of legal interpretation, an Enlightenment that is intent upon keeping the social and legal order open and loose, which looks—*blickt*—always for an opening, a little crack or crevice in the system, through which the fragile shoots of freedom, novelty, and difference can make their way. "Deconstruction" is not skepticism and nihilism, but an openness to the beyond, a threshold of the possible, of the *mère/mehr*, of "the radical difference of the not yet" (Cornell 1992, 110), a delimitation of the tendency of the present to close over and close off the future.

Deconstruction: *viens!* Deconstruction: *oui, oui!*

Cornell's work, which is a badly needed counterpoint to the rash distortions and angry denunciations of deconstruction by which we are still being visited, is marked throughout by an acute appreciation of the proximity of Derrida to Levinas. She makes it clear that Derrida's notion of difference and alterity is driven by a Levinasian sense of the claim of the Other, of the disruption of the same by the transcendence of the Other, and hence by a fundamentally ethical impulse, by a desire for or dream of justice. Thus, for her, the energy of deconstruction is nothing less than the energy of the Good. Distinguishing the Good, or the Law of the Law, from the law as an empirical legal system, she rightly argues that the former prevents the closure of the latter. Every existing legal order is breached from within by the exigencies of Good, by the impossible demands laid upon it by the Good. In "Force of Law," Derrida claims that the law is always deconstructible just because Justice itself—the Good or the Law of the Law—"if there is such a thing," is not deconstructible (FL 14–15).[9] The deconstruction of the law is not bad news. Deconstruction is good news, the good news of alterity, in virtue of which existing legal orders are exposed to continual correction, revision, and alteration in the light of the claim laid upon them by alterity, that is, by what is beyond that code, by what is silenced or excluded by that code. Deconstruction demands the alteration of the law in virtue of the undeconstructibility of alterity. Deconstruction does not leave us with a lack but an opening. Cornell writes:

> The dissemination of convention as a self-enclosed legal system does not leave us with a fundamental lack, but with an opening. What I am suggesting is that the dissemination of convention, through *différance* as the nonfull, nonsimple, and differentiating origin of differences, disrupts the claims of ontology to fill the universe, and more specifically the legal universe. (Cornell 1992, 110)

To be precise, we should say that Cornell's philosophy of the limit is organized around Derrida's intervention upon Levinas in "Violence and Metaphysics" (Cornell 1992, 83–85). There Derrida insists that the Other is not wholly other, not absolutely and utterly other, for in that case the Other would not be an other human being, an other self or subject or person. As such the Other would lack the only real transcendence that Levinas allows and, robbed of her transcendence, would be vulnerable to the worst violence. So, unless the Other is also just so far the same, the Other is not Other. Cornell calls this the principle of symmetry, and it plays a central ethical, political, and legal role throughout *The Philosophy of the Limit* where it is called upon to establish the symmetry of women and of homosexuals—they are always treated together in *The Philosophy of the Limit*—before the laws of heterosexual men, the Monster which dresses itself up as Justice and "The Law."

Innumerable Goods, or Too Good to be True

Deconstruction: a philosophy of the Good. I love the impudence of that for-mulation, the scandalized look on the faces of the officials of anti-decon-struction, the shocked expressions of the self-appointed defenders of the Good and the True when they wake up in bed with the Great Deconstruc-tor. Still, as much as I love the Good and savor this impudence, this is one point on which I would want to reformulate Cornell's use of Derrida, and this in the name of justice and in the name of Cornell's own argument, in the name of the view from Cornell. The Good may be too Good to be true, too True to be of any good to deconstruction and to deconstruction's dream of justice. This may be one award *honoris causa* that "the philosophy of the limit"—and hence, by extension, deconstruction which is at least its ances-tor, predecessor, or *provocateur*—is forced to decline.

I understand the delicious justice of slipping this highly Levinasian expression into the pocket of the philosophy of limit. The Good is some-thing Cornell wants in order to convince the officials of anti-deconstruction that deconstruction is not bad news for the law, that deconstruction is jus-tice in itself, if there is such a thing, that deconstruction does not abandon lawyers and judges to the wolves of nihilism or paralysis. She introduces the notion in connection with two stories about postmodernism. The first, the received story, is that postmodernism has given up on the Good; there is not, there never has been, a Good because there is not, there never has been, an Origin or Presence of which the Good is but another name. Conse-quently, there is no "horizon of the Good, projected out of the principles embodied" in concrete legal systems, "to which one can appeal for guidance in evaluating competing legal interpretations." The result of this first story is legal nihilism, or legal positivism, which is helpless in distinguishing bet-ter and worse legal codes; the result is injustice.

The other story is the one Cornell is telling, a Levinasian-Derridean story of justice, that "the Good remains as the disruption of ontology that con-tinually reopens the way beyond what 'is.'" Existing legal systems operate under the influence of a definite, albeit implicit, conception of a good life. But there is always a distance—a gap forming the very site of deconstruc-tion—between these concretely embodied goods and "the call of the Good." For the Good divests any existing system of its claim to finality, to being the final good, good once and for all; the Good pulls any legal code, however good it may be, beyond itself to a future that is undreamt of, or better, a future of which we all dream, which is what makes radical transformation possible (Cornell 1992, 93–94).

As I love the Good and the use to which Drucilla Cornell puts it here, I also love this distinction between the two postmodernisms.[10] Still, I do not think one needs "the Good" to work this distinction out and hence to serve and save justice. Nothing is gained by pointing out that, as a textual matter, Derrida does not speak of the Good, at least not in his own name, since Cornell is making an interpretive, not a textual, claim, and she is redescribing deconstruction for the purposes of feminist legal theory. But I do not think that it is an accident that Derrida avoids this locution. That is because, contrary to Cornell, I take this expression to be trapped by its premodern provenance and unable to find a home in postmodernism. Postmodernists have good reasons against the Good. The notion of the Good is too strong for Derrida. It is too Platonic, on the one hand, i.e., too idealistic, too suggestive of a regulative ideal, of "projecting" a "horizon"—a locution that, following Derrida, Cornell elsewhere rejects but uses here—of a beyond that exceeds the present as the ideal exceeds the real, as the perfect exceeds the imperfect; and too Aristotelian, on the other hand, too suggestive of a communitarian unity, of a consensus about a shared paradigm, an agreement about the "good life" which "all men" desire with masculine desire. And if Derrida had any more hands, I would say it is also too neoplatonic—and finally, ultimately, too Levinasian.

Cornell is very sensitive to the notion that the Good is not a "horizon" or a "regulative ideal," and she offers numerous, sensitive, and convincing accounts of why that is so. Justice in itself, if there is such a thing, is not a pure ideal that we can never reach but only hope to approximate, an "ought" with which "is" will never catch up. Rather, she points out, for Derrida justice is an aporia, a perplexing and complex undecidability that brings us up short and forces to choose, in this concrete and complex, knotted, and undecidable situation (FL 22–29). Justice compels us to decide what to do, to invent the law for the situation, which is always different. Justice is not an Ideal or a paragon but a parergon, and the law without parergonal justice is a monster. That is good Derrideanism, as good as it gets, but Cornell's recurrent talk of the Good creates a tension with this good Derrideanism. For I think that all of her arguments against the "ideal horizon" of Justice tell equally against projecting the horizon of "the Good" and that the needs of Derridean justice are better served by giving up on the Good (and by not capitalizing "justice").[11]

Historically it is worth noting that, for its contemporary advocates, the "Good" is the antidote to the modern malaise of "value theory," to the subjectivism of valuing that is decried by anti-modernists as different as Heidegger, MacIntyre, and Allan Bloom. The Good, says its defenders, is not the flimsy effect of the will willing but something substantive "out there" that brings me up short. Not "my values" but *the* Good, capitalized, like a good German noun. The term has made its way into Cornell's work by way of Levinas for whom the Good means the Other *(autrui)*, the Infinite One *(l'infini),* the Other over and beyond all being-other, beyond all being *(epekeina tes ousias),* and, more deeply still, the "other than Other *(autre qu'autrui),* God Himself [sic], who is the other infinite one. In Levinas, the other is a positive infinity, like the Cartesian God, or like a neoplatonic excess that wells up from an infinite source and flows towards me. Within this classical discourse a "philosophy of the limit" would be atheism, the denial of the infinite, of positive infinity. In Levinas, too, the Good is a way to displace modern subjectivism and value theory—it is the truth of modern anti-humanism, Levinas says—by a radical substitution by which the subject is handed over to the Other before all consciousness and freedom.

Now while Derrida agrees that the Other comes to me with the shock of transcendence, that the alterity of the *tout autre* is no subjectivistic value posited by the ego, still he does not speak of "the Good," if only because, in his radically postclassical view, the Good has been disseminated. There are "innumerable" goods, too many to count, too many ways to be and not-be, to be otherwise and to be different. I would say that, at most, at best, the Good, "if there is any" *(s'il y en a),* for Derrida is a radically negative and deeply pluralistic notion that bears almost no resemblance to its classical ancestors. On the point of the Good, Derrida is more like the Enlightenment, albeit a new Enlightenment, an *augenblickliche* neo-*Aufklärung,* which also rejects a substantive or strong conception of the Good. This does not mean that Derrida has recourse instead to "the Right." Derrida does not want either to love the Good or to be in the Right. He does not defend a pure autonomous Subject whose Rights flow like water from its pure rational Subjectivity. A little, perhaps a lot like the Enlightenment, Derrida rejects the Good and sides with a justice that differs over the Good. He cannot avoid thinking that the Good, like every *arche,* suffers dissemination, that it has been irretrievably pluralized, localized, and multiplied. On this point, Derrida is a little more modern than classical, and if this is postmodernity, then this postmodernity is a continuation of modernity by another means. By reason of its distinctive notion of alterity, deconstruction emphasizes not my rights but the right of the Other One to be different, the right to be left alone, as Justice Blackmun says (Cornell 1992, 162; 208, n.39), even as it is moved by the plight of the one who is left out, ground under, excluded, erased, or silenced, and hence by that Other's right to be heard, to be addressed, to be given standing "before the law." And to that claim of the Other, corresponds the responsibility of deconstruction.

If you pressed Derrida about what the Good is, he would be a little non-plussed, at least as much as Socrates, but instead of telling us the allegory of the Sun, he could give us an allegory of the simulacrum, of the lowest of the low on the line. Like Socrates he would tell us what the Good is not, not because the Good is so surpassingly beyond Being, *epekeina tes ousias,* but because the Good is so entirely negative, more like the *chora* than the *agathon.* The Good, if there is any, is *in principle,* if it has a principle, something negative. Deconstruction does indeed disturb all existing legal systems by posing an alternative to the present order—that is the central point of *The Philosophy of the Limit.* This it does not in virtue of "the Good" but in virtue of a parergonal analysis of what the present order is leaving out, excluding, erasing, or silencing. The Good, if there is any, is at best something parergonal, nothing else, nothing more.

Furthermore, if we pressed Drucilla Cornell about what the Good is, her answer too would always be something negative; that is, she is much more likely to tell us what is evil than what is Good. She does not, in truth, defend the Good, but keeps on telling us to avoid the evil of enforcing the Good on the bodies of women and homosexuals. For her, too, justice demands that we give up on the Good. For it is the defenders of heterosexuality who claim to know the Good, to know that heterosexuality is *the Good,* a good gift given to us by God or nature which obliges us to be good (heterosexuals) in return, in accord with the binding logic of the gift (GT ch.1). Cornell is clearly making a weaker, "alternistic"[12] claim, not that homosexuality is the Good, for that would be very homogenizing, but that homosexuality is a difference that should be protected, one of many alternative goods, in the plural, among a vast and unheard of panorama of "innumerable" goods. Homosexuality belongs among the parergonal, polymorphic possibilities that the Other (than the heterosexual), the "sexual otherwise," has the right to embrace. Homosexuality is at best *a* good, and this because it is not evil, and it is in the end nobody else's business if someone considers it good, and certainly not the business of the state of Georgia. It is precisely because there is no such thing as "the Good" that the state of Georgia should stay out of the bedroom of "[t]wo men peacefully making love"—or even two men noisily and stormily making love, for that matter—which is one among many innumerable goods (Cornell 1992, 159).

By the same token, it is the opponents of abortion who hold that the preservation of life under all circumstances is *the Good,* that life is a good given us by God and that it flies in the face of God or nature to take life away, even embryonic or fetal life. But Cornell's argument is that the law must be loosened and deconstructed, that it must relearn who women are, that it must lift women out of the prelegal silence and invisibility to which women have been historically consigned by the law, that it must treat women as fully constituted, symmetrical legal agents. And after that the law must let women make their own considered choice—for better or worse, but not for the Good. Justice—not the Good—demands that women be let alone to decide, symmetrically with the law, what they think is good, to decide for themselves whether it would be good for them to have an abortion or not to have one (Cornell 1992, 162).

So even Cornell's theory of the Good is entirely negative: avoid evil, avoid violence, where evil arises precisely when someone—the Same—tries to inscribe his [sic] conception of the Good on the bodies of the Other—above all, for Cornell at least, on the bodies of homosexuals and of women. As Robert Cover says, the law is "a field of pain and death," i.e., of evil, and it is the minimization or reduction of evil that concerns us, while leaving people the space to decide what they think is good. That indeed is why Cornell begins with evil, not the Good, i.e., with a remarkable account of the ethics of sympathy in Schopenhauer and Adorno, of an ethical materialism which is organized around carnal violence to the bodies of the Other.[13]

One way to see the significance of my stand against the Good is to see that Levinas would have no sympathy at all for Cornell's quite Derridean stand for homosexual rights, given that for him the instantiation of the Same and the Other *par excellence* is the Macho Man and the Modest Maid. Levinas would have still less sympathy for Cornell's Derridean stand on abortion rights—indeed he might be quite angry with her—given that for Levinas the offspring of the Good is offspring, the child, indeed the Man-Child born of this loving couple (Levinas 1969, 254–80). When Cornell writes "Of course, the fetus can itself be recognized as Other, with infinite right" (Cornell 1992, 152), she reproduces the position that Levinas would take on this issue which, as she says in the next sentence, would allow "the rights of women"—their symmetry with the fetus and with the law—"to go unnoticed."

My concern is this: homosexual and abortion rights are not protected by "the Good," but only by disseminating the Good in the name of nameless and innumerable goods, of polymorphic, polysexual possibilities that the "monster of the law" wants to close off. Only such a Derridean pluralism of goods will provide the approach to law upon which Cornell insists and that render these rights intelligible. In deconstruction, it is necessary to disseminate the Good in order to make room for justice. Insisting on "the Good" is at least confusing and possibly dangerous to these rights—although I do love the consternation it causes to the officials of anti-deconstruction.

What I find in Cornell is, in fact, a good account of why there are too many goods, too many to enumerate, classify (*glas*), or legislate, and of why there is no Good. If Derrida were of a more apocalyptic frame of mind, he would claim that the age of the Good is over, that it is necessary to deny the Good in the name of the dissemination of many goods, to negate or disseminate the Good so that the Good no longer has any identity. For at that point at which "the Good" congeals into something identifiable, at which it acquires a positive identity, it becomes, like the law, a monster, a terror which terrorizes difference. The Good is the Monster's claw, the teeth with which it chews the morsels of difference. Derrida would say of the "pure Good" what he says of the "pure Gift": the pure good, if there is one, is something utterly disseminated, devoid of all identity, so that at just the moment it is recognized or identified as the Good it goes bad, and the gift turns to poison. As soon as someone says "here is the Good," it has gone bad and turned into a monster.

Cornell is at her Derridean best when she talks about monsters, not about the Good, when she stops talking about the Good and instead calls Derrida a ragpicker (*chiffonier*). Ragpicking does not sound very good. On this account, deconstruction keeps its neo-Enlightenment eyes peeled for the fragments, the leftovers, the leftouts, the remains, the morsels, the outsiders. Deconstruction is the scavenger of the Other. The disreputability of this image, its slightly shocking incongruity, is what makes it good for Derrida and good for deconstruction. The Good is much too respectable, too powerful, too prestigious, too Ideal, too good for deconstruction. Deconstruction is bad, not good; it is disruptive, troublemaking, Socratically disturbing, possessed of a negative *daimon* not a positive *eu-daimonia*. Deconstructive vigilance, as Drucilla Cornell shows again and again, keeps a look-out for a little break, a crack, or a crevice through which something different can break out, for a little spark that might be given off by the system, a spark that will perhaps, if we are lucky, ignite a bigger blaze.

Justice, if such a thing exists, has to do with these little bits and fragments that have escaped the Look of the Monster, with the least among us, the outsiders and the excluded. If justice is "beyond" the law, that is not because justice is too big for the law but too little, because it has to do with the little fragments and remains, the *me onta* who are before the law, beneath the law, too trivial or worthless or insignificant for the law to notice, with rags and litter, the nobodies, the outsiders.

With the "shit." Deconstruction deals with shit. I hasten to say that this is a scholarly reference, an erudite mention, not a rude use. I am citing Derrida citing a text from Genet, not trying to be vulgar (G 1a). Deconstruction deals with the ones that the law treats like shit. And it is Cornell's constant contention, if I may say so, that the law is a monster that treats women and homosexuals like shit. That is much better than the rhetoric of the Good, which is far too edifying, too sanitary, a little misleading and idealizing, neoplatonizing, and even vaguely patriarchal—since the Good is the Father of us all. Even if young Socrates could persuade old father Parmenides that there is an *eidos* for dirt and maybe even one for shit, he would never dare to argue before the old man that the Good is shit. And for good reason. The Good suggests an ideal that we cannot instantiate, realize, or actualize—a "horizon" of infinity that nothing finite can replicate. But the "justice" Drucilla Cornell has in the mind, if there is any, is the singularity that is too small, too finite, to be lifted up into the grandeur and universality of the law, too powerless and impotent when it is brought "before the law."

Dreaming of the Innumerable

One of the numerous strengths of Cornell's feminist alliance with Derrida is that it shows in such a convincing way the utterly affirmative character of deconstruction. So when I take issue with the Good I do not want to be understood as saying say that deconstruction is something negative. On the contrary, while I deny the Good is anything positive, I hold that this denial is very affirmative, indeed that it is doubly affirmative, *oui, oui* (NY 120–133). I have found it necessary to deny the Good in order to make room for affirmation. For deconstruction is the affirmation of innumerability, of innumerable goods, of alternity and all the alternatives, all the polymorphic, pluralistic possibilities (so long as they are good, i.e., not evil) that are left out by the monster of the law. But deconstruction is affirmative without being positive, without identifying positively and definitively what it wants, without wanting the Good. Deconstruction is the affirmation of justice; indeed Derrida says it *is* justice. Derrida does not think that only a God or *the* Good can save us; on the contrary, he thinks that our only hope is that they never show up. As Cornell shows so convincingly, deconstruction settles into the intricacies of the situation—legal, political, social, artistic, academic, etc.—in which it always already finds itself, and looks around, parergonally, alternistically, for the possibility of something different. It does not know what it wants, even and especially when it wants something else, when it affirms something different. Deconstruction cultivates the possible as the possible, as *the* impossible.

It goes to the heart of Derrida's position to delimit "identification," to resist reducing things to something "rigorously or properly identifiable," to resist placing or locating someone or something in its proper place. That is why Derrida says that it is not so much a question of finding a new concept of woman as of questioning the very concept of "concept," of the whole order or operation of fixing and locating, defining and confining, which can only serve to repress and suppress the *mère/mehr* (CH 175).

In *Beyond Accommodation*, commenting on this text, Cornell rejoins that, if it is not a question of a new concept of woman, there can at least be a new "metaphorizing" of woman, which corresponds I think to Irigaray's call for a "feminine imaginary."[14] Derrida's "hesitancy" about this, Cornell says, "may be my central disagreement with him" (Cornell 1991, 110, 118).

> If we do not allow for the broad intervention of the power of refiguration through metaphor and, indeed, fantasy and fable, we can potentially participate in the repudiation of the feminine.

As I have argued elsewhere, any demythologizing must be replaced by *new* mythologies, and feminism in particular is better served not merely by "demythologizing patriarchal myths, but [also] by inventing a new, empowering mythology of the maternal and feminine . . ." (Caputo 1993b, 215). That of course runs the risk of reinstating, not displacing, oppositional schemata, but that is a risk worth running, part of the aporetics or risky axiomatics of the question of sexual difference. Who ever said that things could happen without risk or anxiety? Indeed, I would say that Derrida's dream of justice, his dream of the innumerable—along with Levinas' dream of the justice due "*l'infini*" and with Lyotard's dream of a "sublime" justice—are all just such new, more salutary, empowering myths, postmodern myths, if that is not too paradoxical, myths of justice that inspire *another* postmodernism.

Derrida's strategy is radically utopic, as Cornell insists, or perhaps better atopic, inasmuch as this utopia is thoroughly negative, completely free of any positive—and hence of any positional, positionalizing, thetic—Ideal. His strategy is always to insist on the possibility of being otherwise, on a possibility—an impossibility!—to come, on a "beyond," by which he means not a paragon but a parergon, not a transcendent ideal but rather a little chance for something different or new, something unforseeable, unprogrammable, unchoreographable in advance, a new "dance," a new step—*pas*, which is also a new "not."

It is important to see that this step (*pas*) is not only a step in a Nietzschean dance (WM 27),[15] but an (almost) Levinasian call of the other, the call for something different, here, for the "sexual otherwise," of new possibilities for gender and sexual difference. It is a call for the invention of the other, of new possibilities that will open up alternatives within the present gender-traps, the lures that draw us into repeating again and again well-worn sexual roles and sexual stereotypes, that form and conform us to regularized patterns and expectations. It is a call for justice from and for the sexually otherwise, and a call to find ways to be otherwise than the present tolerances permit.

That is why making a place for women in structures or institutions that hitherto had no room for women—the workplace, the academy, the professions, etc.—represents an important but incomplete feminism for Derrida, a reversal, however urgent, of the desire to confine women to the home, that as such remains within a binary scheme. It is a gesture, however necessary, that still belongs (as its other side) to the most classical topo-eco-nomy of man vs. woman which identified the *oikos* as a woman's place. The more radically Derridean gesture, beyond all reversal and replacing, is to dis-place or disseminate or dislocate this topographical desire, this "law of the proper place" (CH 168), to thwart it—with a dance:

> The most innocent of dances would thwart the *assignation à résidence*, escape those residences under surveillance; the dance changes place and above all changes *places*. (CH 169)

None of this is to be construed, Derrida hastens to add—and this point is directed at his critics—as an excuse for skipping the urgent, difficult, laborious work of reversal, for "deserting organized, patient, laborious 'feminist' struggles," the "incessant, daily negotiation" (CH 168).[16] The "*real* conditions in which women's struggles develop on all fronts (economic, ideological, political) ... often require the preservation ... of metaphysical presuppositions that one must ... question in a later phase—or another place ..." (CH 171; Cornell 1991, 96).

It is never a question of having to choose *between* reversal and displacement, both of which are integral, even simultaneous, phases of the movement of deconstruction. The "feminist alliance with deconstruction," I think, is rather a matter of adjusting deconstruction's velocities: insofar as it advocates displacement, deconstruction needs to be slowed down; insofar as it advocates reversal, deconstruction needs to be given a push. So granting Cornell's precaution about these texts, which is also Derrida's own precaution, that there is a danger of moving too quickly here, of jumping too quickly into this new choreography, we should not lose sight of the "ultimate" "theoretical"—if this is a theory and if it is ultimate—tendencies of deconstruction, which means we should not lose sight of its dream. Deconstruction is deeply anti-essentialist, deeply resistant to the "essentializing fetishes" of "woman" or "feminine sexuality." Deconstruction refuses to let sexuality or gender, or anything else—masculine or feminine, or both, or neither, or both and neither—contract into an identity and settle into a proper place. Deconstruction loves the *mère/mehr*.

This displacement of sexual difference is not intended to make its way back to a neutral terrain, prior to sexuality, to a neutered, generalized, presexual, or asexual human essence, devoid of sexual markings, the upshot of which, ironically, is always to assure a masculine victory. This victorious masculinity is visible in both Heidegger and Levinas, in the crypto-masculinity of a supposedly neuter "Dasein" or "spirit" (CH 178–79). The displacement of sexual difference in deconstruction is rather a displacement of the *binarity*, of the two sexes, of the figure 2, of the oppositional polarity, of the male/female opposition, which is the very form of the "war between the sexes," regardless of the victor's identity, regardless of whether the spoils go to phallocentrism or gynocentrism. The dream of justice for and among the genders is not a dream of a neutral presexuality but of a sexuality that goes all the way down, a sexuality that, to use Heidegger's vocabulary, is ontological and not merely ontic. That is why Derrida can have recourse to terms like "hymen" and "invagination," not in their "widely recognized sense" (CH 181), which means their strictly localized, anatomical sense, which would make them reductionistic and masculine images of women, but in a quasi-transcendental sense. As quasi-transcendentals, hymen and invagination are intended to sexualize or resexualize the hitherto strictly "neutral" territory of the transcendental, while not collapsing into a binary scheme. But Derrida "dreams" of a sexuality free from the start of the classical oppositions, which is how he reads Heidegger's originary *Geschlectlosigkeit*, a sexuality, let us say, not of sexual "difference," but of the strewing of sexual "differences," not a binary but a polymorphic sexuality, a disseminated "polysexuality" (CH 183).

Derrida "dreams"—this is the "desire" of deconstruction—or "thinks"— that is its utopic or atopic thought or aspiration—of justice as something impossible, something "innumerable." In terms of the question of sexual difference, this is a dream of a "sexuality without number," not marked by opposite sexes or identifiable opposites, not stamped with two opposing "classifications," man and woman, submissive to the classificatory law of genre and gender. That dream is meant to protect us from a tragic fate that would assign us like an "implacable destiny" to the straits of one gender: to each "man" or "woman" one gender only, and there are only two to choose from. But instead of loving this fate *(amor fati)*, Derrida speaks of "dreaming of the innumerable," a dream which, by a certain theory of intentionality, is self-validating, for where there is a dream "something dreamt of must be there in order for it to provide the dream" (CH 184–85). He dreams of a "dance," of a "choreography," to replace and displace the reigning "topography," a choreography that is not merely a matter of "exchanging" places, but a choreography that improvises, that creates new steps, new moves, new dances, new styles, that invents new and unheard of combinations and mutations. He dreams of "incalculable choreographies" meant to enact innumerable possibilities, unheard of, more than are dreamt of in our philosophies, impossible and innumerable genders, born of a quasi-transcendental desire and quasi-transcendental dream of an innumerable *mère/mehr.*

That is why Derrida's "thought" and "desire" culminate in what is "to come," in a future, *à-venir*, in a "come," a *viens*, and an incoming (*invention*) of the other, of the *tout autre*. That is why he speaks of a democracy to come, or a Europe to come, of a woman or a man to come—without being able to say who or what is coming. Joining hands with Cornell, as many hands as possible, not merely two, I would say—Derrida would say, Drucilla Cornell would say—it is neither a man nor a woman who is coming, but something new, some odd kind of a new being, a new step, an effect yet to be produced, some new sort of s/he or wo/man, something innumerable and unclassifiable, something unforeseeable and unclassifiable, something unprogrammable, *the* impossible. Maybe what is coming is nothing as simple and unambiguous as an hermaphrodite or an androgyne, but something undecidably miscegenated, something that has not happened yet, something singular, something possible, something impossible, something unimaginable and innumerable.[17]

The deep strand in Derrida's work, as Cornell's work shows, the thought that does not contradict but reorients his Nietzschean side, is the "thought" of the "beyond," of justice as the "impossible" something that will create an alternative and free us all from the straits of identity. Derrida's feminism, then, takes the form of the delimitation of gender, a philosophy of the limits of the two genders and of the law of gender, of the limits "on the proliferation of sexual voices, each with its own unique notes" (Cornell 1991, 98). That, in my view, is where gender theory is led by Derrida and that is the good Derrida can do for feminism.

The two genders, masculine and feminine, not one more, not one less, to which each of us, one by one, is implacably destined: Are they not walls by which we are all confined, men and women, by which we are all "imprisoned" (Cornell 1991, 84–85), "trapped,"[18] and straitened? Do they not dominate and manipulate us all, narrow us and confine us, making us all less than we can be, blocking off the "beyond" and an absolute future to come?

What is coming? Who knows? Who can count? Maybe what is coming will be good (almost). Maybe we are about to visited by the most marvelous and innumerable goods, by the most amazing transformations of gender, in the blink of an eye, by a dance of innumerable steps.

Viens! Oui, oui!

Notes

1. A "quasi-transcendental" is a condition for the possibility—and impossibility—of a thing. As opposed to a straightforward transcendental condition, which sets forth the borders within which a thing may appear, a quasi-transcendental is the condition of a field without closure, for effects that overrun their borders.

2. "It is important to note," Cornell writes, "first just how fundamentally misunderstood Derrida has been by his feminists critics. Derrida has been accused of advocating women's non-identity within patriarchal society." Since Derrida's position is so anti-essentialist, since he denies that there is an identifiable truth of woman (or men, of course)—most notably in notoriously difficult *Spurs: Nietzsche's Styles*—he tends to provoke criticism along these lines; see Rosi Braidotti, *Patterns of Dissonance* (New York: Routledge, 1991). For an interesting and appreciative account of Derrida and feminism, see Peggy Kamuf's "Introduction: Reading Between the Blinds," in *A Derrida Reader: Between the Blinds*, ed. Peggy Kamuf (New York: Columbia University Press, 1991).

3. "However—it is woman who will be my subject" (S 37). But then again, some pages later (121), by virtue of his relentless anti-essentialism, that there is no single truth of *the* woman, Derrida says: "so woman then will not have been my subject." For a commentary, see Gayatri Chakravorty Spivak, "Displacement and the Discourse of Woman," in *Displacement : Derrida and After*, ed. Mark Krupnick (Bloomington: Indiana University Press, 1983), 171.

4. Derrida speaks of writing like a woman in the discussion following "La Question du style," in *Nietzsche Aujourd'hui*, 2 vols. (Paris: Union Generale d'Editions, 1973), I, 299.

5. That is one of the principal points of *Spurs*; see 101–103.

6. On Spivak's interpretation of Derrida's *Spurs*, "woman" is the name, not for being and identity (the transcendental signified), but for dissimulation, style, and artistry, for the play of *différance*, and this because "a man cannot fake an orgasm." See "Displacement," 170 et passim. But that is all the more reason to deny that "hymen" is the name of an absence. See Cornell's critique of Spivak in Cornell 1993, 85. On Cornell's use of *mère/mehr*, see Cornell 1993, 2, 84, 94.

7. Having originated in a 1994 American Philosophical Association, Central Division, panel on *The Philosophy of the Limit*, my attention in the present study is largely given to this work. But I have found Cornell's "The Feminist Alliance with Deconstruction," in Cornell 1991, equally valuable. While more concerned with Derrida's intervention on Lacan than Levinas, in *Beyond Accommodation* Cornell makes use of "Choreographies" to very much the same ends as do I. See also *Transformations: Recollective Imagination and Sexual Difference* (New York: Routledge, 1993), passim.

8. Cornell is fond of calling the law a "monster."

9. In a recent piece, which contests Rorty's claim that the other's suffering is something about which we can be ironic, Simon Critchley wonders whether Derrida's remark about justice in itself constitutes a certain foundationalism; see "Deconstruction and Pragmatism—Is Derrida a Private Ironist or a Public Liberal," *European Journal of Philosophy* 2 (1994): 1–21.

10. I have attempted to work out an analogous distinction between two postmodernisms, but in such a way as precisely to avoid having a theory of the Good, in Caputo, 1993a, chaps. 2–3.

11. For a theory of obligation that has given up on the Good and turned to a life of evil, see Caputo 1993a, chaps. 2–3.

12. On George Steiner's term "alternity," as what is "other than the case," see (Cornell 1992, 111).

13. For the Cover quote, see Cornell 1992, 94 and on Schopenhauer and Adorno, chap. 1.

14. See the discussion of *parler femme* in "Questions," and the critique of Derrida in *"Cosi Fan Tutti,"* in Luce Irigaray, *This Sex Which is Not One*, trans. Catherine Porter with Carolyn Burke (Ithaca: Cornell University Press, 1985); cf. Cornell, *Beyond Accommodation*, 101–102.

15. For an attempt to bring together, to fuse and confuse, these Nietzschean and Levinasian figures, see my discussion of the "dionysian rabbi" in Caputo 1993a, chap. 3.

16. It is for neglecting these struggles that Spivak criticizes Derrida in "Feminism and Critical Theory," in *In Other Worlds: Essays in Cultural Politics* (New York: Routledge, 1987).

17. E.g., although Neil Jordan's *The Crying Game* remains shut up within many classical gender stereotypes, it does engage in some interesting "gender-bending" with Fergus (Stephen Rea), who gradually sheds his unambiguous macho heterosexual identity in order to enter into a humane and nicely ambiguous relationship with Dil (Jaye Davidson). For an interesting analysis of the "essentializing" limitations of the film, see Kristin Handler, "Sexing *The Crying Game*: Difference, Identity, Ethics," *Film Quarterly*, 47 (1994): 31–42.

18. As Cixous says, "It is impossible to see what will become of sexual difference—in another time. . . . But we must make no mistake: men and women are caught up in a web of age-old cultural determinations that are almost unanalyzable in their complexity. One can no more speak of 'woman' than of 'man' without being trapped within an ideological theater . . ." Cited in Cornell 1991, 110.

Works Cited

Caputo, John D. 1993a. *Demythologizing Heidegger*. Bloomington: Indiana University Press.

———. 1993b. *Against Ethics: Contributions to a Poetics of Obligation with Constant Reference to Deconstruction*. Bloomington: Indiana University Press.

Cornell, Drucilla. 1991. *Beyond Accommodation: Ethical Feminism, Deconstruction, and the Law.* New York: Routledge.

———. 1992. *The Philosophy of the Limit.* New York: Routledge.

Derrida, Jacques and McDonald, Christie. 1988. "Interview: Choreographies," trans. Avital Ronell. In *The Ear of the Other: Otobiography, Transference, Translation,* trans. Peggy Kamuf. Lincoln and London: University of Nebraska Press. Copyright: "Choreographies," Johns Hopkins University Press, 1982. Cited as CH.

Derrida, Jacques. 1979. *Spurs: Nietzsche's Styles,* trans. Barbara Harlow, Chicago: University of Chicago Press. Cited as S.

———. 1982. "White Mythology" in *Margins of Philosophy* trans. Alan Bass. Cited as WM. Chicago: University of Chicago Press.

———. 1983. "The Principle of Reason: The University in the Eyes of Its Pupils." *Diacritics* 13: 3–20. Cited as PR.

———. 1986. *Glas,* trans. John Leavey and Richard Rand. Lincoln: University of Nebraska. Cited as G.

———. 1988. "A Number of Yes," trans. Brian Holmes. *Que Parle.* 2: 120–133. Cited as NY.

———. 1992a. "Force of Law: The 'Mystical Foundations of Authority.'" In *Deconstruction and the Possibility of Justice.* Ed. D. Cornell, et al. New York: Routledge. Cited as FL.

———. 1992b. *Given Time: I Counterfeit Money,* trans. Peggy Kamuf. Chicago: University of Chicago Press. Cited as GT.

Irigary, Luce. 1985. *This Sex Which is Not One,* trans. Catherine Porter with Carolyn Burke. Ithaca: Cornell University Press.

Levinas, Emmanuel. 1969. *Totality and Infinity,* trans. Alphonso Lingis. Pittsburgh: Duquesne University Press.

Spivak, Gayatri Chakravorty. 1987. *In Other Worlds: Essays in Cultural Politics.* New York: Routledge.

Where Love Begins 8

Sexual Difference and the Limit of the Masculine Symbolic

Drucilla Cornell

I. Introduction

It is commonplace to note that Sigmund Freud "discovered" another reality, the reality of the psychic life. The meaning of its unconscious underpinnings surfaces in the other world of dreams and in the slips of the tongue that indicate a beyond to the day-to-day life given to us by convention. Certainly, Freud always returns us to the problematic of *Jenseits*, the other side, the beyond of the unconscious, which leaves its traces and marks on so-called "real objects," but which can never be simplistically identified with them.[1] An obvious example of this mistake is the conflation of the penis with the phallus. Another is the identification of the unconscious fantasy object, the Phallic Mother, with actual mothers. Indeed, the ferocity of the debates between different schools of psychoanalysis can, at least in part, be attributed to the idea that unless one remains "true" to the unconscious as the beyond to "reality," there is no psychoanalysis at all, only the crude fix-it therapy that invests in the "world" of purportedly real familial objects as if these objects should serve as the basis for analysis. Simply put, psychoanalysis begins with the differentiation of unconscious from conscious objects.

In recent times, there may have been no more fierce and persistent thinker of the analytic significance of the *Jenseits* in Freud than Jacques Lacan. For the Lacan of his later seminars his "return to Freud" involved the attempt to re-think the beyond to the pleasure principle, what Lacan himself called the Real.[2] To my mind if there is a lasting contribution of Lacan it lies precisely in his insistence on the relationship between psychoanalysis and the problematic of the beyond, *Jenseits*, the other side. Furthermore, Lacan, in characteristically provocative fashion, connects this problematic not only with the Real (which for him is the absolute Other to the web of significance given by the symbolic order), but also with the re-thinking of the Kantian analysis of the transcendental conditions of morality and of the moral will. For Lacan, the very project of psychoanalysis should be understood as a preliminary to moral action. Thus, for him ethics is not a side issue for analysts in the practice of their profession. Instead, psychoanalysis must be understood as moral practice as Lacan insists that, for psychoanalysis, ethics is the very heart of the matter.

I want to give this project of re-thinking the relationship between radical alterity, what Lacan refers to as the Real, the limit of the symbolic, and what I call the ethical relationship its due. Yet, of course, the very use of the phrase "ethical relationship" which I borrow from Emmanuel Levinas signals my central disagreement with Lacan and his concern with an explanation of how the moral law is established. In Levinas, my responsibility to the Other demands that I guard her alterity against her appropriation by any system of cognition including a system of morality when it is established as moral law. As we will see, both Lacan and Levinas argue, if for very different reasons, that the ontological elaboration of the Sovereign Good[3] that classical ethics attempted is philosophically unjustifiable, and even *unethical*. This rejection turns Lacan to his "Freudian" re-reading of the inevitability of the imposition of the moral law because of the very impossibility of there being a Law of law in the sense of an actualized sovereign Good. Levinas, on the other hand, rejects any identification of the ethical relationship and the moral law, whether understood as the ten commandments or the Kantian categorical imperative, two examples of the establishment of the moral law that Lacan discusses in his seminar on the ethics of psychoanalysis (S VII, 82). For Levinas, the Good which provides the sanctity for the Other can never be reduced to a set of commandments because the Other calls me only as herself. Since her call is unique to her, how to heed it cannot be known in advance or simply through her identification with me as another moral subject. To reduce her to a set of definable categories would violate her alterity. This is a simple way of explaining why for Levinas the recognition of the Other as truly other to any system of cognition, including one of the moral rules, imposes infinite responsibility.[4] My responsibility is infinite because the Other is unique and therefore I cannot know her in advance of my encounter with her through any in-place system of cognition. It is precisely because the Good is the good of the Other that it cannot be fully actualized. It is, then *as The Other* that the Sovereign Good is always beyond any of our conventional systems of morality.

But it should now be becoming apparent that not only do Levinas and Lacan reach very different conclusions about the ethical significance of the unrealizability of the Sovereign Good, they do so because of different philosophical positionings before radical alterity or what Lacan calls the Real. The purpose of this essay is to return to the problematic of the *Jenseits*, through a challenge to Lacan's understanding of the Real, as the Real in turn establishes the moral law through its very foreclosure by the symbolic order that sloughs it off through the necessary erection of the barrier that guards the world of meaning and sense.

Lacanians frequently attest to the failure of "poststructuralism" to adequately grapple with the Real.[5] It will be my contention that Derrida continuously grapples with the Real, *as radical alterity*. His deconstruction of metaphysics including his engagement with the Heidegger after "the turn" has at its heart the "matter" of the Real.[6] Ironically, Derrida's own deconstruction of Lacan is that Lacan does not fully apprehend the otherness of the Real as "truly" beyond the symbolic.[7] We will return to that deconstruction shortly and its relationship to Levinas's philosophy of alterity. My emphasis will be on the relationship between the radical alterity of the Real and the ethical relationship, as opposed to Lacan's attempt to found the moral law through the other of the Real.

My argument proceeds as follows. First, I will summarize Lacan's understanding of the relationship between the pleasure principle and the beyond of the Real. My focus will be on how Lacan's elaboration of this relationship could only make sense within his conceptualization of the radical foreclosure of the "positive" symbolization of the feminine within sexual difference. As we will see, Lacan conceptualizes the beyond of the Real through the logic of castration: it is the logic of castration and the foreclosure it demands that establishes the law. Simply put, for Lacan the moral law grounds itself through an always, already established foreclosure of Woman. This is my reading of the ethical significance given to the *le point de capiton* by Lacan in his seminar on the ethics of psychoanalysis. Thus, I will argue that the debate over how to adequately address the Real, which is how I would understand the debate between Derrida and Lacan, necessarily has ethical significance, beyond the obvious implications for those of us marked as women within gender hierarchy.

The second move in my argument sets the stage for re-thinking the relationship between the Real and the limit of the symbolic, conceived without the moral implications of foreclosure. I will return, then, to Derrida's deconstruction of the status of the phallus as the transcendental signifier. What is often missed in Derrida's deconstruction is how it proceeds through the deconstruction of the distinction between *Sinn/Beudeutung* upon which Husserl relied to justify the very concept of a transcendental signifier. In psychoanalytic terms, the result of this deconstruction is that the phallus is redefined as a partial object and thus returned to the chain of signification and of metonymic deferral. Simply put, if the phallus cannot be maintained in the position of the transcendental signifier, its meaning can always be reinterpreted. It is only within the context of the establishment of the phallus as the transcendental signifier that we can understand how Lacan can justify conceptualizing the limit of the symbolic as a foreclosure necessitated by the very "nature" of the symbolic itself.

A further result of this logic is that the Real can only be grasped as lack. Thus, I will argue that the conclusion we can reach once we understand the significance of Derrida's deconstruction of the status given to the phallus within Lacan's logic is that Lacan fails to adequately address the alterity of the Real. Lacan, in other words, ultimately roots the Real in the meaning of the symbolic. I will argue that with this failure to adequately address the Real comes the unjustifiable notion of destination which guarantees the masculine symbolic against the intrusion of the feared feminine Other. It is this notion of destination which keeps the feminine Thing in its place, "out there," that is the basis for Lacan's confusion of a positive conception of what is *impossible* with a quasi-transcendental analysis of the significance of the limit of any possible symbolic order. Lacan, in my own terminology, mistakenly conflates the "impossible" with "impossibility."

In conclusion, I will turn to how the limit understood as impossibility demands that we re-think the very notion of impossibility as it in turn operates to always remind us of the fallibility of any moral law that seeks to establish itself as a barrier to continual challenge and change. The classic example, of course, of such a barrier is the erection of the phallus as a transcendental signifier that forever blocks the symbolization and re-imagining of feminine sexual difference. By "impossibility" I mean to remind us of the ethical significance of the insight that the quasi-transcendental conditions that establish any system as a system always implies a beyond to it. No system can turn in on itself so as to completely encompass its outside. Derrida has shown us again and again that the very attempt to enframe a system[8] and therefore define it as a system necessarily generates a supplement as it delimits itself. As we will see, the promise of fidelity to what remains other to the system informs Derrida's writing whenever he addresses Levinas's philosophy of alterity. Indeed, for Derrida the promise of fidelity to what remains Other, what Lacan would call the Real, is inseparable from the ethical relationship. But the impossibility of the full inscription of the Real into any system of meaning does not yield the inevitability of the Lacanian law of destination, but rather opens up the endless transformative possibility that attempts to eradicate injustice demands. In this sense the end of conceptual knowledge in the strong sense is forever the beginning of hope.

II. What is Lacking in Lacan

A. *The Real, The Pleasure Principle and the Feminine Other*

1. *Lacan's Dialectic of Desire*

In this section, I argue that *ultimately* Lacan can only grasp the meaning of the Real by ironically signifying it as the imaginary feminine Other, the repressed maternal "thing." In Lacan's system,[9] the Real cannot be known except as what is not there, *apart* from reality. But as *a part* of the symbolic reality, the lack in the Real is represented as the Thing. This is a paradox Lacan's analysis of the Real sets up. My argument is that he cannot resolve it. In other words, in his own terms, he cannot give the Real the difference from the Imaginary and the Symbolic that he himself attests marks the Real as an unreachable beyond. If the Real is unimaginable and unknowable, why is what is not *there* for us signified as "no-thing" but lack? Lacan continuously struggles to provide a satisfactory answer to that question. He answers it by linking the pleasure principle and the resulting inevitability of sublimation to the paradoxical representation of the Thing as "Nothing," and then defines Nothing as emptiness. To quote Lacan:

> The Thing is accessible in very elementary examples, which are almost of the type of the classic philosophical demonstration, including a blackboard and a piece of chalk. I referred last time to the schematic of the vase, so as to allow you to grasp where the Thing is situated in the relationship that places man in the mediating function between the real and the signifier. This Thing, all forms of which created by man belong to the sphere of sublimation, this Thing will always be represented by emptiness, precisely because it cannot be represented by anything else—or, more exactly, because it can only be represented by something else. But in every form of sublimation, emptiness is determinative.[10]

But how can emptiness be determinative unless "the Thing that suffers" in the Real is inescapably associated with the logic of castration? And what is it that causes this association if not the symbolic order that cannot give significance to the feminine as Other than the lack, the horrifying gaping hole? Lacan's theoretical apparatus is ultimately not up to answering these questions without presupposing the very act of determination that he must explain if the Real is not simply to be reduced to the meaning given by the symbolic. And the images of the Woman produced by the physical fantasy of Woman. His reasoning turns in on itself because it cannot explain the determination without denying the alterity of the Real which is exactly the presupposition he is attempting to justify.

As is well known, Lacan distinguishes the Imaginary, the Symbolic, and the Real. In his early seminars, his focus was primarily on the relationship between the Imaginary and the Symbolic, and the transition between the Little and the Big Other (S II, 215–47).[11] For Lacan, the little other is the ego itself. Through an act of identification with the other who mirrors it, the ego sees himself as the "a." The ego, in other words, imagines the little other as itself so as to believe that the ego is "him."

The Big Other in Lacan is the symbolic order. This Big Other marks us as the speaking beings we are fated to become. I use the word marks deliberately, because human beings—or more precisely "man" for women cannot be *signified* as *human* in the sense that they can both be *human*, speaking beings, and "women" at the same time—do not create the symbolic order; it stamps us. Our entire reality is given to us by this symbolic order. But how and why are we mandated to subject ourselves to this Big Other? For Lacan the answer lies in the most basic desire "to be" at all, to become an existent. In the unique sense of temporality that Lacan gives to the human "being," we only are as we have already been spoken for. The symbolic order and only the symbolic order provides the process in which we come to be spoken for. To quote Lacan:

> The fundamental relation of man to this symbolic order is very precisely what founds the symbolic order itself—the relation of non-being to being. What insists on being satisfied can only be satisfied in recognition. The end of the symbolic process is that non-being come to be, because it has spoken. (SII, 38)

We need to analyze why and how we subject ourselves to the symbolic, why it gives us our only chance "to be." The obvious answer—that it is language that gives us the complex reality of objects and relationships we know of as our world—would not be a psychoanalytic one. Lacan is not just repeating the insight of the philosophy of language that what we know as the existing world is given to us in language. From a psychoanalytic perspective we would still need to know why we invest in this order. Why do we invest in ourselves as speaking beings? Why do we endure the burden of the subjection imposed upon us by the symbolic and how does it save us from engulfment by non-being?

According to Lacan, the answer lies in his re-interpretation of the Oedipal complex. He assumes that we initially invest in the Big Other because of a primary narcissistic wound. For Lacan, the genesis of linguistic consciousness and with it the inscription into the Symbolic order occurs when the infant is forced to register that the Mother is separate from himself. She is not just "there" as the guarantor for his identity. The registration of the

Mother's desire and separation from her are thus inseparable, and such registration is, of course, inevitable since mothers are also actual women. There can be no desiring "Mommy" in the imaginary infant/Mother dyad, and it is therefore fated to be broken up by the third, the one the mother desires. But does this third necessarily have to be the Father or if not the actual Father what the Father symbolizes? An answer "true" to the Oedipal complex would have to be yes. To understand why Lacan would argue that the third will inevitably be unconsciously identified as the Father we need to explore the effects of this primary and inevitable narcissistic wound. The terror of the threat that the Mother presents in her separateness, initiates the struggle to overcome dependence of the need the infant has of her. The move from need to demand, "Give me," is in part the infant's expression of resistance to the vulnerability of his need.

This resistance will be against the Mother because it is her desire that is registered as robbing the infant of his security. Of course, this kind of absolute security is a fantasy. The condition of this fantasy is that the Mother not "be" sexed. Thus, it is inevitably associated with the pre-Oedipal phase, the time before the registration of the significance of sexual difference. The fantasy of absolute security then rests on the corresponding fantasy that the Mother is whole in herself and thus a "being" unscathed by the rending of desire. This fantasy figure on whom the infant is totally dependent in its need is the Phallic Mother. Once the fantasized mother/child dyad is shattered, the Phallic Mother "remains" in the imaginary as all-powerful and threatening in her power to both bestow and take away life. Awakening to the Mother's desire is thereby marked by a terror of otherness.

The terror of and yet the longing for a return to this imaginary Other accounts for the repression of this figure into the unconscious. This terror can also potentially explain the drive to enter into the symbolic realm so as to seek the fulfillment of desire that can no longer be guaranteed by the fantasy of the Phallic Mother. Desire is for the one other who can always, and forever guarantee the fulfillment of my desire. Registered as separate from the infant, and as therefore incomplete, the Mother comes to be abjected for her lack which is inseparable in the unconscious from her failure "to be" the fantasy figure who can guarantee the fulfillment of the infant's desire.

This primordial moment of separation is experienced not only through terror and the fear of loss but also as the gaining of an identity separate from Her. The attempt to negotiate the ambivalence of a loss that is also the gaining of identity is beautifully demonstrated in the *fort/da* game of Freud's grandson, Ernst. The game enacts the fantasy that the child is separate but still in control of the Mother/Other. But this negotiation in turn demands an unconscious identification with the One who is at least imagined to be able to bring the mother back because He is the site of her desire. The narcissistically wounded infant thus turns toward the Imaginary Father because the Imaginary Father is whom "Mommy" desires. But what is it that Daddy has that Mommy desires, that symbolizes what "Mommy" wants?

The identification with the imaginary Father is inseparable from the projection of the power to control the Mother, to literally give her a name and in that sense guarantee that she and correspondingly the infant are spoken for. This Big Other that keeps the Mother as "his" in the specific sense of stamping her with his name is imagined as the guarantor of identity that is established, though only precariously, through the loss of the fantasized Mother/child dyad. The terror is that he who is not spoken for slips through the cracks of social life into figurative non-existence. With the crumbling of the fantasy that the Mother is phallic, with recognition of separateness, comes the desire to turn to the third to guarantee the infant's identity since he can no longer count on the Mother to secure his being through unity with her.

Thus, it is the name of the Father and the symbolic register of his potency that is the basis for the identification with him and not the simple "fact" that he has the penis. The biological penis takes on the significance it does only through its identification with the Big Other that secures identity through the power to control the Mother/Other. This power cannot be separated from the symbolic register established by patrilineal lineage which identifies the Father as the one who names and thus can secure identity, and in this sense, the "being" of the infant. On this account it is the symbol of the phallus and its reinforcement by the law of patrilineal lineage that accounts for the meaning given to the penis and the corresponding significance given to the initial "sighting" of sexual difference. Sexual difference or more precisely, the registration of feminine sexual difference as lack would, then, be the result of a prior *citation* in the unconscious. It would be this prior citation that would explain why it is *the lack in the mother* that has structural consequence for the castration complex. To quote Lacan,

> Clinical practice demonstrates that this test of the desire of the Other is not decisive in the sense that the subject learns from it whether or not he has a real phallus, but inasmuch as he learns that the mother does not. This is the moment of experience without which no symptomatic or structural consequence (that is, phobia or *penisneid*) referring to the castration complex can take effect. It is here that the conjunction is signed between desire, in so far as the phallic signifier is its mark, and the threat or nostalgia of lack-in-having.[12]

This lack-in-having is both a threat and a nostalgia because it is the only way in which the primordial loss of the Phallic Mother can be signified. Thus, the phallus stands in as a bar to the return to the phallic Mother. But as the representation of what is not there, the lack in both "sexes" the phallus can only play its role as veiled. Again to quote Lacan,

> All these propositions merely veil over the fact that the phallus can only play its role as veiled, that is, as in itself the sign of the latency with which everything signifiable is struck as soon as it is raised (*aufgehoben*) to the function of the signifier.
>
> The phallus is the signifier of this *Aufhebung* itself which it inaugurates (initiates) by its own disappearance. This is why the demon of Aiowc (Sham, shame in the ancient mysteries rises up at exactly the moment the phallus is unveiled (*cf.* the famous painting of the Villa of Pompeii).
>
> It then becomes the bar which, at the hands of this demon, strikes the signified, branding it as the bastard off spring of its signifying concatenation. (Lacan 1982, 82)

On this interpretation of how the phallus comes to be "cited" as the signifier of lack in both "sexes"—an interpretation consistent with Lacan's own understanding of why the phallus can only play its role as veiled—there would be no necessary basis for the identification of the phallus with the penis aside from the automatic reading of an already registered citation, and therefore, there would no biological or even representational reason for the phallus to be appropriated to the side of the masculine. It would just be a matter of a reading even if that reading would be so automatic that it would appear as inevitable. Nonetheless Lacan struggles to draw a more direct connection between the penis and the phallus when he explains why the phallus cannot be totally separated from its representation by the penis:

> The phallus is the privileged signifier of that mark where the share of the logos is wedded to the advent of desire. One might say that this signifier is chosen as what stands out as most easily seized upon in the real of sexual copulation, and also as the most symbolic in the literal (typographical) sense of the term, since it is the equivalent in that relation of the (logical) copula. One might also say that by virtue of its turgidity, it is the image of the vital flow as it is transmitted in generation. (Lacan 1982, 82)

But even if one rejects the attempt to find a representational explanation for the inextricable association of the phallus with the penis, the unconscious identification of potency with the Imaginary Father will yield an automatic reading of the "sighting" of sexual difference. Thus, even if the phallus represents the lack that triggers desire in both "sexes" the two "sexes" will be differentially positioned before this bar precisely because of the identification of the penis with the phallus. The significance of this differential positioning engenders each one of us as "man" or "woman."

The consequences of this engendering of "man" is that it provides a fantasy of masculinity that can compensate for the primordial loss of the Phallic Mother and the resulting inevitability of symbolic castration. In fantasy, the condition of phallic deprivation gives rise to the necessity for phallic restoration. This fantasy arises in the psychic life of both "sexes." The one with the penis, however, can engage in a projective identification with the Imaginary Father who has the power to bring the Mother back by satisfying her desire. But this identification strategy is an impossibility for the little girl because she does not have the penis. Its lack is identified as a secondary disempowerment that leans on the primary narcissistic one. Deprived of the penis, the little girl is also deprived of the fantasy that she has the "phallus." She is left only with the masquerade of "being" it which is not "to be" at all. The cut from the feminine imaginary imposed by the Name of the Father and the masculine symbolic renders Woman beyond expression, and what cannot be expressed does not exist. Hence, for Lacan, Woman does not exist. Ultimately, Woman as the castrated Other "is" only as the symptom of "man," the inevitable return of the truth that he is inevitably marked as the "lack-in-having." "Man" endures this symbolic castration "to be" at all in the sense of having his identity as a speaking being secured by the Name of the Father against the ever-threatening if Imaginary Other. Woman is denied this guarantee that secures "man." What then is her investment in the symbolic?

Lacan is always returning to Woman, his symptom at least as long as he is a "man," and re-visiting the question of why we must always return to Woman. Is it because Woman is the repressed imaginary figure that will forever be "out there" as the unknowable object of desire, repressed so that "man" might exist and secure his existence through entry into the symbolic order? Or is the return to Woman a signal of a more fundamental lack, a "hole" in reality itself which is represented by Woman through the process of substitution? If there is "a turn" in Lacan it involves the shift in emphasis from the repressed imaginary Woman to Woman as the signifier of the cut—often indicated for Lacan by metaphors of the vulva[13] (Lacan 1982, 82)—of what is missing in the reality given to us by the symbolic.

2. The Significance of das Ding in Lacan's Reading of Freud

From the beginning, Lacan's answers to these questions revolved around his reading and re-reading of Freud's own writing on *das Ding* and the functioning of the pleasure principle. This rereading can only be understood against "the dialectic of desire"[14] Lacan staged, and more specifically against the transcendental position Lacan attributes to the phallus as " the privileged signifier of that mark in which the part of the logos is joined with the advent of desire" (Lacan 1982, 92). Against this background we can now return to the paradox of why the unknowable Real is represented for Lacan as the cut that marks what is missing, the Woman's "sex." We can also understand why the Real must always remain beyond, given our subjection to the pleasure principle, and yet will operate to forever reestablish the moral law.

According to Lacan, the true pleasure principle as it functions in Freud is the dominance of the signifier (S VII, 134). The symbolic order which defines us as human in the sense of speaking beings is what separates animals from "man" in Lacan. Consciousness and the drive to symbolization are, under Lacan's view, inseparable and uniquely "human." To quote Lacan,

> I don't want to begin developing a theory of knowledge here, but it is obvious that the things of the human world are things in a universe structured by words, that language, symbolic processes, dominate and govern all. When we seek to explore the frontier between the animal and the human world, it is apparent to what extent the symbolic process as such doesn't function in the animal world—a phenomenon that can only be a matter of astonishment for us. A difference in the intelligence, the flexibility, and the complexity of the apparatuses involved cannot be the only means of explaining that absence. . . . The word is there in a reciprocal position to the extent that it articulates itself, that it comes to explain itself beside the thing, to the extent also that an action—which is itself dominated by language, indeed by command—will have separated out this object and given it birth. (SVII, 45)

The "I" begins by splitting itself off from what is other. This splitting results from the intensity of need and the resistance of the outside world. But it also takes the form in "man" of giving birth to the world of experience through the words to make it "his." The splitting combined with the resistance and the effort to control the otherness of things also renders the outside strange, *Fremde*, or even hostile. To quote Lacan,

> The whole progress of the subject is then oriented around the *Ding* as *Fremde*, strange and even hostile on occasion, or in any case the first outside. It is clearly a probing form of progress that seeks points of reference, but with relation to what?—with the world of desires. It demonstrates that something is there after all, and that to a certain extent it may be useful. Yet useful for what?—for nothing other than to serve as points of reference in relation to

the world of wishes and expectations; it is turned toward that which helps on certain occasions to reach *das Ding*. That object will be there when in the end all conditions have been fulfilled—it is, of course, clear that what is supposed to be found cannot be found again. It is in its nature that the object as such is lost. It will never be found again. Something is there while one waits for something better, or worse, but which one wants. (S VII, 52)

The need to control the outside cannot be separated from the attempt to see to it that the object returns to us as that which will always be *there*. That something which is there prior to and yet demanding our engagement with it, is what drives us in to the world of signification. Significance gives us the world of our reality, but, since that reality is marked by our intervention it cannot give us "the thing in itself." Lacan here is just repeating the Kantian insight that knowledge both gives us our world of experience and keeps us from reaching beyond it to what is just "there."[15] The thing is lost as soon as we give it significance. But what is added is the psychoanalytic insight into what motivates us to keep up the search for the lost object and the inevitability of our continuing it. Again to quote Lacan,

> The world of our experience, the Freudian world, assumes that it is this object, *das Ding*, as the absolute Other of the subject, that one is supposed to find again. It is to be found at the most as something missed. One doesn't find it, but only its pleasurable associations. It is in this state of wishing for it and waiting for it that, in the name of the pleasure principle, the optimum tension will be sought; below that there is neither perception nor effort. (S VII, 52)

The desire to control, to find the object again, is connected not only to the desire to recover the original lost object but to stabilize reality so as to guarantee satisfaction. It is the pleasure principle which sets up the conditions of the search not in the least through this effort at stabilization. Lacan writes,

> That is something which even prior to the test of this search, sets up its end, goal, aim. That's what Freud indicates when he says that "the first and most immediate goal of the test of reality is not to find in a real perception an object which corresponds to the one which the subject represents to himself at that moment, but to find it again, to confirm that it is still present in reality. (S VII, 52)

Since the drive for consistency stems from the pleasure principle what is sought is not an actual object that corresponds to the representation but a world that allows the subject to minimize displeasure.

The ultimate object, *das Ding* is an unconscious object. We find "it" only in its substitutions and through its displacements. For Lacan, topographical representations of "it" are the result of signifying chains produced either by metaphor or metonomy.[16] To confuse its substitutions and displacements and the signifying relations around it with actual objects is the mistake of Anglo-American objects relations theory. Lacan always insists on the beyond of *das Ding* which in turn cannot not be separated from the "stranger within" of the unconscious.

> Simply by writing it on the board and putting *das Ding* at the center, with the subjective world of the unconscious organized in a series of signifying relations around it, you can see the difficulty of topographical representation. The reason is that *das Ding* is at the center only in the sense that it is excluded. That is to say, in reality *das Ding* has to be posited as exterior, as the prehistoric Other that it is impossible to forget—the Other whose primacy of position Freud affirms in the form of something *entfremdet*, something strange to me, although it is at the heart of me, something that on the level of the unconscious only a representation can represent. (S VII, 71)

For Lacan, this understanding of the relationship between so-called knowledge and the world of perception is Freud's addition to Kant's transcendental analysis of the conditions of experience. Lacan's explanation of how, through the functioning of the pleasure principle, we are cut off from *das Ding* accounts for why it is so difficult for rational men "to see" the world in the same way. There is an hallucinatory element in the very condition of representation since it fills in what is absent.

3. The Path of Analysis

According to Lacan, it is to the subject's initial orientation to *das Ding* to which his *Neuronenwahl,* or the choice of neurosis can be traced.

> It is then in relation to the original *Ding* that the first orientation, the first choice, the first seat of subjective orientation takes place, and that I will sometimes call *Neuronenwahl,* the choice of neurosis. That first grinding will henceforth regulate the function of the pleasure principle. (S VII, 54–55)

Since the pleasure principle functions to seek satisfaction precisely through stabilization and with it the avoidance of excess, the analyst can successfully differentiate between different psychic systems of organization precisely because they will be stabilized around this initial orientation.

Lacan makes a distinction between the obsessional neurotic and hysteric so as to exemplify this mode of analysis:

The behavior of the hysteric, for example, has as its aim to recreate a state centered on the object, insofar as this object, *das Ding*, is, as Freud wrote somewhere, the support of an aversion. It is because the primary object is an object which failed to give satisfaction that the specific *Erlebnis* of the hysteric is organized.

On the other hand—this is Freud's distinction and we don't need to give it up—in obsessional neurosis, the object with relation to which the fundamental experience, the experience of pleasure, is organized, is an object which literally gives too much pleasure. (S VII, 53–54)

It is the connection drawn between Kant and Freud that provides Lacan with his unique understanding of the beyond of the Real and the Thing which suffers in it. We can only understand this relationship between the Real as the ground of law and the foreclosure of Woman if we return to Lacan's dialectic of desire which rests on the abjection of the phallic Mother and the resultant turn toward the One who in fantasy has the phallus. Even if *das Ding* is "on the level of the unconscious something only a representation can represent," (SVII, 71) why would that representation mimic the characteristics of the creature stamped by the masculine symbolic as the castrated Other? Why, in other words, in all our sublimations would lack or emptiness be determinative?

4. The Law of the Hole

We should remember that the Thing in Lacan is not simply identical with the Real. The Thing is that which "suffers in the Real from the signifier," suffers in the sense that "it" is fated to be subjected to representations which cannot be faithful to it. The use of the word "suffers" clearly has ethical overtones; for Lacan there is an inevitable connection between his emphasis on the Thing as an unconscious object and his insistence that psychoanalysis is inevitably an ethical practice.

It is only through the trauma of the suffering of the Thing that we run up against the Real; the Real has operational force because of the trauma that "is," the Thing. Or, to reinforce the circularity of Lacan's argument, the Thing is the trauma mandated by the impossibility of inscription faithful to the Thing. Through this failure of symbolization, we are brought up against the barrier of the Real. We only know the Real through the barrier which enforces a re-turn. We are always forced by the Real to go back to the trauma which is the Thing we cannot escape—a trauma inseparable from our enforced entry into the symbolic. It is only if we grasp the Real *as trauma* that we can understand how it is that the Real enforces a return so as that "it" is always found again. Thus Lacan argues that "The real, I have told you, is that which is always in the same place" (S VII, 70). There can be nothing lacking in the Real because the Real for Lacan is what remains beyond the scar left by inscription into the symbolic: "the fashioning of the signifier and the introduction of a gap or a hole in the real is identical"(S VII, 121). To differentiate, to cut, is the very process by which some-thing is there, because something exists only as it is given significance. What is not cut is by definition fullness in itself, but then it is not there for us. The pleasure principle functions so as to foreclose the very Thing we seek. The drive to know is inseparable from the drive to cut, which is in turn inseparable from our enforced entry into the symbolic—a symbolic which grounds itself only through the cut from the other, the Phallic Mother.

On this analysis the unconscious connection between Woman and the Thing is the result of an unconscious identification. If the Thing is what is cut out by man's knowledge of it and if Woman must be cut out from the symbolic for there to be knowledge at all, then through unconscious identification Woman comes to be imagined as the representation of the cut that can function to represent, the Thing which by definition can only be known through its substitutions. It is only because Woman through substitution stands in for the Thing that Lacan can explain to his own satisfaction "the incredible idea" that man places in "this beyond a creature such as woman" (S VII, 214). Lacan continues,

> Rest assured that I am in no way passing a derogatory judgment on such beings. In our cultural context, one isn't exposed to any danger by being situated as absolute object in the beyond of the pleasure principle. Let them go back to their own problems, which are homogenous with our own, that is to say, just as difficult. That's not the issue.
>
> If the incredible idea of situating woman in the place of being managed to surface, that has nothing to do with her as a woman, but as an object of desire. (S VII, 214)

More precisely, there is *nothing* in actual women to desire. Lacan himself offers us the best possible explanation for why the identification of oneself as an "object of desire beyond the pleasure principle" carries within it a serious danger. He continuously reminds us that courtly love poetry is the classic example of men confusing their object of desire with an actual woman and therefore designating it as a woman with an actual name. Lacan writes that this,

> explains the extraordinary series of ten line stanzas by the poet Arnaud Daniel that I read to you. One finds there the response of the shepherdess to her

shepherd, for the woman responds for once from her place, and instead of playing along, at the extreme point of his invocation to the signifier, she warns the poet of the form she may take as signifier. I am, she tells him, nothing more than the emptiness to be found in my own internal cesspit, not to say anything worse. (S VII, 215)

Yet Lacan does not seem to be able to stop himself from filling in the emptiness with a "positive" description of Woman. It would be more consistent with Lacan's own "logic" to refuse the description of Woman as refuse. If woman stands in only as the substitute for the cut, the trauma which "is" the Thing, then her non-being cannot be described as Other than non-being. In other words, Woman cannot be described at all, not even as the refuse of the "internal cesspool." Is this attribution to women of "positive characteristics" separable from her historical and fleshy reality as "man" imagines it? Can the so-called Real ever be separated from the masculine imaginary and its embodiment in a masculine symbolic?

5. The Unconscious Identification between Woman and the Thing

Lacan's analysis of the Imaginary Phallic Mother and Her abjection could explain why it is that women as the substitutes for this unconscious and abjected object are identified as "internal cesspools." What is always, already abjected is identified in the conscious mind as "yucky" and this "yuckiness" would have nothing to do with actual women but with male fantasy. But if the Real is already emptiness "prior to" to the abjection of the imaginary Woman, why and how can this be the case since, as we have seen, it is the symbolic, through the trauma of the Thing, that marks the Real as a lack?

If it is not the abjection of the Imaginary mother, what then explains "man's" drive to imagine the Real and the Thing as lack, and to mark both with the form of Woman as emptiness. Lacan's insistence that it is not as women, even as fantasized objects of the flesh, that gives woman the form of the signifier of emptiness would at first glance seem consistent with the so-called "turn" in Lacan from an emphasis on the Imaginary to the emphasis on the Real. It is the Thing as the trauma that returns us to lack, that is the Real. It is on this analysis the horror of the lack in the Real that *causes* the abhorrence of Woman, and not vice versa, our projection of our terror of women onto the Real. We thus need to spell out the logic for the "later" Lacan of how Woman comes to take the form of the signifier of emptiness, through a different process of substitution not based in the first order on the abjection of the Phallic Mother.

This other logic would argue as follows. Women as the castrated Other can take the form of the object beyond the pleasure principle because they share with the Thing the impossibility of being known. "Man" is driven by the pleasure principle to signify the Thing. He looks around and finds woman, but why Woman? Lacan's only answer can be that Woman has the form of this signifier of emptiness precisely because they cannot *signify* as creatures of the flesh. How can such a creature take the form of the signifier of emptiness? How can a creature that cannot "be" at all as herself and as feminine stand in as the *ex nihilo*, the ground of being? More importantly why would "man" signify woman as *ex nihilo* since it is "man" and "man" alone who introduces the signifier into the world? The answer to this paradox for Lacan is in "the lack" in our reality of Woman. Woman stands in for the Thing because she cannot signify as Woman, just as the Thing cannot signify as The Thing. Lack of significance is thus shared and can function as the basis of an unconscious identification.

This lack of significance of Woman as an actual creature of the flesh turns her into the signifier of emptiness or the hole. Woman signifies the hole from out of "which" man can fashion his world. Lacan re-interprets Heiddeger's fable of the vase to help us see his point. For Heidegger, the vase unites the celestial and terrestrial powers around it, as the signifier of the way in which emptiness and fullness are linked. In Lacan, fullness drops from sight as it must since what is full of itself, the very form of the Real, cannot be known. The vase can only be filled because it is empty. It is this emptiness that determines the filling, and therefore there is no difference between emptiness and fullness. Thus, the vase is no longer pregnant with the meaning of the togetherness of emptiness and fullness. To quote Lacan:

> This nothing in particular that characterizes it in its signifying function is that which in its incarnated form characterizes the vase as such. It creates the void and thereby introduces the possibility of filling it. Emptiness and fullness are introduced into a world that by itself knows not of them. It is on the basis of this fabricated signifier, this vase, that emptiness and fullness as such enter the world, neither more nor less, and with the same sense. (S VII, 120)

Like the vase, Woman signifies as the hole out of which man can fill in his world. As the hole she can represent "the existence of the emptiness at the center of the real that is called the Thing" (S VII, 121).

But does the form of Woman as a signifier of the hole have nothing to do with the "fleshy and historical reality" of woman? If the answer is that Woman takes this form on the basis of an unconscious identification and, therefore, one which is not an historical identification in any simplistic sense, there would still have to be an analysis of why this identification happens. Indeed, why cannot it be dislocated? My own argument will be that this unconscious identification turns on the engraving of a particular path of repression mandated by a symbolic order established through the positioning of the phallus as the transcendental signifier. For now we need to take note of Lacan's own attempt to reverse the order of the relationship between the abjection of woman and the definition of the Real as lack.

6. Psychoanalysis as Moral Practice

We can now turn to the way in which the Real grounds the law in Lacan and how this law is inseparable from the foreclosure of the significance of Woman as a being with historical reality. For Lacan, the Real grounds moral action because we are fated to "bang our heads against the wall." The Real is the barrier that guarantees the Thing as the beyond to the pleasure principle.

Ethics involves the establishment of order (a return to the same place) and Lacan repeats Levi-Strauss's insight that order itself is based on elementary structures of kinship and exchange. Levi-Strauss gives to the exchange of women a central role in the establishment of these primordial ethical structures. According to Lacan, these structures allow for the arising of human culture, a culture based on speech and on the ability of man to turn himself into the sign of the creator of significance. This reproduction of man as a speaking being is inseparable from the pleasure principle. The pleasure principle is what drives us into the search for the impossible object. For Lacan, it was Kant's world historical insight to make of ethics itself an impossible object. In Kant, the moral law demands that we rid ourselves of all of our desires; if we do good because we desire to do good we have not acted according to the dictates of duty.

Lacan's argument is that psychoanalysis makes a crucial contribution to Kant's insight by explaining why we are forced to turn ethics into an impossible object, one that is forever sought but never achieved. The Freudian answer for Lacan turns on the way the functioning of the pleasure principle operates so as to foreclose the object of *jouissance*. It is this foreclosure that makes the moral law possible because it separates the law absolutely from the Good. The antimonic structure between law and desire that is the very basis of Kantian ethics can then be traced back to the functioning of the pleasure principle. The ultimate law organizes our inaccessibility to the ultimate object of *jouissance*, the Thing. It is this law that we cannot transgress precisely because we are destined to be castrated from that ultimate object.

For Lacan, if we look at any moral code we will be returned either directly or indirectly to questions of sexuality and the lack around which the law organizes itself. "Men" become signs themselves only by entering the symbolic which has as its basis the enforced regulation of sexual difference or more precisely its lack. "Men" become "men" against the feminine object.

When men thus regulate women and their relations to this object, they are expressing the fundamental foreclosure which is the basis for the law itself. Any moral code will be built around the fundamental law of the unconscious, the foreclosure of the Thing and with it our enforced entry in to the symbolic.

It is in his discussion of the commandment that addresses itself to the property of one's neighbor that Lacan most directly spells out his understanding of Woman, the Thing and the Law. The commandment reads as follows: "Thou shalt not covet thy neighbor's house, thou shalt not covet thy neighbor's wife, neither his man servant, nor his maid servant, neither his ox, nor his ass, nor anything that belongs to thy neighbor." Lacan's focus is on the part of the commandment that forbids the coveting of the neighbor's wife. The covetousness that is forbidden is "Not addressed to anything that I might desire but to a thing that is my neighbor's Thing." (S VII, 121) Desire flares up precisely because of the law that marks the Thing as Other and therefore as what is most desirable. The law enforces our desire for it precisely as it enforces its otherness. But if we were to have "it," we would not be "men"—speaking beings. The commandment thus expresses for Lacan the condition in which we become "men."

The elimination of the Imaginary is inseparable from the abjection of the Phallic Mother, the Other marked by the law as the Thing. It is only through her abjection that "man" can "be" at all. Thus, we are returned to the very fundamental idea in Lacan that castration is the price "man" pays for being. To be tempted by Woman is the temptation of the death of "man" as a speaking being, of psychosis. As the fundamental command then we are forced to turn away from the Mother, accept our castration from Her, our only real object of desire. As we do so we find "life" through the Imaginary Father.

Lacan understands the fundamental ethical message of psychoanalysis to be there can be no ontological grounding of the Good. The dominance of the signifier forever cuts us off from the Good. And psychoanalysis tells us why and how we are cut off from the good by the Oedipal complex:

> Well now, the step taken by Freud at the level of the pleasure principle is to show us that there is no Sovereign Good—that the Sovereign Good, which is *das Ding*, which is the mother, is also the object of incest, is a forbidden good, and that there is no other good. Such is the foundation of the moral law as turned on its head by Freud. (S VII, 70)

This foundation of the moral law gives us the battlefield of our experience built as it is around a fundamental lack, the hole which is always at the center of desire. We can thus not help but be forever returned to the "impos-

sible" sexual relationship, because Woman cannot take the form of the signifier except as emptiness. Very simply put, no "man" can have a "relationship" to this "no-thing." Man cannot not "relate" to what is beyond the
pleasure principle although he is fated to encounter "it" precisely as what
cannot be known. His "existence" as a speaking being depends on his cut
from the Thing, the object of *jouissance*. The temptation is always there precisely because she is what we are cut from, and yet the barrier *must* be maintained. That *must* is the moral law imposed by the name of the Father, which
is why Lacan argues that psychoanalysis is inherently moral, since it illumi-
nates the moral law and how we must exist if we are to be "men."

But on Lacan's own analysis of Freud "men" are given to be "men" only by
being damaged, damaged by their very castration. Thus, according to Lacan
the question of the impossible sexual relation and how one lives with this
"it" as impossible has always been at the center of ethics, the question of
how to regulate the "damage" of inevitable castration so as to live with the
absolute otherness of the Thing. On this complex understanding of the battlefield of men's moral experience, psychoanalysis has a crucial role to play
precisely because it must return ethics to the hole that is at the center of
moral life, the lack of love and of the sexual relation. Lacan writes,

> Freud placed in the forefront of ethical inquiry the simple relationship
> between man and woman. Strangely enough, things haven't been able to
> move beyond that point. The question of *das Ding* is still attached to whatever
> is open, lacking, or gaping at the center of our desire. I would say—you will
> forgive the play on words —that we need to know what we can do to trans-
> form this dam-age into our "dame" in the archaic French sense, our lady.
> (S VII, 84)

Lacanian analysis is driven by the drive to transform this "damage," this
"damn age." But isn't there something contradictory in Lacan's suggestion of
what must be accomplished in the transformation? On Lacan's own analysis this transformation cannot truly be accomplished precisely because of
the effects of the sublimation demanded by the project itself. Was it not
Lacan that taught us that lesson? What remains for us to do, if we are to
escape this law imposed on us— if we are to be "men"? Lacan always
reminds us that we cannot think at all beyond the conditions imposed by
the law of the Real. But is the battlefield of experience he so profoundly analyzes truly our fate? Or is there a beyond which operates precisely as the
reminder of the limit of our experience? Must the Real ground the law, or
does it instead forever operate to disintegrate its basis? We must address why
Lacan necessarily fails on his own terms to faithfully address the Real.

9. Lacan's Infidelity to the Beyond of the Real

As we have seen for Lacan, it is only the symbolic which scars the Real as lack. It is this symbolic which in turn signifies the Woman as the castrated Other. Even if this is an unconscious identification between the Thing and Woman based on a primordial lack that marks "man's" desire, the very significance given to lack cannot be separated from the symbolic. The Real *appears* in Lacan, it is given form as Woman. It is the appearance of the Real, its identification with its representation as lack, that Lacan analyzes. Lacan's infidelity to his own argument lies here: he takes the appearance of the Real *mandated* by this drive to representation as the Real. But by the terms of his own argument there would be no basis for knowing what the Real in *it-self* mandated.

On this reading, Lacan is arguing about how the symbolic operates as law to give us the reality of our sexual difference, which in turn is read back into the Real itself because of the functioning of the pleasure principle. That would be the law that could account for why emptiness is determinative of all our sublimations. But that would be an account of the law of the symbolic that inscribes the Real as lack, not an account of what the Real mandates. Lacan recognizes that the signifier of the form of emptiness is introduced by man because all signifiers are introduced by man.

> The fact is man fashions this signifier and introduces it into the world—in other words, we need to know what he does when he fashions it in the image of the Thing, whereas the Thing is characterized by the fact that it is impossible for us to imagine it. The problem of sublimation is located on this level. (S VII, 125)

To know why man is driven to imagine the invisible in a particular way is exactly that; an explanation about why "man" is driven to imagine "it" in that way. Without an explanation of the unconscious identification between Woman and lack through the elimination of the feminine imaginary, there is no analytical basis for this identification. The analytic basis for Lacan is how the Oedipal complex operates through the Name of the Father to foreclose the symbolization of the mother and through her lineage the significance of feminine sexual difference. If we cannot imagine the Real in itself, then we cannot imagine "it." What we have is an explanation of why "men" imagine it in the way they do. Lacanian analysis on this reading would give us an explanation of why for "men" emptiness is determinative of all their sublimations.

Thus, what *remains* after Lacan is his very project of re-thinking what *remains* beyond the symbolic, and with it the question of whether the symbolic is guaranteed by its own law to endlessly re-establish itself as a system? Given that the Lacanian law of the symbolic is inseparable from the foreclosure of Woman, to answer these questions we will once again find ourselves returned to Woman and to the name of the Other, Woman.

III. The Poststructuralist Release of the Real

A. *The Deconstruction of The Status of the Phallus*

For Lacan, the symbolic is guaranteed against the feminine Thing which threatens his very existence as a speaking being, by the establishment of the phallus as the transcendental signifier. This transcendental signifier cannot be known in and of itself; "it" can only be known through its displacement. For Derrida, in Lacan's seminar on Poe's story "The Purloined Letter," the story is used to demonstrate the decisive orientation which the subject receives from the itinerary of a signifier. It is the itinerary of the signifier that allows us to reconfirm the status of the phallus since we cannot know it directly. It is the truth of the itinerary which is the economy of the fiction, in this case Poe's story. Thus, Derrida interprets Lacan's statement that "truth inhabits fiction,"

> Truth inhabits fiction" cannot be understood in the somewhat perverse sense
> of a fiction more powerful than the truth which inhabits it, the truth that fic-
> tion inscribes within itself. In truth, the truth inhabits fiction as the master of
> the house, as the law of the house, as the economy of fiction. The truth exe-
> cutes the economy of fiction, directs, organizes, and makes possible fiction: "It
> is that truth, let us note, which makes the very existence of fiction possible."
> (PC 426)

Ironically, Derrida's interpretation is "true" to Lacan's insight that "man" is the creature of fictions in the general sense that his reality is given by a symbolic order. This reality is inevitably encoded in a chain of significance inseparable from metaphoric substitution and metonymic deferral. The underlying disagreement between Derrida and Lacan is over how the itinerary of the signifier is established as truth. How is the itinerary of the signifier guaranteed so that the letter necessarily will return to its proper place? How can we *know in advance* that the letter will always return to its place? Indeed, how did Lacan come to give the letter the significance he gives to it as the truth of the itinerary of the signifier that points back to the phallus as the transcendental signifier?

The Lacanian answer is that the phallus as the transcendental signifier is always in its place by definition, and thus the truth of the Being as non-being will always be unveiled as a Woman. The Thing is that to which man is always returned and that Thing can only be figured as a hole. But the key word here, as I discussed, is figured. That the Thing must be figured is exactly what Derrida argues is the basis for the deconstruction of Lacan's truth claim about inevitable destination that allows us to know in advance the itinerary of the signifier. For Lacan, it does not shake his claim to truth that the Thing must be figured because that figure will *necessarily* be Woman. That is the law of foreclosure. The figure of non-being has to be Woman and she will remain the *only* object of substitution and displacement for the truth of the Real; it is only on this basis that Lacan's claims about how truth inhabits fiction can stand up. But it is a fiction, in the sense of representation, that Woman "is" the Thing. We "see" woman this way because she is designated *a priori* as the castrated Other, as the site of the lack of the penis. Derrida writes,

> This proper place, known to Dupin, and to the psychoanalyst, who in oscillating fashion, as we shall see, occupies Dupin's position, is the place of castration: woman as the unveiled site of the lack of a penis, as the truth of the phallus, that is of castration. The truth of the purloined letter is the truth, its meaning is meaning, its law is the law, the contract of truth with itself in logos. Beneath this notion of the pact (and therefore of adequation), the notion of veiling/unveiling attunes the entire Seminar to the Heideggerian discourse on truth. Veiling/unveiling here concerns a hole, a non-being: the truth of Being as non-being. The truth is "woman" as veiled/unveiled castration. (PC 439)

Not only is Woman the substitution of the hole, this hole can be known and indeed described, so that the entire itinerary of the subject is organized around it. Without this knowledge of the contours of the hole there could be no accurate description of the economy of desire that could be analyzed as a regulated circulation which will necessarily replace the letter in its proper place. Again to quote Derrida,

> *The proper place, first of all.* The letter has a place of emission and of destination. This is not a subject, but a hole, the lack on the basis of which the subject is constituted. The contour of this whole is determinable, and it magnetizes the entire itinerary of the detour which leads from hole to hole, from the hole to itself, and which therefore has a *circular* form. In question is indeed a regulated *circulation* which organizes a return from the detour toward the hole. (PC 437)

Thus, even if the "later" Lacan reverses the order of how Woman comes to represent the lack in the Real—the Real is not imagined as lack because of the abjection of the Mother, instead Woman is the substitution for the always, already there hole in the Real, The Thing—her form as a signifier still turns on an unconscious identification of Woman as emptiness, as *ex nihilo*. This unconscious identification can in the end not be separated from a particular trajectory of repression which is inseparable from the foreclosure of the sexual difference in the symbolic order. It is this foreclosure and the unconscious identification that designates Woman as lack that purportedly allows us to know the contours of the hole. This foreclosure is the law, but how is this law guaranteed? Without the law we cannot even know what the proper place of the letter is, let alone that it will return there. When Lacan says that the letter has no proper meaning of its own, as Woman has no meaning in herself, he is still counting on another meaning by which he can know that; know that the letter has no meaning of its own. To know that Woman has no proper meaning in her self is to know her as the sign of Truth, if not as Woman.

This knowledge can only be guaranteed by a transcendental which semantics can analyze exactly how the cut in reality will take place. Knowing just how the Real will be cut is what gives us knowledge of the contours of the hole. If we didn't know how the Real will necessarily be cut, we couldn't know why the letter is put into circulation in the first place. The place of woman, of the hole which is Woman, as "it" is always designated as what is missing in its place, is also the lack that is never missing from it. To quote Derrida,

> This is where the signifier (its inadequation with the signified) gets underway, this is the site of the signifier, the letter. But this is also where the trial begins, the promise of reappropriation, of return, of readequation: "the search for and restitution of the object." The singular *unity* of the letter is the site of the contract of the truth with itself. This is why the letter *comes back to, amounts to* [*revient à*] woman (at least in the extent to which she wishes to save the pact and, therefore, that which is the King's, the phallus that is in her guardianship); this is why, as Lacan says elsewhere, the letter amounts to, comes back to Being, [*la lettre revient à l'être*], that is to the nothing that would opening itself as the hole between woman's legs. Such is the proper place in which the letter is found, where its meaning is found, where the minister believes it to be in the shadows and where it is, in its very hiding place, the most exposed. (PC 439)

1. The "Place" of the Phallus

Thus, this place which is not "there" in reality is not "there" because it is a transcendental "place" deduced from a reading of a particular path of repression which always leads back to the object we set out to find, The Thing. Derrida's deconstruction of Lacan's concept of destination is itself put into circulation by Lacan's insight into how Woman's "place" as veiled/unveiled of castration gets the signifier underway. The destination of the letter is only guaranteed if the status of the phallus is that of the transcendental signifier and this status, too, can be clearly established. Lacan himself always insists on the materiality of the signifier, even if he never gives any explanation of why this is the case. Derrida has already argued the letter as the letter can only return to its place if it is indivisible, if it is one. This very idea of oneness can only be guaranteed by a transcendental semantics which stamps the phallus as an ideal object. Only as an ideal object can the phallus be one, the barrier which guarantees the circular logic of castration. Thus, before we even get to Derrida's own re-thinking of the beyond of the Real, his deconstruction of Lacan shows in its first movement that the phallus can only operate to guarantee the law of the foreclosure of Woman if it is justified as an ideal object. To give this status to the phallus negates Lacan's insistence on the materiality of the signifier. A signifier marked by materiality can always be fragmented, and this fragmentation would open up alternative trajectories for the letter itself. Thus, the law of the hole can only be established through a system of meaning guaranteed by an ideal object. It is his necessary commitment to ideality that opens up Lacan's phallic logic to Derrida's deconstruction.

> This determination of the proper, of the law of the proper, of *economy*, therefore leads back to castration as truth, to the figure of woman as the figure of castration *and* of truth. Of castration as truth. Which above all does not mean, as one might tend to believe, to truth as essential dislocation and irreducible fragmentation. Castration-truth, on the contrary, is that which contracts itself (stricture of the ring) in order to bring the phallus, the signifier, the letter, or the fetish back into their *oikos*, their familiar dwelling, their proper place. In this sense castration-truth is the opposite of fragmentation, the very antidote for fragmentation: that which is missing from its place has in castration a fixed, central place, freed from all substitution. . . . The phallus thanks to castration, always remains in its place, in the transcendental topology of which we were speaking above. And this is why the motivated, never demonstrated presupposition of the materiality of the letter as *indivisibility* is indispensable for this restricted economy, this circulation of the proper" (PC 441)

It is the phallus as the indivisible one that cuts the Real so as not only to provide us with knowledge of the contours of the hole, but to also foreclose the possibility that Woman as a substitution can in turn be substituted and ultimately returned to the chain of significance and metonymic displacement. If she could be so returned, the letter would not necessarily be returned to its proper place. There would be no guarantee. But if the logic of the signifier has always already been castrated by the phallus that establishes its logic, then Woman will always be returned to her place as the truth of "the never had it." That return results from the circular logic of the law of castration only. Only on the basis of such reasoning can Lacan avoid the danger that if Woman stands in for the Thing she could always be re-presented. If the phallus cannot be kept in the position of the transcendental signifier, there *can be* no firm boundaries which would fix the hole's exact contours. Without the "stricture of the ring" there can be no guarantee that the signifier would not continue to slide.

There is a further difficulty associated with the very idea of the phallus as a transcendental signifier. Transcendental signifiers can only be known deductively through their representations precisely because they are transcendental. In the masculine imaginary the penis stands in for the phallus but as the stand in, the penis is not it. Indeed, the penis marks the failure to be "it" because "it" only "is" as a stand in. What is marked in both "sexes" by the absent phallus, known only as a bar, is castration. Lacan's appeal to the turgidity of the penis in reproduction as the basis for the unconscious identification of the penis with the phallus doesn't stand because that turgidity "comes and goes." Indeed, it is precisely the "coming and going" of this turgidity that marks the penis itself as the mark of the failure of the "man" to have "it." If the penis is only the stand in for castration, couldn't "it" be the signifier of what is for ever lacking? If there is no firm connection between the phallus and the penis, if it, too, could represent castration, then there would be no rigid divide between the "sexes" since both would be viewed as having "sex" organs that marked their castration and of course, on the contrary, the woman and her body could be re-signified as the One with the imaginary phallus. Judith Butler has brilliantly argued that on this reasoning the lesbian phallus is not only possible, it could disrupt the very logic of castration by dis-locating the association of Woman alone, as the castrated Other. The very status of the phallus as an ideal object means that it cannot be protected from contamination by its representations. This contamination makes it inevitable that it be fragmented in the sense of given "body." This "body" as we have seen, is an imaginary identification of the penis with the phallus, but the underlying unconscious truth belies this fantasy, undermines this identification. The unconscious registration that no "no-body" has phallus means that the penis can be dis-located from this identificatory structure and that other possibilities besides Woman can stand in for the figure of castration. These possibilities would in turn mean that the letter would not necessarily be returned to its proper place because some figure besides Woman could be "it," and the "it" itself could be re-signified as the phallic lesbian. It should be noted that these possibilities are based on the significance given to the phallus itself as the "lack-in-having" which marks desire in both "sexes" and therefore can never be actually identified with the penis.

Derrida also makes the point that the phallus as a transcendental signifier cannot escape the deconstruction of the divide between *Sinn and Bedeutung*, a divide which must be maintained in any transcendental semantics. A transcendental signifier must be true to is own form. But since we cannot know it directly but only in its expression and representations, it cannot achieve that purity. The very project of purifying the concept of form gets bogged down by the very productivity of language in which it must be carried out and explained. The phallus can only be maintained in its position if it can escape the ellipsis inevitably associated with linguistic expression and representation. But how could "it" and "it" alone be uniquely salvaged from the fate of the transcendental signifier. Lacan's only answer has to be an appeal to the ideality of meaning in the *unity of speech*. As Derrida argues,

> We are always led back, from stage to stage, to the contract of contracts which guarantees the unity of the signifier with the signified through all the "*points de capiton*," thanks to the "presence" . . . of the *same* signifier (the phallus), of the "signifier of signifiers" beneath all the effects of the signified. This transcendental signifier is therefore also the signified of all signifieds." (PC 465)

The phallus guarantees the unity of the symbolic order and the unity of the symbolic order guarantees the phallus. The reasoning, as Derrida demonstrates, is circular.

2. Lacan's Fallback Position

There would seem to be a fall-back position for Lacan which would attempt to explain why it is that phallus continues to be reinstated in the position of the lack for both "sexes" but in such a way as to guarantee that Woman will remain in her proper place as the representation of the hole. That position would rely on the circularity of the argument itself to guarantee that the "effects," the establishment of the law of the Father and with it the appropriation for the phallus to the side of the masculine, would forever re-instate the "cause," the phallus as the "signifier of all signifiers." This is the retroactive performativity that Slavoj Žižek attributes to Lacan. In accordance with Lacan's argument about the role of the pleasure principle in the drive towards significance itself, the lost object would be produced by the search for it. The *cause* of the object then would be the search itself, which is why the effects of the search could become the cause. Žižek describes the paradox of retroactive performativity as follows: "First we have the paradox of a signifier which is part of the representation of reality (filling out a void, a hole in it). Then we have an inverse paradox of an object which must be included in the signifying texture."[17]

But even if we accept this idea, we would still have to ask why that object takes the form it does, why it is one particular search and only one possible object as the "result," why it is "emptiness that is determinative of all of our sublimations." Why is it a particular signifier that fills out the hole in reality? Lacan argues that it will be Woman that figures castration and will stand in for the Thing which is sought. But we can only know that this substitution will take place and therefore that the letter will be put into a regulated circulation, if the phallus is already in the position of the transcendental signifier so as to guarantee the unity of speech and the foreclosure of Woman. The response that desire produces an "object a" does not answer the question because the question addresses the inevitability of the *form* of the object that will be produced. The question does not address whether there will be an "object a," a residue that will be produced by desire. We need to have a specific answer as to how the feminine object gets marked as it is for Lacan as "the letter" and how it circulates in a regulated manner. Of course, Žižek's answer following Lacan is that it is the Real that guarantees the designation and the destination of the letter.[18] But this Real as inevitable trauma for Žižek, "must be constructed afterward so that we can account for the distortions of the symbolic structure."[19] A Real defined in this way is deduced from the symbolic and as such it fails to adequately address the Real.

Thus, even if we give Lacan his fall back position, we are still returned to the question of how the establishment of the phallus can be firmly established and the structures of its effects sedimented as reality. Even if the argument were presented that the citation of the phallus in the unconscious will determine how the "sighting" of the Mother's difference will be viewed—this is the interpretation I would give to Lacan's description of the circuit as a machine—this would still be a reading based on a past reading. Thus, there is an irony in the very idea of retroactive performativity. It is precisely the inevitability that language will "perform" on is objects that makes it impossible to guarantee the distinction between *Sinn* and *Bedeutung* and with it the closed circuit that will always, return the "effects" to their "cause" as Žižek suggests. The very temporality of the Lacanian symbolic depends on the phallus always already being in place as the transcendental signifier. But it is precisely that position that cannot be maintained because of the very conditions in which an ideal object must be "presented."

As Derrida shows us, the very idea of a conceptually generalizable form gives way to the fragmentation of its expression. The phallus as a purportedly indivisible, and thus, ideal object cannot be spared this contamination. As a result, there can be no security against this fragmentation and with it the possibility of a multiplicity of meanings given to the phallus, Woman, and sexual difference. As a fragmented object, the phallus is returned to the chain of meaning and more specifically of metonymic displacement and deferral. If the ultimate meaning is deferred then we will never be able to know for sure the pathway by which "the object a" is constructed, and therefore we will not be able to determine the destination by retroactively giving the "effects" a "cause." In place of the ideal, ever-rigid phallus there is only the dissemination of its meaning which overruns the neatly contoured "hole."

The only guarantee against the dissemination of meaning of the phallus and with it the law of the hole, is the obedience of Woman, or in the case of the Purloined Letter, the Queen to the law. As Derrida reminds us,

> The letter—[the] place of the signifier—is found in the place where Dupin and the psychoanalyst expect to find it: on the immense body of a woman, between the "legs" of the fireplace. Such is its proper place, the terminus of its circular itinerary. It is returned to the sender, who is not the signer of the note, but the place where it began to *detach* itself from its possessor or feminine legatee. The Queen seeking to reappropriate for herself that which, by virtue of the pact which subjects her to the King, i.e. by virtue of the Law, guaranteed her the disposition of a phallus of which she would otherwise be deprived, of which she has taken the risk of depriving herself, that she has taken the risk of dividing, that is of multiplying—the Queen then, undertakes to reform, to reclose the circle of the restricted economy, the circulatory pact. (PC 440)

On this reading the circuit is a "pact" that depends on Woman. And what guarantees her compliance? Her compliance to the law is only the result of her fear of being detached from the only position in which she could dispose of the phallus, the position of the King's wife. But what makes this the only position by which she can dispose of the phallus? The answer is, the system in which Woman can only be as lack. If that system cannot be guaranteed, if there are other positions in which Woman can dispose of the phallus then there would not be the same risk of non-compliance with the law. Queens could start to re-interpret what it means to be queens.[20] If the whole edifice turns on Woman's compliance with the law so as to secure the pact, then the true foes of Lacanism are the feminists and deconstructionists. But they are foes because they undermine the law, not because they deny the Real.

If the symbolic cannot be secured against the slippage of the signifier, then we cannot replace knowledge of the Real with knowledge of the law of the cut established by the barrier of the phallus. As a result, the distortions of the symbolic cannot be read back into a definition of the Real so that the Real becomes the impossibility of escaping those distortions. The distortions of the symbolic cannot be read as the inevitable trauma of castration, a trauma which for Lacan is our destiny: "man" is destined to be "man" and thus, castrated. Derrida's deconstruction of Lacan's transcendental semantics shows us that that truth cannot hold up as the law that establishes the unity of the symbolic. As Derrida writes, "the lack does not have its place in dissemination" (PC 441).

B. The Neographism of Differance

The above quote could be interpreted to prove the "truth" of the criticism that Derrida denies the Real. On this reading of "dissemination" there is nothing other to this endless process by which meaning slips away from itself in the sliding of the signifier. By returning everything that is to the field of the signifier, Derrida purportedly denies the beyond of the Real. But for Derrida, on the contrary, the dissemination of the order of the symbolic is mandated by the attempt to be "just" to the alterity of that which remains Other to all conceptual systems. "Deconstruction is justice" in precisely this sense; deconstruction gets underway as an address to the Other that proceeds though the promise of fidelity to the remains.[21] As we have seen in Derrida's deconstruction of Lacan, what slips away from itself in the effort to maintain the phallus in the position of the transcendental signifier is the ultimate meaning of the logic of castration. Dissemination disperses the unity of speech that is the symbolic order. It is the ordering of the Real through the logic of castration that is deconstructed. What is left after that deconstruction is precisely what is left over, beyond any symbolic system. In Derrida, too, the limit of all symbolic systems is that to which we are always returned as the impossibility of the full inscription of the otherness of what Lacan calls the Real.

But this "Real," this ~~Being~~, operates against the attempts of man to ensnare alterity and secure himself against it. The very conditions of presentation of what comes to be defers any static definition of the Real.[22] The Real or in the Heideggerian terminology adopted by Derrida, ~~Being~~ as it is presented, as beings, as objects is Other to these forms. Derrida radicalizes the very idea of the *es gibt* through the introduction of temporization. It is, then, not just the difference between ~~Being~~ and beings that keeps ~~Being~~

other to reality. The very presentation of being in time introduces a fundamental multiplicity and complexity which displaces any lingering stasis inherent in a notion of a beyond that "is," even as it disappears in what "is."

For Derrida we encounter the Real through the operational force of *differance*. This "Real," however, as a *force* has none of the properties associated with the Real defined in Western metaphysics, including in Lacan, as a substance, subject only too limited divisibility. As we will see, the challenge to Lacan by Derrideans is not that there is no Real, but that the Lacanian notion of the Real is to limited. The debate, then, between Derrida and Lacan is how to adequately address the Real and how one "knows" its operational force including in the effects of sublimation. Once the debate is re-defined in this manner we can re-examine its ethical significance. Indeed, we are called to return to the ethical precisely because we cannot separate the ethical from competing modes of address to the Real. If we think in terms of fidelity to the *Jenseits*, which for Lacan was the very heart of the matter of psychoanalysis, Derrida's promise to the Real and to the ethical is always a promise to what remains beyond any symbolic system.

1. Differance as a Disordering, Ordering "Principle"

Before we return to the ethical we need to examine the disordering, ordering "principle" that disrupts any conception of the law of law including that introduced by Lacan's phallo-logocentrism. Derrida heeds this disordering, ordering "principle" as *differance*, which is not a principle in any strong philosophical sense. For Derrida, by definition one cannot know the Real by conceptualizing it because what would be known would only be the concept, not the Real. Thus, he insists that *differance* is "literally neither a word nor a concept" (D 3).

Differance cannot be separated from the becoming time of space and the becoming space of time. This becoming space of time and the becoming time of space is always already underway, as soon as anything "is." Thus, there cannot be an adequate pictorial representation of a "before" this presentation of what is, because what "is" is already, always temporalized. The idea of temporalization undermines the pictorial representation of an empty space as "nothing" in which something comes to be in that space which is already "there." As a result, the traditional notion of the separation of time and space is philosophically undermined, and with the idea of a "prior" nothing. As is only too evident, Lacan's metaphors of the "Nothing," as the Other, indeed, even as the origin clearly partakes of an older world view in which there is a "there of nothing" before the symbolic world of things. It is that Nothing which remains Real in Lacan which is precisely why we know "it" as Woman.

But if Being is always, already in intervals, and thus temporalized, there can be no absolute past that was just there "before," even as Nothing. Such past would not be presentable because as things are presented they are always, already in time, or more precisely things only are through time. Again to quote Derrida,

> In constituting itself, in dividing itself dynamically, this interval is what might be called spacing, the becoming—space of time or the becoming time of space (*temporization*). And it is this constitution of the present, as an "originary" and irreducibly non-simple (and therefore, *stricto sensu* nonoriginary) synthesis of marks, or traces of retentions and protentions (to reproduce analogically and provisionally a phenomenological and transcendental language that will soon reveal itself to be inadequate) that I propose call archiwriting, archi-trace, of *differance*. Which is (simultaneously) spacing (and) temporization. (D 3)

But is *differance* as "the non-full, non-simple, structured and differentiating origin of differences" (D 11) itself just another conception of the Law of law as an originary causality that causes things to be in a certain way, or, more precisely, gives us another law of limited divisibility? I would argue that *differance* is not a Law of law in the strong sense of an original causality because the line between the "before" and "after," active and passive cannot be maintained. A differentiating origin of differences cannot be known as an origin that is "there." What is always already differentiated and in a web of relationships that is constitutive of the things themselves undermines the traditional notion of an original law of causality. Objects are not caused to be differentiated by *something other* so that we can know exactly how they will be differentiated. They are as differentiated and in a web of relationships in which what was the cause and what was the effect can be read differently because "nothing" can be taken out of the knot of reality and put absolutely in the prior position of the cause. As a result, there would not be a neat line that could distinguish cause and effect because what was there would be the relationality of what Derrida calls the sheaf. For Derrida, the word sheaf seems to mark more appropriately that the "assemblage to be proposed has the complex structure of a weaving, an interlacing which permits the different threads and different lines of meaning—or of force —to go off again in different directions, just as it is always ready to tie itself up with others" (D 3).

This idea of a sheaf of differentiations which are knotted and reknotted, but not in accordance with any prior law, goes beyond the idea of limited divisibility to introduce multiplicity and complexity into the very heart of the Real itself. Once one has introduced the idea of multiplicity and complexity into the very heart of the Real there can be no way to predict absolutely according to Law of law how things will next be cut. In Derrida's language there will be "retentional traces and protentional openings" (D 21) rather than any simple pictorial representation of cause and effect. Given the complexity and multiplicity of the figure of the sheaf we cannot reassure ourselves, if there are those of us who would find it reassuring, by appealing to the inevitability of any order. The Real cannot, as Lacan would like to maintain, be "there" as the inevitability of order. Instead as Derrida reminds us, "Not only is there no kingdom of *differance*, but *differance* instigates the subversion of every kingdom. Which makes it obviously threatening and infallibly dreaded by everything within us that desires a kingdom, the past or future presence of a kingdom" (D 22).

C. No Real Guarantee

On my interpretation of Lacan, it is the symbolic that reigns and effectively establishes the kingdom of reality in spite of what we do. This explains why some disgruntled feminist can scream out the King has no clothes and it won't matter because all the "men" will still see him dressed as the King no matter what he is actually wearing or not wearing. But Lacan would reject this idea that it is the symbolic that reigns as a self-perpetuating system. For the "later" Lacan, as we have seen, the Real is the ultimate guarantee of the kingdom. Derrida's sheaf of differance clearly challenges the idea that Lacan's notion of the Real can serve as that guarantee or indeed, that the Real can be conceived as a "hard kernel," or the barrier which paradoxically is "no-thing." As I have already argued, Lacan's Real is irreducibly stamped by the symbolic and envisioned through the masculine imaginary.

This Lacanian Real is embedded in the logic of repetition and circularity. As Lacan says,

> [I]t seeks what ever is repeated, whatever returns, and guarantees that it will always return, to the same place—and it has driven us to the extreme position in which we find ourselves, a position where we can cast doubt on all places, and where nothing in that reality which we have learned to disrupt so admirably responds to the call for the security of the return. (S VII, 75)

The Real, as we have seen, is the inevitability of an irruption that signals the incompleteness of the symbolic. It is, of course, a paradox, that the Real is marked by an inevitable "accident":[23] "the real is beyond the automaton, the return, the coming back, the insistence of the signs, by which we see ourselves governed by the pleasure principle."[24] The ultimate cause is the gap known only through its irruption of the automoton of the pleasure principle. That gap Woman represents will always be there as the *causa nomenon*. This is still a cause of a cause of sorts and one that marks its effects as inevitable, if through Žižek's retroactive performativity. The gap will always and effectively resist any challenge to its displacement precisely because it will be reconstructed as the cause of "Man's" condition. I would replace the Lacanian idea that impossibility functions as antagonism with this rendition of a psychoanalytic law of inertia. It is this psychoanalytic law of inertia that accounts for Lacan's "positive" statements about what is and is not possible in the reality governed by the so-called Real.

But we also need to ask whether this psychoanalytic law is truly beyond the pleasure principle? Indeed, isn't it for Lacan its ultimate expression? As I have already argued, this law could not be beyond the pleasure principle since it is only the functioning of the pleasure principle that gives us this law of limited divisibility of the Real as the Thing. It is, as I argued earlier, only if we understand the forbidden *jouissance* unconsciously associated with the Thing that we can understand why and how it is the Real will always be cut in exactly this manner.

Thus, ironically for all of Lacan's claims to the contrary that the Real is beyond the pleasure principle, "it" should instead be grasped as its ultimate expression, at least as the pleasure principle is understood by Lacan. Lacanian analysis always returns to Woman. But we are once again returned to the question of how do we know that she will always be "there" in her proper place?

D. Derrida's "Beyond" to the Pleasure Principle

1. "Cinders There Are"

Derrida "knows" that he cannot know that, the truth of Woman. This allows him to theoretically *open up* a possibility of a "Real" *beyond* the automaton of the Lacanian pleasure principle. That opening that cannot be closed is inseparable from the Real, if a Real given to us by *differance*. The difference between an opening and a gap is that one cannot know what awaits on the other side, what "is" over there. In other words, "man" cannot know the contours of the opening or into what he will fall. This suspicion of Lacan's truth is inseparable from Derrida's profound awareness of how the unity of masculine symbolic has marked the tradition of Western metaphysics. Derrida is thus in earnest when he questions whether or not one can even think the *es gibt*, "before" sexual difference since the form of being has been inseparable from the metaphors of Woman. In his insistence that Western metaphysics is phallologocentric the question of woman is elevated to philosophical status in a very traditional sense. We need to know how and why these metaphors of Woman have shaped the very conditions of knowledge and our most basic experience of what is. Thus, the deconstruction of phallologocentrism also always returns us to Woman, and more importantly to the limit of her meaning as imposed by a masculine symbolic. It is precisely this emphasis on the limit of the meaning of Woman that has been misunderstood in Derrida as one more attempt to put her in the place of the mysterious, unknowable Other. For Derrida, the question of Woman is ineradicably associated with the question of how to adequately address the "real" alterity of the Other, an alterity which is by definition beyond the masculine symbolic. This project depends on the disruption of the economy of desire described by Lacan.

Let me turn then to the question of how for Derrida there can be a beyond to the automaton of the pleasure principle particularly as this automaton guarantees that emptiness will be determinative of all of our sublimations. The first step is to re-think the law of the pleasure principle. To do so we are once again returned to the operational force of *differance* and more specifically to the way the deferral of *differance* disrupts the specific itinerary of the destination of desire given to us by Lacan.

For Derrida, as we have seen, objects, all objects, are constituted through a temporalization that disrupts the very idea of a "past," even one that is only there as the automatism of repetition. To quote Derrida,

> All the differences in the production of unconscious traces and in the processes of inscription (*Niederschrift*) can also be interpreted as moments of differance, in the sense of putting into reserve. According to a schema that never ceased to guide Freud's thought, the movement of the trace is described as an effort of life to protect itself by deferring the dangerous investment, by constituting a reserve (*Vorrat*). And all the oppositions that furrow Freudian thought relate each of his concepts one to another as moments of detour in the economy of *differance*. One is but the other different, one differing and deferring the other. One is the other in *differance*, one is the *differance* of the other. This is why every apparently rigorous and irreducible opposition (for example the opposition of the secondary to the primary) comes to be qualified at one moment or another as a "theoretical fiction." Again, it is thereby for example (but such an example governs and communicates with everything that the differance between the reality principle and the pleasure principle is only *differance* as a detour (D 18).

It is the deferral of the ultimate meaning of any of the principles since they can only be understood through *differance* that keeps Freud's work from being turned into the ultimate theoretical justification of a restricted economy of desire. The detour that Derrida ascribes to *differance* could be the detour of the more traditional understanding of what the pleasure principle demands. Do we have to save ourselves only by cutting ourselves off from our pleasure? Is the choice between calculated pleasure and death? For Derrida the other to the pleasure principle with its restricted economy is only death if we already accept that we are fated to be in that economy. The either/or is created by the way in which the pleasure principle and the reality principle are read together in traditional readings of Freud, including Lacan's, rather than read through their difference from one another so as to leave open the possibility of a risk of oneself to the other that would not just be an unconscious investment in absolute loss. But for Derrida,

> [T]he economic character of *differance* in no way implies that the deferred presence can always be found again, that we have here only an investment that provisionally and calculatedly delays the perception of its profit or the profit of its perception. Contrary to the metaphysical, dialectical, "Hegelian" interpretation of the economic movement of *differance*, we must conceive of a play in which whoever loses wins, and in which one loses and wins on every turn. If this displaced presentation remains definitively and implacably postponed, it is not that a certain present remains absent or hidden. Rather, *differance* maintains our relationship with that which we necessarily misconstrue, and which exceeds the alternative of presence and absence (D 20).

Derrida understands the unconscious to be exemplary of the excess of the dichotomy of either present or absent. It is other to consciousness, neither there as lost or as found. Thus, for Derrida there is no such "thing" as an absolutely lost object that can be known in its very loss. Psychoanalysis proceeds down the path of aftereffects, which are "the traces of unconscious traces" (D 21). It is precisely the deferral that leaves only aftereffects that disrupts the very idea of the retroactive reconstruction of the unconscious *cause* as "The Thing" that is lost. The irony is that in Lacan's attempt to know the unconscious Thing, even as what is lacking, he once again reinstates an identity between the unconscious and a present entity. A hole known in its contours is *something present.* Thus, through his analysis of the Thing, Lacan is "untrue" to his own insistence on the otherness of the unconscious. Retroactive performativity still renders what is absent present in order to present us with the Thing as *cause.* It is only through this presentation that Lacan can establish the Real as inevitable trauma which guarantees the restricted economy of the psyche Lacan describes as the destination of the letter. It is within this restricted economy which is an expression of the law that we are forbidden access to the object of our desire which is lost always, already. The *law of the detour* of *differance* replaces the law of inertia of Lacan's automatism. *Differance* endlessly defers the law which makes the "sexual relationship impossible." The impossibility of knowing absolutely what "sex" is or what it cannot be, which is a knowledge dependent on knowing what "sex" is, does not foreclose possibility, including the possibility of "hetero"-sexual love. But a love for the *heteros* demands that the other remain other beyond the knowledge of gender. This is why for Derrida homosexuality and heterosexuality are dichotomous opposites dependent on the gender hierarchy. To challenge the restricted economy of gender also then necessarily implies a challenge to the rigid line between homosexuality and heterosexuality.

E. The Impossibility that Gives Possibility

Love for the Other as the *heteros*, as other begins where any system of knowledge that attempts to capture the Other, leaves off. Lacanians "know" that "Woman" is the symptom of man. If Derrida knows anything at all he knows that he cannot know that that representation of Woman is her truth. The renunciation of that knowledge is not an attempt to transgress the law. If it is based in anything, it is based in the knowledge that there is ultimately "no-thing" out there that we can know in its contours. The knowledge that one cannot know the truth of "sex" is not a moral law in that it prescribes anything like a rule we can follow. But this lack of knowledge that inevitably refuses lack is a crucial moment in the ethical relation, that lets the other remain beyond, as Other. Thus, the impossibility of full inscription of the reality of the Other, and yes as the Other, Woman does not function as a foreclosure in Derrida. Indeed, impossibility if one is consistent with the very idea of impossibility, cannot function as a foreclosure. Put differently, love is the possibility kept open by the impossibility of knowing the reality of the "sex" of the Other or, indeed, knowing the other at all.

> No literature with this, not with you my love. Sometimes I tell myself that you are my love: then it is only my love, I tell myself interpellating myself thus. And then you no longer exist, you are dead, like the dead woman in my game, and my literature becomes possible. But I also know—and for me, moreover, this morning this is the definition of knowledge, I should publish it—that you are well beyond what I repeat as "my love," living, living, living, and I want it so, but then I have to renounce everything, I mean that love would come back to me, that turned toward me you let me even hear what I am saying when I say, say to you or say to myself, my love. . . ." (PC 29)

The paradox of this renunciation is that it makes pleasure possible. The search for the lost object is still a secure investment of energy as long as one can determine that the object will remain lost. But the renunciation of knowledge is also to give up the guarantee that one will not find her again.

> In the beginning, in principle, was the post, and I will never get over it. But in the end I know it, I become aware of it as our death sentence: it was composed, according to all possible codes and genres and languages, as a declaration of love. In the beginning the post, John will say, of Shaun or Tristan, and it begins with a destination without address, the direction cannot be situated in the end. There is no destination, my sweet destiny . . . The condition for me to renounce nothing and that my love comes back to me, and from me be it understood, is that you are there, over there quite alive outside me. Out of reach. And that you send me back. . . ." (PC 29)

If she remains other, she remains. The other that remains Other is the beyond to the pleasure principle. This Other that remains cannot be even retroactively analyzed as the cause that makes "emptiness determinative of all of 'man's' sublimations." The effect of the loss of "my love" is evoked differently by Derrida, as the secret of what was there and is still, the Cinder.

> Who is Cinder? Where is she? Where did she run off to at this hour? If the homophony withholds the singular name within the common noun, it was surely "there," *là*; someone vanished but something preserved her trace and at the same time lost it, the cinder. There the cinder is: that which preserves in order no longer to preserve, dooming the remnant to dissolution. And it is no longer the one who has disappeared who leaves cinders "there"; it is only her still unreasonable name. And nothing prevents us from thinking that this may also be the nickname of the so-called signatory. Cinders there are, the phrase thus says what it does, what it is. It immediately incinerates itself, in front of your eyes: an impossible mission (but I do not like this verb, to incinerate: I find in it no affinity with the vulnerable tenderness, with the patience of the cinder. The verb is active, acute, incisive). (CI 35)

The "Real" other remains a secret. She can only be evoked as what has been given, recalled through another memory that does not reduce her to what I remember of Her. The name figures but only to remind of the inadequacy of any representation of the Other.

> It is obviously a figure, although no face lets itself be seen. the name "cinder" figures and, and because there is no cinder here, (nothing to touch, no color, no body only words, but above all because these words, which through the

name are supposed to name not the word but the thing, they are what names one thing in the place of another, metonomy when the cinder is separated, one thing while figuring another from which nothing remains." (CI 71)

The vulnerable tenderness of the Cinder can be heeded as the trace that points beyond itself. It is in this trace of otherness, that always remains beyond that calls us to the ethical relationship.

In his engagement with Levinas, Derrida argues that the alterity of the Other cannot be separated from her being:

> If to understand being is to be able to let be (that is to respect Being in essence and existence, and to be risible for one respect) that the understanding of being always concerns alterity, and par excellance the alterity of the Other in all its originality: one can have to let be only that which one is not. If Being is always to let be, the Being is indeed the other of thought." (WD 141)

This respect for the being of the other cannot be separated from the promise of fidelity to what remains other. This respect for being, this aspiration to fidelity to the remains is inherently ethical which is why it shares an affinity with Levinas's ethical philosophy of alterity. For Derrida, Levinas suspicion that any reference to the being of the Other is reducible to ontology misses the fundamental point that it is precisely the "thereness" of the Other that keeps her as other. It is this "thereness" that remains that must be respected in the ethical relationship and in love.

But the specific evocation of the "thereness" of the Other as Cinder makes another contribution to Levinas's ethical relation. The figure of responsibility upon which Levinas frequently relies is the pregnant Woman who completely gives her body over to the son. This sentimentality expresses what Lacan calls the physical fantasy of Woman. The feminine is evoked as the figure of the ethical relation but only as the good mother. But this is hardly to evoke the otherness of the Other but to once again imagine her within the structure of masculine fantasy. The identification of the Cinder as the feminine là' marks the unconscious association of the feminine as Other but only through the impossibility of embodying her. The paradoxical figure of the Cinder marks the otherness of the Other as beyond any of her fantasy embodiments. In this manner, Derrida's re-reading of the beyond of the pleasure principle makes a significant contribution to re-thinking how the "thereness" of the other, and more specifically of the Other Woman, is what marks the other as the *heteros*.

But this "thereness" of the Other also demands the recognition of the singularity of her being. It is her uniqueness, her singularity, her being that constitutes her alterity that calls us to justice. It is the Lacanian law that woman must be denied the otherness of her being for man "to be" man. It is only if we dislocate this meaning imposed upon Woman that we can even begin to re-capture a feminine imaginary and struggle to re-collect and remember a feminine symbolic.[25] Deconstruction is justice precisely as it enacts the deconstruction of the Lacanian law that ultimately denies the beyond of the "real" Other.

References

1. What is at stake in the debate between "object relations" theorists and so-called Lacanian feminists is frequently missed precisely because the beyond, the other side, of the unconscious has been erased in the conflation of "unconscious objects" with "real objects." The most obvious example is the conflation of the phallus, which does not exist except through the anxiety of what has always already been lost, with the penis. The conservative bias of even feminists object relations theory is exemplified by the continuing hold of this conflation which gives too great a role to the actual significance of "real Daddys" in the development of the identity and individuality of little girls. (See for example the critique of Jessica Benjamin for exactly this mistake and how this mistake has implications for the treatment of women patients by Graciela Abelin-Sas in "The Sheherzade Complex"). As sociology, this "new" objects relations theory has made acute observations about how gender identity is formed in white middle class families in which certain roles and relationships to young children are played out on the basis of whom is identified and has internalized the identity of man and woman. Its failure is that it fails to see the fantasy structures that fill in as so-called real objects. The result is a literal mindedness that reduces women to a set of descriptive characteristics that not only buys the world of a system of gender as solid truth rather than as a representations that always point beyond themselves it also by so doing undermines the utopian, radicalism of feminism. For a political critique of objects relations theory, see *Beyond Accommodation: Ethical Feminism, Deconstruction and the Law* (Cornell 1991).

2. Throughout this text I will rely primarily on the seventh seminar of Lacan both because of its focus on the relationship between the pleasure principle and the Real and because this relationship is crucial for how Lacan understands the connection between the conditions for the establishment of moral law and order and correspondingly his own version of the ethics of psychoanalysis. See generally, *The Seminar of Jacques Lacan, Book VII: The Ethics of Psychoanalysis*, (hereinafter cited in the text as S VII).

3. The classic example of an ethic of the good is Aristotle's *Nicomachean Ethics*. A modern example of the elaboration of the Good as the truth of the actual is Hegel's *Science of Logic* which is why Levinas positions Hegel as his major philosophical foe.

4. See generally *Totality and Infinity: An Essay on Exteriority*, and *Otherwise than Being or Beyond Essence* for Levinas' ethical and philosophical rejection of any ontological ethics which attests to the actualization or even argues for the possibility of the actualization of the realized Good.

5. Slavoj Žižek is a noteworthy example of a thinker who distinguishes post-structuralists from Lacanians because the former refuse the Real. To quote Žižek because his work is exemplary of this line of criticism:

> Post-structuralism claims that a text is always "framed" by its own commentary: the interpretation of a literary text resides on the same plane as its "object." Thus the interpretation is included in the literary corpus: there is no 'pure' literary object that would not contain an element of interpretation, of distance towards its immediate meaning. In post-structuralism the classic opposition between the object- text and its external interpretative reading is thus replaced by a continuity of an infinite literary text which is always already its own reading; that is, which sets up distance from itself. That is why the post-structuralist procedure par excellence is not only to search in purely literary texts for propositions containing a theory about their own functioning but also to read theoretical texts themselves as literature—more precisely, to put in parentheses their claim to truth in order to expose the textual mechanisms producing the truth effect. As Habermas has already pointed out, in post-structuralism we have a kind of universalized aestheticization whereby truth itself is finally reduced to one of the style effects of the discursive articulation (Žižek 1989, 153).

The central intent of this paper is to, in particular, clear Jacques Derrida from this misreading of his work. But an important aside to my central argument is that Habermas often accuses his predecessor in the Frankfurt school Theodor Adorno of making this same mistake of universalized aestheticization. It is true that Adorno and in a similar manner Walter Benjamin argued that art had a unique and irreplaceable role in heeding the otherness of the other that had been buried by what Adorno called identity logic thinking. I have argued that the question of innovative writing styles within philosophical discourse was motivated in Adorno by an ethical impulse to heed the call of the suffering physical. Benjamin was nothing less than obsessed by what approach to the object would be true to "it." Derrida, too, is obsessed with exactly the same quest; how to position oneself before the otherness of the Other so as to be true to her. The prominent place that Derrida, and Adorno and Benjamin before him, gives to the place of what simplistically is referred to as the aesthetic by Habermas has to do with this ethical insistence on the extraordinary difficulty of being "true" to the otherness of the Other. The charge of aestheticization by Habermas misses the ethical moment entirely. Ironically in terms of the debate with Žižek, Derrida's so-called innovative writing style, his emphasis of the limit of philosophy has little to do with turning philosophical texts into literature but instead with respect for the absolute otherness of what Lacan calls the real. It is because the Other is "really" Other that we are called upon to heed our fidelity to

Her through a different approach than her reduction to an object
defined by a system of cognition. For two of Derrida's texts which seek
out a style that could attempt faithfulness to the Otherness of the Other,
see *Cinders* and *Glas*.

6. See, e.g., Derrida, "Differance".

7. Ibid. See also Jacques Derrida, "Le Facteur de La Verite", in *The Post Card: From Socrates to Freud and Beyond* and "Outwork" in *Dissemination*.

8. There are interesting intersections between Derrida's philosophy of the limit and Niklas Luhmann' systems theory. See *The Philosophy of the Limit* (Cornell 1992a), chapter 5.

9. I am using system in the specific sense given to that term in the work of Niklas Luhmann. I have argued that the gender hierarchy as elaborated in the work of Lacan should be understood as a system as Luhmann defines it. See my essay, "The Philosophy of the Limit, Systems Theory, and the Ethical Relationship," in *Deconstruction and The Possibility of Justice* (Cornell 1992b).

10. See *The Seminar of Jacques Lacan, Book II: The Ego in Freud's Theory and in The Technique of Psychoanalysis*, (hereinafter cited in the text as S II), p. 38.

11. In Lacan the imaginary is inherently connected to the pre-genital mirror stage in which the ego is formed on the basis of an other that is erased in its otherness through the specular identification in which the ego imagines itself as the other. For Lacan the ego is the little other. The status of the ego as an object which is dependent on the mirroring of the other is thus denied. This is why Lacan links the ego directly with paranoia. The precariousness of the status of the ego is only unconsciously recognized in the fear of the other who can always take it a way from me. Teresa Brennen in an original argument has connected the ego and the corresponding terror of the power of the other to deprive me of it with the abjection of Woman as the primary other who initially mirrors the child and upon whom the infant is dependent for the projective identification that allows the infant to imagine itself as its own mirror. See *History after Lacan* (Brennan 1993).

12. *Feminine Sexuality* (Lacan 1982, 83).

13. Lacan openly speculates about the use of slang expressions associated with the term vulva as these also indicate castration. Lacan asks, "Why is it the image of the vulva that surfaces to express a number of different acts, including those of escaping, of fleeing, of cutting and running (*se tailler*), as the German term in the text has often been translated?"

    Lacan then goes on to speculate that the metaphorical uses to which the word vulva are associated are interesting in the attempt to show the origins of how the female sexual organs come to be identified with what has already been cut, and therefore are designated by nouns while the male sexual organs continue to be given a verbal form.

    One takes note of the fact that the use of a term that originally meant "coitus" is capable of being extended virtually infinitely, that the use of a term that originally meant "vulva" is capable of generating all kinds of metaphorical uses. And it is in this way that it began to be supposed that the vocalization presumed to accompany the sexual act gave men the idea of using the signifier to designate either the organ, and especially the female organ, in a noun form, or the act of coitus in a verbal form. The priority of the vocal use of the signifier among men is thus supposed to find its origin in the chanted calls that are assumed to be those of primitive sexual relations among humans, in the same way that they are among animals and especially birds.

The idea is very interesting. But you can sense right away the difference that exists between the more or less standardized cry that accompanies an activity and the use of the signifier that detaches a given articulatory element, that is to say either the act or the organ". Lacan is speaking of an article by Sperber in his comments. Yet in spite of his recognition of a "gap" in the his own speculations on Sperber's article he never the less finds the article significant for "making us see the way in which what is essential in the development of our experience and in Freud's doctrine may be conceived, that is to say, that sexual symbolism in the ordinary sense of the word may polarize at its point of origin the metaphorical play of the signifier" (S VII, 168–9).

14.   The phrase "dialectic of desire" is obviously reminiscent of Hegel. Although Lacan uses the phrase he militantly rejected the idea that he was a Hegelian. To quote Lacan himself,

It is clear that we put the accent on the irreducible element in the instinct, on that which appears at the limit of a mediation and that reification is unable to encompass. But in encircling that something whose limits we explore, we are encircling the empty image.

The deliberate intention to emphasize this notion has never been absent from what I have said thus far. If you look up the texts I referred you to on this subject, you will see that there is no ambiguity. That Hegelian radicalism that was rashly attributed to me somewhere by a contributor to *Les Temps Modernes* should in no way be imputed to me. The whole dialectic of desire that I developed here, and that I was beginning at the very moment the rash individual was writing that particular sentence, is sharply distinguished from such Hegelianism. It is even more marked this year. The inevitable character seems to me to be especially marked in the effect of sublimation (S VII, 134).

On the surface at least, Lacan's rejection of Hegel for failing to mark the limit, and the "outside" of the system of mediation of absolute knowledge shares with Derrida a recognition of the inevitability of the "Outwork" (See *Dissemination*) to any symbolic system. Both thinkers engage seriously Hegel's own attempt to achieve a truly circular philosophy which cancels

out its own presuppositions so as to overcome the divide between phenomenology and ontology and ultimately achieve absolute knowledge of the
truth of the Real. Derrida's questioning of Lacan is whether or not Lacan
does not re-instate his own version of circularity in his conception of destination. See "Le Facteur de Verite," in *The Post Card*. We will return to this
text in the body of this essay. For now I simply want to note that Lacan
explicitly argues that any attempt to adequately address the Real demands
the rejection of the circularity of Hegelianism. I agree with Lacan in this
conclusion. Thus, I disagree for example with the attempt of Slavoj Žižek to
give a Hegelian reading to Lacan's account of the Real in *For They Know Not
What They Do* (Žižek 1991, 99–137).

15. Lacan's emphasis on *das Ding* as the excluded Other beyond mediation is
    Kantian not only in the explicit replication of Kant's own language. Again I
    am returned to my agreement with Lacan that, particularly in his later semi-
    nars, his dialectic of desire is not Hegelian. For Hegel's own rejection of
    Kant's analysis of *das Ding* see *The Science of Logic*.

16. For a detailed discussion of Lacan's unique understanding of the centrality
    of metaphor and metonomy in the constitution of topographical represen-
    tations of the unconscious object, *das Ding*, see my chapter "What Place in
    the Dark", in *Transformations* (Cornell 1993, 170–194).

17. *The Sublime Object of Ideology* (Žižek 1989, 161).

18. Žižek develops a subtle Hegelian reading of Lacan to try to philosophically
    justify the paradoxes in Lacan's account of the Real. (Žižek 1989, 169–173.)
    My disagreement with his reading of Hegel is beyond the scope of this
    paper. But it should be noted again that Lacan himself explicitly addressed
    the question of his own Hegelianism. His rejection of the comparison
    between his own dialectic of desire and that of Hegel's was based on his
    analysis of how the effects of sublimation could not be mediated. Although
    my own critique of Lacan is directed towards the way in which, in spite of
    his intent, the effects of sublimation are mediated by his dialectic of desire,
    the rejection of Hegelianism clearly has to do with the correct recognition
    that in Hegel the "effects" of the Infinite's necessarily contradictory expres-
    sion in the finite must ultimately be sublated into the truth of absolute
    knowledge.In other words, Lacan correctly recognizes that any dialectic of
    desire that would be faithful to the Real and the otherness to the system of
    the effects of sublimation could not be Hegelian. Žižek discusses in detail
    the" post-structuralist" critique of Hegel's "philosophy of reflection". I agree
    with him that there is a reading of Hegel that can free absolute knowledge
    from the "tain of the mirror" (Žižek 1991, 85–89). But ironically the very
    heart of Derrida's deconstruction of Hegel begins with the same premise as
    Lacan that in Hegel all the effects, or in Derrida's terminology the remains,
    of the Concept must ultimately be sublated into absolute knowledge, even
    as this sublation demands that we increasingly enrich the idea of the

Concept itself. Matter for Hegel cannot be exterior to the Science of Logic.

For both Lacan and Derrida, truth must be veiled precisely because matter remains "external to form." The effects of sublimation at least in Lacan's own understanding of his dialectic of desire "matter" as the mark of the Other, the thing of the system. For Derrida, too, the remains matter as other to the system. Thus his deconstruction of Hegel proceeds as an "outwork" which moves to show that "matter" remains other to the pure form of thought, even thought that thinks "matter" as the truth of its content (See Derrida, "Outwork" in *Dissemination*). In their insistence on the otherness to the system that "matters" precisely as "it" thwarts a system of thought in which every-thing is included in the system, Lacan and Derrida share a form of argument. The difference lies precisely in whether or not Lacan's attempt to know the contours of the hole can be reconciled with his own insight that the effects of sublimation cannot be mediated. As I have argued sublimations determined by emptiness are mediated. The question the becomes "what it takes" to adequately address the Real so both thinkers agree that Hegelianism ultimately denies the Real in the magnificent attempt to think "it" and know it as the truth of the Infinite's embodiment as the content of all that is finite. Absolute knowledge is the heart of the matter for Hegel, the absolute Truth of being.

19. *The Sublime Object of Ideology* (Žižek 1989, 162).

20. For an excellent analysis of why queens taking themselves seriously as "queens" would disrupt the law of gender hierarchy see *Gender Trouble* (Butler 1990).

21. I have figured Derrida as the ultimate chiffoner to bring into focus the ethical relation that is promised to the remains by deconstruction. See *The Philosophy of the Limit*, Chapter 3, "The Ethical Significance of the Chiffoner" (Cornell 1992a).

22. Thus, although there are clearly important affinities with Theodor Adorno's negative dialectic there are also important points of divergence in the philosophical positions of the two thinkers. For a more lengthy discussion of the differences between Adorno and Derrida, see *The Philosophy of The Limit*, Chapter 1, "The Ethical Message of Negative Dialectics", and the conclusion,"The Ethical, Political and Juridical Significance of the End Of Man," (Cornell 1992a)

23. For an excellent discussion of how Lacan philosophically grapples with causality and how his conception of causality is inseparable from the symbolic foreclosure of Woman, see Emanuela Bianchi, "Causation, Justice, and Feminist Politics" (unpublished lecture originally presented at The New School for Social Research, New York on June 1, 1993).

24. *Four Fundamental Concepts* (Lacan 1978, 53–4).

25. See *Beyond Accommodation* (Cornell 1991) for a detailed analysis of "The Feminist Alliance with Deconstruction," pp. 79–118.

References

Abelin-Sas, Graciela. "The Sheherzade Complex." Unpublished manuscript.

Brennan, Teresa. 1993. *History after Lacan.* New York: Routledge.

Butler, Judith. 1990. *Gender Trouble: Feminism and the Subversion of Identity.* New York: Routledge.

Cornell, Drucilla. 1991. *Beyond Accommodation: Ethical Feminism, Deconstruction and the Law.* New York: Routledge.

———. 1992a. *The Philosophy of the Limit.*. New York: Routledge.

———. 1992b. "The Philosophy of the Limit, Systems Theory, and the Ethical Relationship." In *Deconstruction and the Possibility of Justice,* eds. Cornell, Carlson, and Rosenfeld. New York: Routledge.

———. 1993. *Transformations: Recollective Imagination and Sexual Difference.* New York: Routledge.

Derrida, Jacques. 1981. *Dissemination,* trans. Barbara Johnson. Chicago: University of Chicago Press. Cited as DI.

———. 1982. "Differance." In *Margins of Philosophy,* trans. Alan Bass. Chicago: University of Chicago Press. Cited as D.

———. 1982. *Glas,* trans. Leavey and Rand. Lincoln: University of Nebraska Press. Cited as G.

———. 1987. *The Post Card: From Socrates to Freud and Beyond,* trans. Alan Bass. Chicago: University of Chicago Press. Cited as PC.

———. 1991. *Cinders ,* trans. and ed. Ned Lukacher. Lincoln: University of Nebraska Press. Cited as CI.

Lacan, Jacques. 1977. *The Four Fundamental Concepts of Psychoanalysis,* ed. Jacques-Alain Miller, trans. Alan Sheridan. New York: W.W. Norton and Company.

———. 1982. *Feminine Sexuality,* eds. J. Mitchell and J. Rose, trans. J. Mitchell. New York: W.W. Norton and Company.

———. 1991. *The Seminar of Jacques Lacan, Book II: The Ego in Freud's Theory and in The Technique of Psychoanalysis,* ed. Jacques-Alain Miller, trans. S. Tomaselli. New York: W.W. Norton and Company.

———. 1992. *The Seminar of Jacques Lacan, Book VII: The Ethics of Psycholanalysis,* ed. Jacques-Alain Miller, trans. Dennis Porter. New York: W.W. Norton and Company.

Levinas, Emmanuel. 1969. *Totality and Infinity: An Essay on Exteriority,* trans. Alphonso Lingis. Pittsburgh: Duquesne University Press.

———. 1981. *Otherwise than Being:, or Beyond Essence,* trans. Alphonso Lingis. The Hague: Martinus Nijhoff Publishers.

Žižek, Slavoj. 1989. *The Sublime Object of Ideology .* London: Verso.

———. 1991. *For They Know Not What They Do: Enjoyment as a Political Factor.* London: Verso.

Contributors

John Caputo is David R. Cook Professor of Philosophy at Villanova University. He is author of a forthcoming volume, *The Prayers and Tears of Jacques Derrida*, as well as *Against Ethics* (1993) and *Demythologizing Heidegger* (1993). He has also served as Executive Co-Director of the Society for Phenomenology and Existential Philosophy.

Tina Chanter is Associate Professor in Philosophy at the University of Memphis. She has held a post-doctoral fellowship at the University of Virginia, and has been a Visiting Scholar at Brown University. Her book, *Ethics of Eros: Irigaray's Rewriting of the Philosophers* was published in 1995, and her articles focus on the figures such as Derrida, Hegel, Heidegger, Kristeva, Lacan, Levinas, and Merleau-Ponty.

Drucilla Cornell is Professor of Women's Studies, Political Science, and Law, Rutgers University.

Ellen K. Feder currently teaches in the Department of Philosophy at Vassar College. She has been a Research Fellow at Wesleyan University's Center for the Humanities, and served as co-editor, with Eva Kittay, of a special issue of *Hypatia* on "The Family and Feminist Theory" (1996).

Jane Gallop teaches in the Modern Studies Graduate Program at the University of Wisconsin-Milwaukee. She is the author of a number of books including *Thinking Through the Body* (1988) and *Around 1981* (1992). She has just completed *Feminist Accused of Sexual Harassment,* to be published by Duke University Press.

Kelly Oliver is Associate Professor of Philosophy at the University of Texas at Austin. Her publications include: *Reading Kristeva: Unraveling the Double-bind* (Indiana 1993), *Ethics, Politics, and Difference in Kristeva's Writing* (ed.) (Routledge 1993), *Womanizing Nietzsche: Philosophy's Relation to the Feminine* (Routledge 1995). Presently she is working on a book entitled *Family Values: Reading Between the Lines* (Routledge 1997) and editing *The Portable Kristeva Reader* (Columbia 1996).

Mary C. Rawlinson teaches philosophy at the State University of New York, Stony Brook. Her publications include articles on Hegel and Proust, as well as a series of essays devoted to the "old quarrel" between philosophy and art over truth. As a frequent contributor to and guest editor for the *Journal of Medicine and Philosophy,* she has published special issues on "Michel Foucault and the Philosophy of Medicine," "The Future of Psychiatry," and, with Norah Martin, issues on reproductive technologies and feminist bioethics. *The Way of Icarus,* an analysis of problems of method and intersubjectivity in Derrida's work, is forthcoming.

Emily Zakin is a member of the Philosophy Department at Miami University. She teaches feminist theory, psychoanalysis, and contemporary French philosophy. Her current work focuses on the relations between ideology, subjectivity, and the politics of sexual difference. Her next project will be an analysis of the structural forces at work in feminine melancholia.

Ewa Plonowska Ziarek is Associate Professor in English at the University of Notre Dame. She has published articles on Derrida, Kristeva, Levinas, Foucault, Kafka, Benjamin, and Joyce. She is the author of *The Rhetoric of Failure: Deconstruction of Skepticism, Reinvention of Modernism.*

Index